TRENSIS
A Capella
B Refectorium
C Hospitium principale
D. L. Fecit
Glocestriam Postmodū vero varijs ædificijs auctū est sumptubus Aliarum per Angliam Monachorum Benedictinorū prop
e vir D. Thomas White Miles & Collegij D. Johannis Baptistæ in ead Universitate fundator Dignissimus pecuniâ sua illud redemit
nunc audiat

WORCESTER

Portrait of an Oxford College

4

WORCESTER

Portrait of an Oxford College

Jonathan Bate and Jessica Goodman

THIRD MILLENNIUM
PUBLISHING, LONDON

Contents

PEOPLE

THINGS

LIFE

Preface

The Provost

The location is a little off the beaten track. We are not on the Broad or the High. We do not nestle by the Bodleian and the Radcliffe Camera. Nor do we stand majestically over St Giles' or St Aldate's. We were once in the country and when you enter the College grounds it sometimes feels as if you still are.

The exterior is unassuming. When in shadow, the façade looms a little starkly, even gloomily. It's on the way to the railway station and there is an old story of a College don on Beaumont Street being asked by a French visitor if it was indeed the station. '*C'est magnifique,*' came the reply, adapting Marshall Bosquet's remark on the Charge of the Light Brigade with a twist on the word '*guerre*' (war), '*mais ce n'est pas la gare.*' Hansard records the following remark in a debate on Industrial Development and Preservation of the Countryside in the House of Commons on 20 November 1959: 'The great thing is that buildings should look what they are and not pretend to be something else. The idea of putting up an unattractive building and painting it green so that it looks like a tree is not successful and tends to inspire the opinions embodied in the famous comment on Worcester College, Oxford, *C'est magnifique mais ce n'est pas la gare.*' And in Jeffrey Archer's 1996 novel *The Fourth Estate,* a lightly disguised narrative of the lives of rival newspaper tycoons Rupert Murdoch and Robert Maxwell, the Murdoch character 'Keith Townsend' – whose career at Worcester, complete with bust of Lenin on the mantelpiece and active role in the University Labour Club, is rather vividly evoked – gets drunk and chalks the phrase on the College's 18th-century walls.

But there are other stories associating the remark with Balliol or Keble. Myth and fact are not always easy to separate in Worcester's history. Was there really a time when the College became a training-ground for Greek Orthodox clergy from Constantinople and Antioch? True, albeit only briefly. Was Lewis Carroll inspired to create the rabbit-hole in *Alice in Wonderland* by seeing the tunnel into the gardens at the end of the main quad? Almost certainly false, but he did write a lovely poem for Provost Daniel's daughter Rachel, and she in turn played the part of Alice in a dramatisation in her father's garden, with rehearsals witnessed from the shrubbery by Carroll himself (at the last minute, old Dodgson expressed his disapproval of the idea of people paying to enter the grounds, so the College agreed that the audience could come in for free but should pay to go out). Did wallabies once roam the College grounds? Yes. Did Rupert Murdoch put them there? No.

The moment you enter, you find yourself in one of Oxford's most photogenic environments. The sunken quad. The juxtaposition of

LEFT: *'The secret garden':* Worcester: cottage orné, *by Mavis Batey (1982).* ABOVE: *Lovers in a boat on the lake, in a Buskins production of* The Merchant of Venice. OPPOSITE: *Fresco in the College Chapel, depicting 'the beasts of the field'.*

cloister, 18th-century Terrace, medieval cottages and garden wall with a view of mature trees beyond: there is nothing comparable in any other College anywhere in the world. And that is before you reach the lake.

When I was elected Provost of Worcester in 2010, the first thing that people would say to me – knowing I am a Shakespeare scholar – was always the same: 'Do you know about Nevill Coghill's 1949 production of *The Tempest,* which ended with Ariel running to freedom across the lake?' A student actor called Charlie Hodgson, who decades later appeared in the first-ever episode of *Inspector Morse,* appeared to run on water (there were slats just below the surface), then sprinted up into a tree to wave his last farewell to Prospero. It was a brilliant coup de théâtre that no one who saw has ever forgotten. So brilliant indeed that I have met many people who swear they did see it, even though they could not possibly have been in Oxford in 1949 (there was at least one re-staging in the 1950s).

A Shakespeare play by the lake at the end of Trinity Term is a longstanding Worcester tradition. In 2013 the Buskins staged *The Merchant of Venice* not just beside the lake but on it. There was a pontoon stage, rowing boats conveying the characters from Venice to Belmont, and the Provost's bridge standing in for the Rialto. Light faded in the interval and dozens of candle-lanterns were lit. One performance night, as I drifted off to sleep in the bedroom high on the northern side of the Lodgings, sounds of music (lute and theorbo) crept in my ears through the soft stillness of the night. 'The sweet wind did gently kiss the trees' and I heard with absolute clarity the words 'How sweet the moonlight sleeps upon this bank' even as the moon illuminated lake, garden and quad. Again, this was a production that no one who saw is ever likely to forget. Especially if they were in their final year before leaving the enchanted garden – or, as 21st century undergraduates call it, the 'Worcester wonderland' – and entering the world of work.

This book is for everybody who has been to Worcester, for all who love and want to remember Worcester. But also for anyone who wants to know *why* Worcester casts its special magic, and indeed for casual visitors, for readers intrigued by a very unusual Oxford College, and for anyone interested in Worcester's people – from the architect and collector George Clarke to the opium-eater Thomas De Quincey to spymaster Masterman to the dons, the staff and the students who have enlivened the College in more recent times. It is a *portrait* of the College in the true sense of the word: not an academic history, but an *impression* of the place, its people and its customs.

A visual as well as a verbal portrait: the pictures are essential to the book. Indeed, you cannot really get to the essence of Worcester without images. At the time of writing I have been Provost for two years and if you asked me to summon up the essence of Worcester as I now see it, I would tell you to go to Mavis Batey's wonderful 1982 book *Oxford Gardens* and take a close look at colour plate 12, which is captioned '*Worcester: cottage orné*. By the addition of curly barge boards to the gable, a trellised porch on the window and a raised garden, an upstairs set of rooms enjoys the effect of a picturesque cottage in a park.' This is the famous set of rooms at the end of the quad, with the private garden above the tunnel. A secret garden and a medieval gable end transformed into an 18th-century rustic cottage: these evoke the charm and the eclecticism of Worcester in an instant. But the image presents a human scene, not an artificially manicured one: Mavis Batey's white handbag is sitting rather obtrusively on the lawn and by the French doors Harry Pitt's black dog Flint is looking quizzically at the camera. Both don and dog have their place in our history, as will be seen. A College is ultimately its people, its community – past, present and future – and not just its architecture and its landscape.

I feel very lucky to have arrived as Provost at the moment when the College was beginning preparations for the 300th anniversary of its re-foundation as Worcester. The year 2014 marks not just a once in a generation but a once in a century opportunity to look back at the last 300 years and lay the foundations for the next 300. All Oxford colleges have their eccentricities – in their characters and in their customs – but only Worcester can claim the oddity of having celebrated its 700th anniversary before its 300th. On 27 June 1983, *The Times* of London carried a photograph of former Prime Minister Macmillan with a caption stating 'Harold Macmillan, Chancellor of Oxford University, celebrating the seven hundredth anniversary of the founding of Gloucester College, the Benedictine college, some of whose buildings are now occupied by Worcester College' (the dinner had been held in a marquee on the Nuffield Lawn two days earlier – on a very hot day with very slow service). Since it is our foundation as *Worcester* in 1714 that we are commemorating here, the emphasis in this book is on more recent history, including such momentous events as the advent of women in 1979. We do, however, begin with accounts of our 'pre-history' as Gloucester College and Gloucester Hall, not to mention that brief interlude as the 'Greek College'.

It was a particular pleasure to receive the first chapter, on Gloucester College, from the incomparable James Campbell. Characteristically, he was the first to deliver, despite suffering a serious illness during the time when he was doing the research for the chapter. Creating the book has been a labour of love. Huge gratitude is owed to all the contributors, but especially to the College Librarian Dr Joanna Parker and the Archivist Emma Goodrum, for all their research, their checking of facts, and their work co-ordinating the pictures. And completion would not have been possible without the Herculean labours and cool efficiency of my co-editor, Dr Jessica Goodman – who, it should almost go without saying, was a graduate scholar of the College effortlessly gaining her doctorate even as she worked on this project.

Jonathan Bate

HISTORY

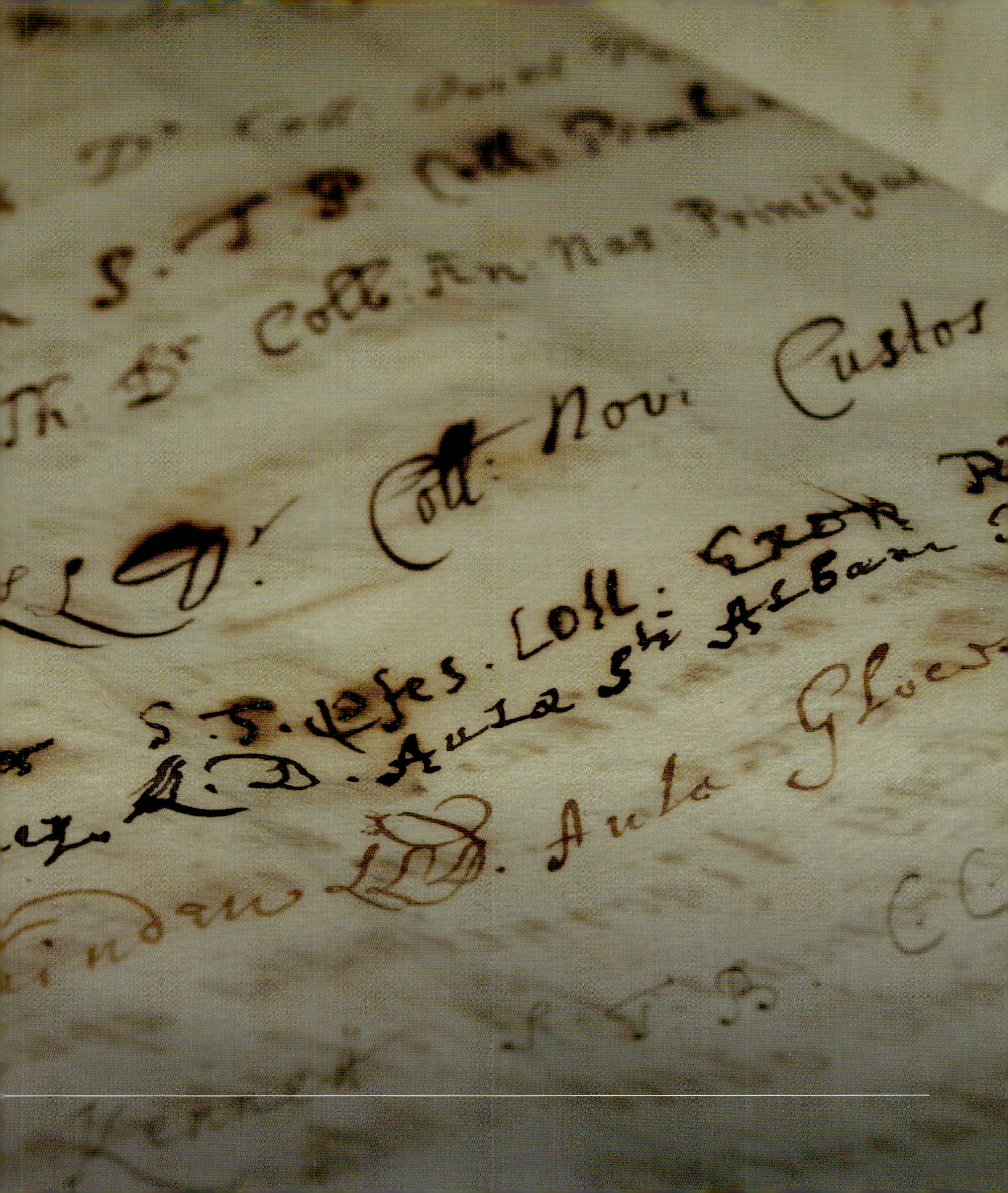

S. T. B. Coll: Pemb:

Th: Dr Coll: Æn: Nas: Principalis

Coll: Novi Custos

LLD. Coll: Exon:

S. T. B. Jesus Coll:

D. Aula Sti Albani

LLD. Aula Glouc:

S. T. B.

1. Gloucester College

James Campbell

Gloucester College was founded in 1283 and perished with the dissolution of the monasteries in 1539. The College was the centre of study in Oxford for Benedictine monks, until 1338 for those who came from the ecclesiastical province of Canterbury, thereafter for those from the province of York also.

In the 13th century the confidence of the great monasteries of England began to be shaken. There was an uneasiness that the world was passing the Black Monks by. Two threats converged. First: the rise of the universities and in particular the rise of Oxford ensured that Benedictine monasteries were no longer what some of them had been for centuries – the principal centres of intellectual life. Second: in the 1220s the Dominican and Franciscan friars came to England and soon flourished. Their way of life contrasted to that of the Black Monks and implied criticism of it. Their popularity among all ranks of society was a galling challenge to the great houses that had for so long been central to the life and piety of England. What is more, the friars soon became deeply and influentially involved in the universities. No longer did an intending benefactor, or a bright young man, think first of a Benedictine house when it came to seeking a home for money or for intellect.

Something had to be done to establish a closer link between the monasteries and the University. At a meeting of the Benedictine chapter in 1277 a crucial decision was taken: to found a house of studies at Oxford for Black Monk students, the project to be financed by a levy of 2d. in the mark (13s. 4d.) on the income of each house.

For some years the project hung fire. No student of the affairs of the Benedictine chapter could be surprised at this. An assembly of the heads of independent institutions, all deeply suspicious of any threat to that independence and quick to feel a slight, was not easy to move to effective action. Some abbeys were cooperative, but others were not. However, in 1283 came a hopeful step forward. A rich Gloucestershire knight, Sir John Giffard, bought a site in Oxford and gave it to St Peter's monastery, Gloucester, to provide a base in the University. Originally intended for just Gloucester monks, it was soon extended to provide for the Benedictines of the southern province. Some complicated choppings and changings followed; at one stage the benefactor seems to have been near to losing his temper and reclaiming his property. The legal position was not fully resolved until 1298.

In that year Giffard decided that not Gloucester but Malmesbury, the abbey at which he was spending his declining years, should be

Mural from the Chapel of a Benedictine monk holding a model of Gloucester College.

the owner of the site. On it were to be built buildings for the common use of the students, to be paid for by the abbeys of the province of Canterbury. Students' rooms were to be built by each abbey for its own men. From then on the College was a going concern, though it still had difficulties to face, not least the reluctance of many houses to pay their due contributions. The name of 'Gloucester College' was retained, though 'Malmesbury College' would have been more appropriate. Names can survive wonderfully. How many of those who board a bus on Gloucester Green know that the 'Gloucester' derives from a pious impulse of a Gloucester knight in 1283?

In 1320 or 1321 came a major stroke of luck: an opportunity to extend the site. The origins of this chance were believed to lie in the Battle of Bannockburn, 24 June 1314. Edward II was in imminent danger of capture by the Scots and vowed to found a house of Carmelite friars if he escaped. After his escape he was as good as his word. He gave the Oxford Carmelites the royal house there (which later antiquaries called Beaumont Palace). Up to this time the Carmelites had been the next-door neighbours of Gloucester College. The site that Giffard had given the College probably comprised most of that which is now occupied by the present 18th-century buildings and by the Front Quad. The Carmelites were immediately to the south, occupying the site of Pump Quad and a large area beyond. The 'Beaumont Palace' was to the east of the present College, on the other side of the road, occupying most of the space now taken up by Worcester Cottage, the west end of Beaumont Street, and part of the area between Beaumont Street and Gloucester Green. The first inclination of the Carmelites was to hold on to both sites and in 1318 they obtained a licence for a tunnel to join them, though such a tunnel was never built. Generations of undergraduates who have stood impatiently at the seemingly interminable red traffic light outside the College may well wish it had been.

In 1320 the Carmelites decided to put their old site on the market. This was too good an opportunity for the Benedictines to miss and the presidents of the chapter snapped up the old Carmelite site for the large sum of 800 marks. A further step forward came with Pope Benedict XII's legislation in 1336 and 1338. This made it compulsory for Benedictine houses to have one in 20 of their monks studying at the University. Hitherto it had been up to each monastery as to whether or not it sent monks to Gloucester College. Now this was not so. Though the legislation was not universally observed, it had considerable effect.

By the middle of the 14th century Gloucester College's constitution was settled much as it was to remain. It was complex. This was not a College in the sense of being a legal entity with corporate powers of owning property. Individual abbeys had accommodation within the College, acquiring licences to build from Malmesbury. The most important officer of the College was the *prior studentium*, responsible to the Abbot President of the Benedictine chapter and usually chosen from among the senior students.

Who came to study at Gloucester College and what did they study there? Some houses were more strongly and continuously represented than others. Westminster sent considerably more monks than it was bound to do. The College could have held over a hundred students and sometimes some were also lodged outside the College. It is likely that in the later Middle Ages the number present was lower. The only date for which we have a list of the monks present is 1537 when there were 32, from 13 or more different monasteries.

A full university course leading to a Doctorate in Divinity took 17 years; eight years for Arts (principally Logic and Philosophy) and nine years for Theology. Most monks were exempted from parts or most of the Arts course on the ground that they had already received the instruction required in their monastery. Many did not proceed beyond a Bachelorship in Theology. A high proportion did not take a degree at all, but simply came for a few years, perhaps above all to learn how to preach. It is worth remembering that those who took the full course received greater learning in a more sophisticated system of instruction than is available to most modern students. That the College was anything but dead in its last years is demonstrated by 14 Benedictines having taken degrees in its final year, 1538–9.

How old were the students? Our best indication comes from records of monks from Westminster (though they may not have been typical). A majority came within six or seven years of entering the monastery, which is to say that they would be in their early or mid-20s. Quite a number were younger; some were much older. In some cases when there was a little group from a monastery, an older monk would be sent to keep an eye on the younger ones. There could have been many considerations in deciding who was sent. It may sometimes have been a question of who could best be spared to keep up the quota, or whose company his confrères could best do without.

On leaving the College nearly all went back to their monasteries. A few went on to grander careers outside the cloister. The most remarkable such career was that of Adam Easton. A monk of Norwich, born in about 1330, he was at Gloucester College, though not continuously, from 1352–3 until 1366 when he became *prior studentium*. In 1369 he went to the papal court at Avignon and became Proctor for the English Benedictines at the *curia*. At about this time he wrote a powerful book, *Defensorium Ecclesiasticae Potestatis*, remarkable not least because in order to make best use of the Old Testament he learned Hebrew, one of the very few scholars of his day to do so. In 1381 he was made a cardinal by Urban VI (two popes were produced by the schism of 1378 and he was the one whom the English supported). Urban VI was, to say the least,

difficult, and deeply mistrustful of many of his own supporters. In 1385 he deprived Easton of his benefices, and had him imprisoned and tortured. In 1389 he was re-instated and he died in 1397. His tomb still stands in his titular church of St Cecelia in Trastevere.

Such grandeur was anything but characteristic of the careers of Gloucester College men. The overwhelming majority led quiet lives in their monasteries when they went down. As men more highly educated than their confrères they provided a considerable proportion of those elected to become heads of their houses or who held administrative offices within them. How considerable a

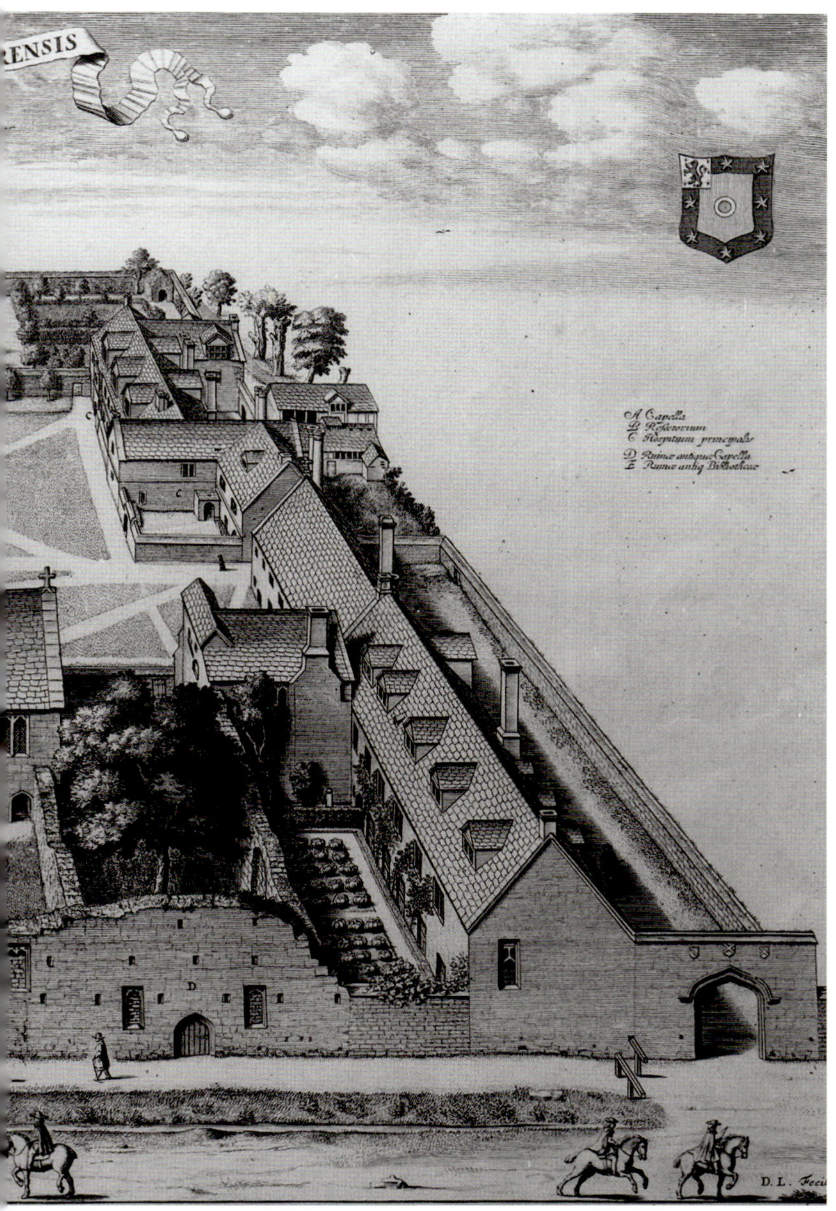

David Loggan, Gloucester Hall, from Oxonia Illustrata *1675.*

proportion became heads is undetermined. At Westminster only half the abbots between 1350 and the Dissolution had been at Gloucester College. None of the monks who had been there wrote a book such as to demand more than brief notice in the history of medieval thought, Easton apart, though some wrote books of one kind or another. But the collective influence of the men who had been to Gloucester College on the Benedictine monasteries of England was probably persuasive and great.

Contrary to what has been often supposed, Benedictine intellectual life and that of Gloucester College quickened in the last years before the Dissolution. The number of monks taking degrees at Oxford increased considerably. A description of intellectual life there is provided by the letter-book of Robert Joseph (1530–3), which casts light on his position as a former Gloucester College student. It not only shows the fairly wide range of his contacts but also the influence of Humanism, not so much on his theological thought as on his strong interest in Latin style.

Gloucester College was a very agreeable place in which to be. Its environs were far more pleasant than they are even now. The College stood somewhat outside the city walls. Between the College and the river stretched marshes, drained by dykes. To the north was open countryside. Opposite the east front of the College stood the buildings of the Carmelites, which were probably somewhat grand. Anthony Wood says they included a 'steeple with bell'. It was one of several monastic establishments scattered round the outside of western Oxford. All except the present Cathedral at Christ Church and the remains of Gloucester College are now totally lost apart from mere fragments. Opposite the College on the west, just on the other side of a branch of the Thames, stood the Cistercian abbey of Rewley. Beyond Rewley lay the house of the Augustinians at Osney. Four hundred yards south-east of the College was the Franciscan Friary; 200 yards beyond that the Dominican Friary; another 300 yards on were the Augustinians of St Frideswide's whose church is now Christ Church Cathedral. All these monasteries had buildings of some, or great, splendour. One of the most abiding memories from Gloucester College must have been that of living within sight, or, not least, sound of the most astonishing aggregation of monasteries anywhere in England.

We have a good idea of the nature of the buildings of Gloucester College particularly from Loggan's print of 1675 showing the College's successor, Gloucester Hall. Loggan's prints are beautifully executed and are enlivened by the life he shows going on in and around them. Thus in his Gloucester Hall print he shows among other living beings a man making his way to the common latrine of the Hall, a woman with a baby on her back, with another infant trailing behind, and a dog, rollicking on the foot-way outside the College. The print shows how relatively impressive were the buildings of Gloucester College, as befitted an institution of some national importance. Two of the major buildings of the College had been demolished, probably in the interval between the Dissolution (1539) and the establishment of Gloucester Hall in 1560. These

Above: *Medieval wagon ceiling from what is now the JCR, re-discovered in 1930.* Right: *Pump Quad wall from Worcester Street.* Opposite top: *Medieval chimney of the old kitchen.* Opposite below: *The medieval* camerae.

were the Chapel (which occupied the site of the present Chapel) and the Library. It is easy to pick out the Hall running north-south from the north side of Pump Quad. It was, says Hearne (writing when it was still standing), 'a noble room', 63 feet by 33. This would indeed have been a noble room, a little bigger than the present Hall. The new kitchen, built in 1423, was the little wing still running on the garden side of Staircase 11 and its great chimney is still there. (The tradition of having the kitchen in this area and at this cooling distance from the Hall has been piously preserved.)

Some of the changes, indeed bodges, brought to Gloucester College buildings in Gloucester Hall or even Worcester College days can be glimpsed in Pump Quad. If one stands on the opposite side of the road from the east side of Pump Quad one can see one of the most interesting walls in Oxford. The top floor of the quadrangle had been added to the medieval buildings in 1824. One sees at once from the window openings that at some stage the road outside had been raised to such an extent that the buildings are obscured knee-deep. The explanation of this is readily to be seen in the Loggan print which shows what appears to be a recently raised foot-way running in front of the Hall. Not the least interesting feature of the wall is the trace of a pointed arch near its right-hand end. There is a corresponding trace within Pump Quad and it could be that here we have the remnant of the entrance lodge of the Carmelite monastery. Consideration of the wall as a whole shows a number of former windows that bear no likely relation to what was there in Gloucester College days, but reflect later efforts to create accommodation. The nature of this somewhat undignified conversion can best be glimpsed by going into the rooms on the south side of Pump Quad. There, we find a series of fine medieval beams, which now bears no relation to the divisions between the rooms and the adjacent staircase. Here we have the remains of the grand ground floor room of the accommodation owned by Glastonbury Abbey.

The most conspicuous, and affecting, medieval survivals are the buildings now called the 'cottages' but in Gloucester College days called *camerae*. A line of six of these forms the south side of the present main quad and the remains of one or more others contain the Senior Common Room accommodation in and beyond the north-eastern corner of that quad. These 'cottages' are the accommodation provided by individual monasteries for their monk students. The identification of the monastic ownership of particular accommodation is sometimes easy, sometimes difficult or impossible, especially given that property could change hands from one monastery to another. The most westerly of the cottages on the south side of the quadrangle undoubtedly belonged to Pershore Abbey in the last years of Gloucester College. The abbey's arms stand to the right of the niche above the door; the rebus (a comb

Opposite (left to right): *Arms of Ramsey Abbey; Arms of St Albans Abbey; Arms of Winchcombe Abbey; The rebus of William Compton, the penultimate abbot of Pershore Abbey; Arms of Bury St Edmunds Abbey, a gift to the College in 1957; Arms of Malmesbury Abbey; Arms of St Augustine's Abbey Canterbury; Arms of Glastonbury Abbey, moved from Pump Quad in 1957; Arms of Pershore Abbey.* Right: *Arms of Sir John Giffard, Founder of Gloucester College, a gift to the College in 1957.* Far right: *Entrance gate to Gloucester College.*

and a tun) and initial of its penultimate abbot, William Compton, stand to the left. The cross over Staircase 11 is that of St Augustine's, Canterbury. Over Staircase 10 is the splendid cross and virgin of Glastonbury. But it does not belong here, having been moved from Pump Quad. The ownership of a number of others can be identified at one stage or another. Thus the L-shaped house towards the west end of the buildings on the north side of the quad belonged to St Albans. The Bury building that lay along the east side of the College is of special interest because a surviving memorandum describes it. This building belonged to the 15th century and included not only the Bury accommodation, but also a library for common use. The Bury rooms were, first, a *camera* 'under the library and next to the chapel', 22 feet or more long, and 18 feet wide, and next to it another room under the library, 24 feet or more long, by 18 feet wide. (Thus we can see that the library was on the first floor and was about 46 feet long and 18 feet wide. Its east windows must have been those standing shattered in the Loggan print.) There was also an *aula*, a hall, 30 feet long and 18 feet wide, and on the ground floor. There was a *camera* above the *aula* and of the same dimensions, then came two *camerae*, one above the other, each 21 feet by 18.

The Bury accommodation was clearly grand. What was that within the cottages on the south side of the main quad like? I can only offer suggestions. It is likely that each of the houses had a big sitting room or Common Room as its ground floor; the present staircase doors entered straight into these rooms, though there could have been a lobby. The actual staircases are relatively modern. Ascent to the first storey in medieval times would have probably been by a narrower winding stair, sometimes lighted by very small windows such as those which can be seen beside the doors of Staircases 8 and 10. Perhaps the upper floors were divided into a couple of rooms; perhaps there was just one big room. The cocklofts shown by Loggan could well have been post-medieval.

It is important to notice that most of the significant buildings in the College date from the 15th century. The demonstrably late date of the Pershore *camera* is significant. The similarity to its architectural style to that of the cottages to its east suggests that they are not much later, and there was another (which must have been later) to the west. The late and fine buildings of the College are evidence (and not the only evidence) that its latter days were not characterised by the indolence and torpor which Victorians attributed to it.

One last aspect of the physical nature of the College may be noticed: the way in. It will readily be seen that there was no entrance corresponding to the present Worcester College lodge. Entrance was by the archway shown by Loggan and which still survives at the extreme north of the medieval buildings. The difference between the medieval ground level and that of the street outside as it had become by the 17th century is clearly observed as one passes the arch. After the arch one went along a lane bounded by a wall on the right and the present Senior Common Room block on the left. After about 30 yards one turned sharp left through a gap between two of the houses (it can just be detected on Loggan). It is the nature of this entry that explains the siting of the Malmesbury arms whose red

John Whethamstede, shown in the Catalogue of Benefactors of St Albans Abbey, *held at the British Library.*

griffin is still the brightest feature of the front quad. Malmesbury Abbey was the owner of the site, so it kept what was, if one thinks of Gloucester College from the inside, the central situation, and ensured that what you saw as you entered the front quad was the Abbey crest, larger than anyone else's, straight ahead of you. The medieval buildings as they survive are in the main, wrecked shells. Much of the pleasure and beauty of the buildings lay in their decoration and furnishing. The Chapel had stained glass showing the Crucifixion, the Virgin, and John the Baptist. Hearne says (he is writing of one of the cottages): 'and in the same windows here as in many other places about the College, several rebuses, mottos, and allusions as also portraitures of saints, bishops and monks with inscriptions under them, were (either by the childishness of students not since long inhabiting therein or by the iniquity of envious times) for the most part blemished and obliterated'. The plate and the Chapel furniture were taken away in early 1539.

The present College has only one thing, stone apart, which belonged to Gloucester College. This is a manuscript: a collection of tracts directed against Lollardy, well-written and illuminated, taken away at the Dissolution, and generously returned by Merton College in 1938. It was given to Gloucester College by John Whethamstede, abbot of St Albans (1452–65). Whethamstede was a conspicuous figure: learned, a kind of proto-Humanist, the reformer of the finances of St Albans, a great builder and organiser. He did much for Gloucester College, rebuilding the St Albans accommodation, and funding the construction of its library and chapel. The book is one of those he gave to the College library. It is mentioned (with a sister volume now in the British Library) in a very long list made at St Albans of *Expensae Abbatis Johannes Whethamstede Notabiles*. It is in as good order as it was when his donative verse was written in it.

Perhaps this manuscript, not strikingly beautiful, but decently elegant, and thoroughly well made from the best materials, tells one something about the ethos of Gloucester College. The abbots who were responsible for its building and furnishing were largely the sons of minor gentlemen or yeoman farmers; all had serious administrative experience, and knew how to get value for money; their nature and that of the institutions they served was such as to leave them to think of future generations and to prize durability. They did not seek great magnificence in their Oxford establishment, for many had magnificence and to spare in their abbey buildings at home. Nor did they wish to provide luxurious accommodation for monk students. They did seek a degree of solid comfort for men who were intended to live disciplined, but not sparse, lives at the University, and who, as monks of ancient and often rich abbeys, were men of some consequence. (The annual allowance of the Westminster monks at Gloucester College was £10, later £6 13s. 4d., a year – a man could be counted a gentleman in the 15th century on £5 a year.) And they wanted the College to be well and agreeably built and to be worthy of the great institutions that it served. The stone of the cottages is, in a sense, of a piece with the manuscript. They are well built of excellent Cotswold stone, so good that it has

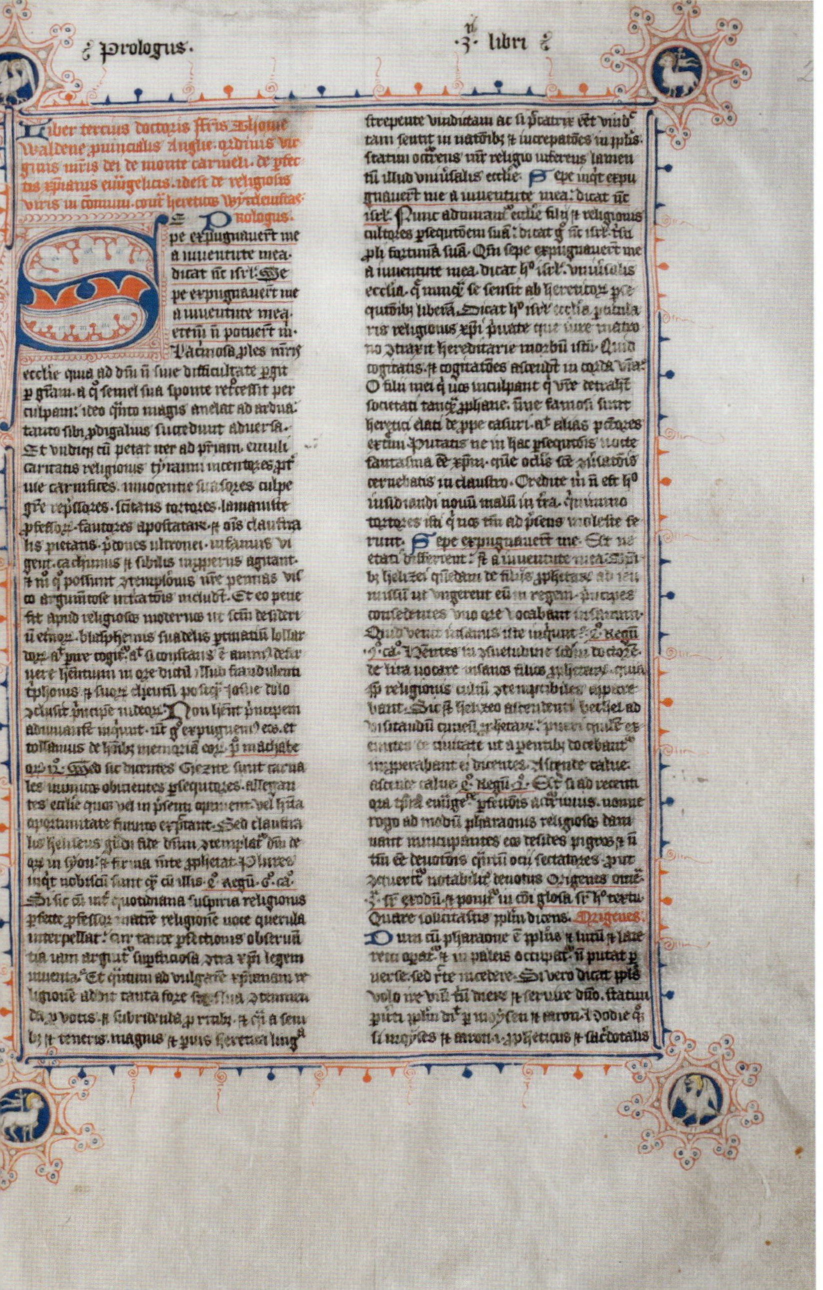

Above: *The Whethamstede manuscript, bound in oak boards with a vellum back.*

Left: *Opening page of the Whethamstede manuscript with lambs and eagles motif characteristic of his books.*

never needed re-facing, while nearly all the stone of the 18th-century buildings opposite has required renewal at great expense.

The cottages say something else about the spirit of the Benedictines. Their very nature is an expression of the particularism of the monasteries. This appears even in the roof-line: one roof up a little, another down a little. Yet the range marries together extremely well. Gloucester College was an extraordinary architectural phenomenon in its combination of unity and diversity. Everywhere it revealed its composite nature; yet there was a real, if strange, pattern and order to it. As it stood in its last, its finest, days, it revealed the good sense and the very good taste of the Black Monks.

2. Gloucester Hall and the Greek College

Roger Ashley

The federal nature of Gloucester College, controlled as it was by the various monasteries that supplied its student body, made it easy prey for Henry VIII's commissioners at the Dissolution in 1539. Three years later, its 'aedifices, chambers, walks and gardens' were granted by the Crown to the new bishopric of Oxford. It was removed from the episcopal endowment in 1547, though that was to be the subject of lengthy, litigious dispute. Subsequently, the Chapel was taken down and the Hall partially demolished. It was in this condition when a detailed survey was made in 1559, which minimised the value of the property and very likely overdid the dilapidations. It also recorded two pensioner monks. In the following year, it was purchased by Sir Thomas White, granted by him to St John's College and, three months later, established as an academic Hall, leased to William Stock, its first Principal, for 20 years at a rent of £7 a year. The rent was not the only benefit in hand; as late as 1581–2, 43 loads of stone were taken from the site to St John's. The College was not to relinquish its freehold until 1714.

There was money to be made in a new Hall; there were rents and fees from the students. Stock would have expected a better living than he had enjoyed as a Fellow of St John's and, with a brief interlude as that College's President, he was Principal for 13 years. But Halls were much more than simply places of residence. Their corporate

Canterbury Quad, St John's College.

Ralph Agas' map of Oxford 1578 from Oxonia Depicta, *by William Williams, 1733. Gloucester Hall is shown on the far right of the map (see detail on p.101).*

activities, worship, teaching, dinner and supper, recreation even, had been codified in 1490. Gloucester, St Mary, St Alban, Hart and St Edmund Halls had tutors and presented to degrees. Moreover, they played an important part in introducing Italian cultural values to 16th-century Oxford and helped change the concept of colleges as institutions for graduates only.

It is likely that the daily routines of the Hall were not dissimilar to those at other institutions within the University, such as Corpus Christi College, about which more is known. If that were so, then the day started with Chapel at four or five in the morning. Although the Gloucester Hall Chapel had been demolished, organised prayer did continue, since there is evidence that it was conscientiously avoided by some. It would have taken place in somewhat improvised surroundings, possibly in the gallery above the screens end of the Hall, where Loggan's view shows a four light window. Private study or lectures took up the hours between six and ten with dinner at 11. Fellows, graduates and undergraduates ate at trestle tables arranged laterally around a central hearth in which fires were rare. Indeed, fuel was a useful benefaction, sometimes given for particular days of the week. The smoke escaped, in a somewhat desultory fashion, through the *louvre* at the apex of the roof, visible on Loggan's engraving. Strict distinctions of status would have been represented in the seating arrangements and table coverings. There was a Fellows' table, which also catered for important visitors, a Master of Arts and Bachelors' table and a 'third for people of lower condition', the undergraduates perhaps. Those gazing about them might have seen panelling, but more likely whitewashed walls with minimal hangings. Instead, at Gloucester Hall, their attention would have been held

Left: *Pump Quad.*

by the great roof and two light windows with four centred heads. Contemporaries attested that it was a splendid space.

The food was hearty, not finicky. The main dish was meat, divided into large portions for each table. After dinner, there was further study until five, followed by a free hour. Supper was at six and was made up of cold meats, 'staples' (that is butter, cheese and beer) and occasionally a pottage of oatmeal and gravy. 'Disputation', when theses were formally defended and attacked, filled the hours between supper and bed at nine or ten. Sleeping accommodation was notoriously chill and the upper chambers or cocklofts were much sought after. It might have been worse. But the Benedictines had built and lived well, and there were substantial grounds, meadows, closes, a hop yard and an orchard. How much the dilapidations were a distraction is a difficult question. Certainly, Principal Stock needed an entrepreneurial spirit. His lease was a repairing one; he had undertaken to spend 100 marks on repairs in the first five years.

A strict and embracing regimen did not necessarily weigh heavily on all the junior members. An official visitation of the Halls in 1582 and 1583 warned students that they must 'stand not idle at the gates of there houses nor walke the streetes or resorte to tavernes but studiously imploye the tyme to the certain increase of learning and vertue'. One parent of a Gloucester Hall student, Bevill Grenville, wrote to his son, Dick, in 1638, 'shun drinking houses & drunken companions as poyson … neither let the view of other youth's liberty or misspending their time diquiett or ensnare you'. Halls had inherent problems as well as advantages. Nicholas Fitzherbert, in 1602, thought that the discipline there was laxer than in colleges and that consequently they attracted the sons of the rich and noble who were more difficult for the authorities to control. His argument has a circular nature to it.

For their part, many of the senior members showed a determined reluctance to conform with the state religion, as it had been defined by the Anglican settlement. Perhaps the Hall was less visible, since it was outside the city walls and somewhat on the University's periphery. The leadership was certainly suspect. Principal Stock, says Anthony Wood, was always '*in animo Catholicus*', coming from a College re-founded in 1555, during Queen Mary's reign. The University as a whole was exempt from the control of the Archdeacon of Oxford, so much in the way of religious discipline depended on the Chancellor, the Earl of Leicester, whose patronage might be eclectic and attitude ambivalent. The consequence was that the Hall enjoyed 20 years of relative freedom, until larger, political forces obliged the authorities to take a firmer line.

It was during that period that a number of Fellows, expelled from their Colleges for their Catholic sympathies, were able to find a haven there. Edmund Reynolds, turned out of his Fellowship at Corpus Christi, came to the Hall in 1568 and stayed there until his death at the age of 92 in 1630. Stock made him deputy Principal. Another was the martyr, James Fenn, who left Oxford for the Continent and returned to be executed at Tyburn in 1584. Some were sleeping dogs who were permitted to lie, remembering the Catholic 'restoration' of the University that commenced in 1553,

Sir Kenelm Digby, engraving by Robert Van Voerst, after Anthony Van Dyck.

Thomas Allen, engraving by J. Bretherton.

hoping the world might turn again. A notable example was Thomas Allen, a 'church Catholic' or outward conformer, highly favoured and regarded. He was expelled from his Trinity Fellowship in 1570, took up residence on the south side of the quadrangle, near the entrance to the park, and was neighbour to Edmund Reynolds for 60 years. If Anthony Wood is to be believed, Allen was on such close terms with Leicester 'that few matters of state passed, but that he had knowledge of them and nothing of moment was done in the university, but Allen gave it to him in writing'. In short, he was useful in more ways than one. Queen Elizabeth consulted him about a star, and Leicester 'offered' him a bishopric, despite his ambiguous religious life.

Serious mathematical and scientific interests in Oxford were maintained by coteries, and one of the most important was that around Thomas Allen. It included men like Henry Savile of Merton, Miles Windsor, Robert Cotton, William Camden and John Selden, and the most talented mathematicians of the day, to whom he was tutor and friend, Philip Sidney, Robert Hegge, Robert Fludd, Kenelm Digby (his pupil, whom he called the 'Mirandula of his age') and Brian Twynne, Fellow of Corpus Christi. Gloucester Hall was on the geographical periphery, but it was intellectually connected, albeit a little unusually.

Theoretically at least, its students attended lectures on set texts by the regent masters, on grammar, rhetoric, logic, arithmetic, geometry, astronomy and music. They engaged in disputations and they took their BA after three years and their MA after seven. The curriculum was in many respects medieval, but at Gloucester Hall the 'other arts' included pure mathematics, history, English and judicial astrology (the casting up of horoscopes for a wide variety of purposes). Numbers were good. There were 73 in residence in

1572; eight MAs, 13 BAs, 43 undergraduates, eight servants and one resident, Sir George Peckham. The one resident is a reminder that Principals stretched for income had the option of offering bed and board. Peckham was a good lodger: Anthony Wood reckoned that he spent £100 on repairs.

Catholicism remained, for the authorities at least, the notorious characteristic of the Hall. They feared 'the contagion' entering the student body. In 1577, it was said that the Hall 'is greatly suspected and yet the Principal there presented nothing'. His critics meant to imply that Principal Russell, newly in post, was keeping quiet about the religious irregularities of his staff, students and lodgers. Sir William Catesby was living in Sir George Peckham's old rooms; his daughter, born there in the same year, had been 'christened not by the vicar but by a popish priest'. There were limits. When Christopher Bagshaw, a well-known Catholic, succeeded Russell in 1580, Chancellor Leicester forced his resignation. Bagshaw became a priest and a great nuisance to authorities both Protestant and Catholic. His successor, John Delabere, was a Leicester placeman. The Hall was visited and questions were asked. Who gives catechism? Is grace said and by whom? How many attend communion? Are there any prohibited books? Are illegal feast days being observed? Despite the turmoil, the Hall continued to matriculate: 36 students in 1576; ten in 1577; 34 in 1578; 19 in 1581.

In the following year, Leicester might have been thinking of Gloucester Hall, when he complained to Convocation 'of secret and lurking Papists amongst you, which seduce your youth and carry them over by flocks to the Seminaries beyond Seas'. Certainly, amongst those flocks were students from the Hall who went on to the English School at Rome, where the account of their interviews in 1600 is instructive. John Faulkner had done some reading in History and English at the Hall, but he had seen his tutor seldom, once a month perhaps, and had kept clear of public and private disputations. He had become less rather than more staunch in his faith, and that was something he now regretted. John Fowler confessed to lapsing during his time at the Hall. Perhaps the need to keep a low profile had resulted in dangers of another kind for him. Thomas Hodgson was older, 38. He had been at the Hall for 17 years, studying astronomy and judicial astrology before he had been licensed to practise medicine. For such as these, the dangers were real. Of a total of 56 Elizabethan martyrs at Oxford, seven came from St John's and four from Gloucester Hall.

There were other Gloucester Hall Catholics, some famous, others less so. George Blackwell was archpriest to the clandestine mission to England, 1597–1607. Nicholas Garlick was at first a schoolmaster.

Above: *Thomas Coryate, engraving by William Hole.* Opposite: *Gloucester Hall benefactors' book, with entries by Degory Wheare and Tobias Garbrand.*

(Three of his pupils became priests; one was martyred.) He subsequently attended the English College at Rheims and took part in two missions to England. He was executed at Derby and beatified in 1987. Robert Catesby, son of Sir William and a prime instigator of the Gunpowder Plot, was shot at the skirmish at Holbeche House, Staffordshire in 1605. John Faulkner became a Jesuit and was a missionary in Oxford in the 1620s. John Davis was one of Thomas Allen's converts. He was a promising mathematician, but joined the army as one of the earl of Essex's men. Lucrative public office, marriage and wardship were lost when he became involved in the rebellion of 1601. He was present at the performance of Shakespeare's *Richard II* that was specially commissioned by Essex's followers on the eve of their abortive uprising. He saved himself

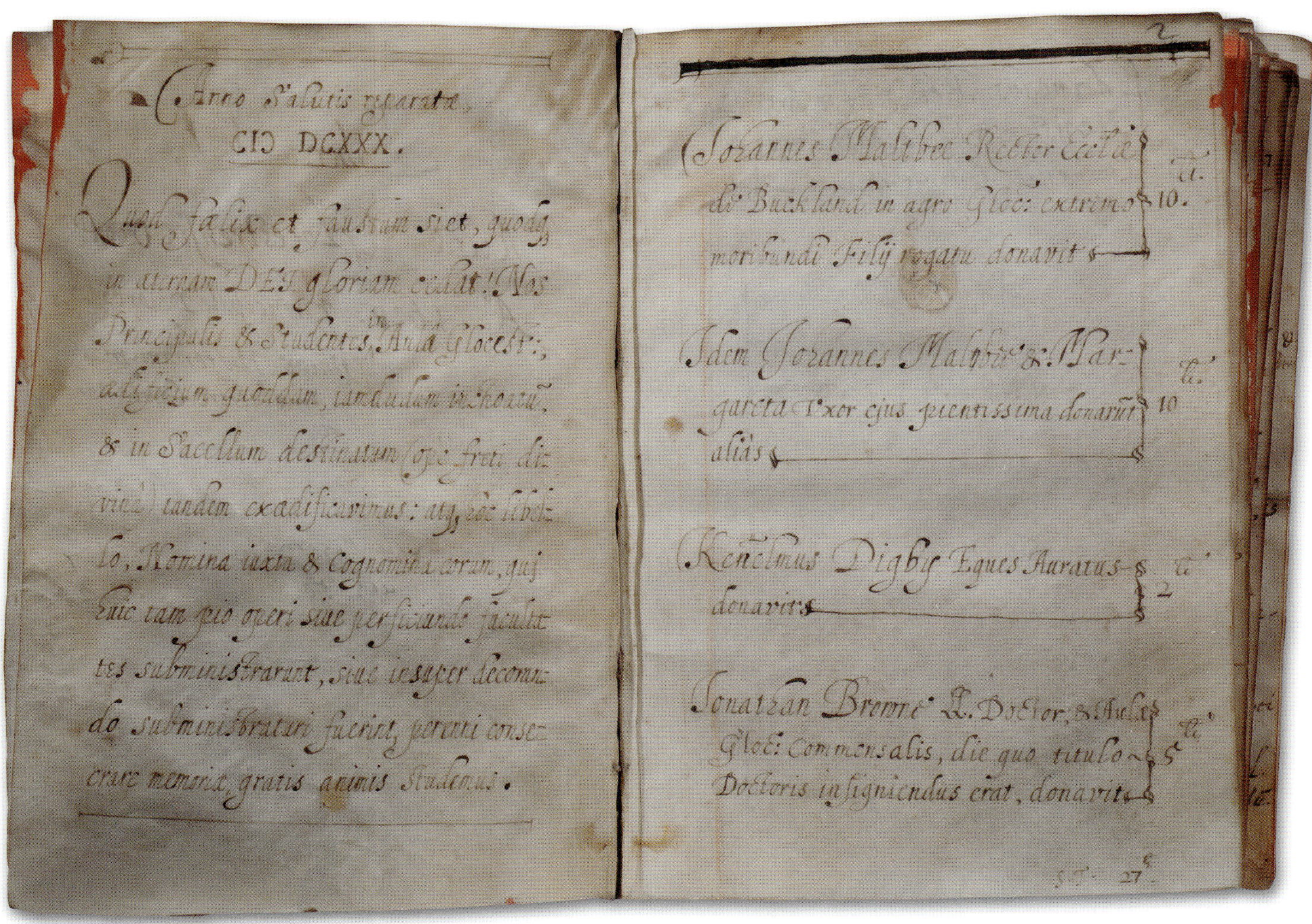
Anno Salutis reparatæ,
CIↃ DCXXX.

Quod fælix et faustum siet, quodq; in æternam DEI gloriam cedat! Nos Principalis & Studentes in Aulâ Glocestr:, ædificium quoddam, iamdudum inchoatū, & in Sacellum destinatum ([illegible] divini) tandem exædificavimus: atq; hoc libello, Nomina iuxta & Cognomina eorum, qui huic tam pio operi sive perficiundo facultates subministrarunt, sive insuper decommodo subministraturi fuerint, perenni consecrare memoriæ, gratis animis Studemus.

Johannes Maltbee Rector Ecclesiæ de Buckland in agro Gloc: extremo moribundi Filij rogatu donavit — li. 10.

Idem Johannes Maltbee & Margareta Uxor ejus pientissima donarunt alias — li. 10

Kenelmus Digby Eques Auratus donavit — li. 2

Jonathan Browne L.L. Doctor, & Aulæ Gloc: Commensalis, die quo titulo Doctoris insigniendus erat, donavit — li. 5

from the scaffold by 'telling who was in with the deepest', and years later re-emerged in an attempt to move the Wadham endowment to Gloucester Hall.

The alumni of this period were not remarkable solely for their Catholicism. Henry Perry took his BA from the Hall, during passage from Balliol to Jesus. Despite the potentially disruptive influences there, he followed a career in the Welsh Anglican church and as a linguist. More curious was Thomas Coryate, 'the Odcombian leg-stretcher' who walked around Europe and, on a subsequent expedition, reached Surat in India where he died. He left record of his adventures, most famously in his *Crudities,* and remains an inspiration to imitators on bicycle or foot.

The Hall lost some of its momentum during John Hawley's tenure of office, 1593–1626. Hawley was a lawyer and career administrator; his interests were elsewhere. He spent much time as the Vice Chancellor's stand-in and supervised the building of the Bodleian quadrangle, a time-consuming task. Furthermore, the supply of distinguished, dispossessed, but Catholic, Fellows from the colleges had naturally dwindled. Yearly matriculations dropped to five and the shortfall was made up by letting the vacant rooms to strangers, who might or might not be less trouble than students. The many separate lodgings made it a pleasant and quiet retreat for elderly men and women. Nonetheless, Hawley's period of office was not devoid of talent. Thomas Wroth, author and politician, was much involved in Somerset politics and colonial enterprise. He supported the impeachment of Charles I, but was pardoned at the Restoration. Walter Rumsey, philosopher, scientist and musician, became Chief Justice of Wales. Matthew Griffin was chaplain to Charles I and engaged in debate with John Milton. Kenelm Digby, another protégé of Thomas Allen, who bequeathed him his library, was a courtier

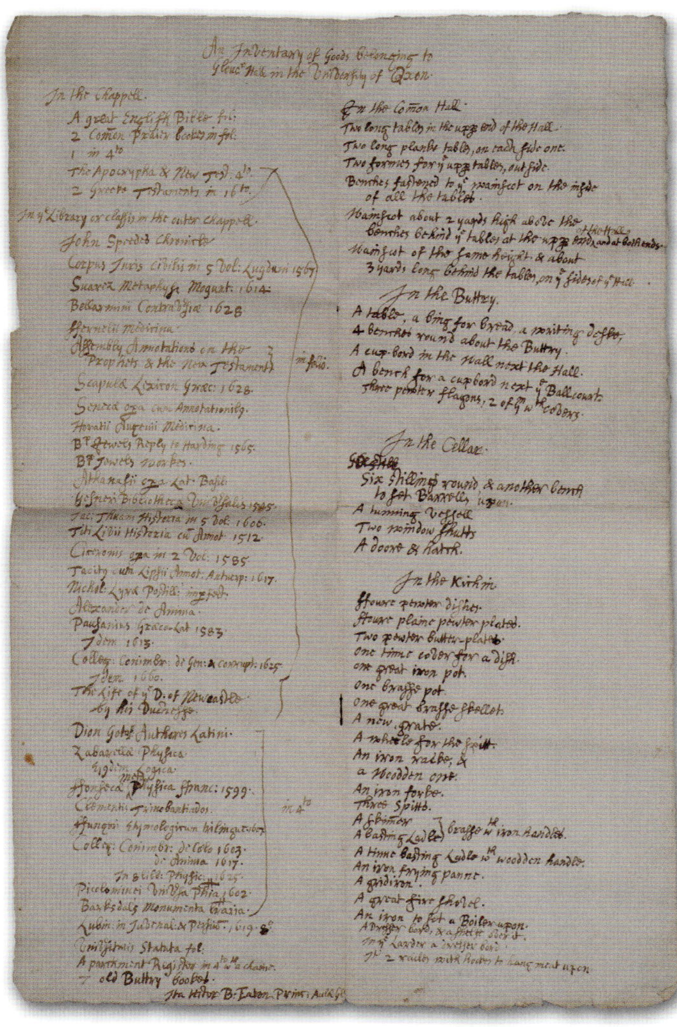

ABOVE: *Inventory of the contents of Gloucester Hall compiled by Byrom Eaton* c.1692.
RIGHT: *Commentary on Aristotle's* De Anima *by Alexander of Hales, printed by Theoderic Rood 1481. It was given to Gloucester Hall by Clement Barksdale, graduated BA 1629. Mentioned in the* c.1692 *inventory above.*

and leading Catholic intellectual. 'Waterworks Sandys' improved the Warwickshire Avon and the Wye for navigation.

Degory Wheare, with his wife and several children, had settled in the Hall in 1621. The following year he became the first Camden Professor of Ancient History. His inaugural address became the basis of his *De Ratione et Methodo Legendi Historias* (1623): in Latin, then English, it became a standard work. When he succeeded Hawley as Principal, the matriculations increased, sometimes to more than 20 a year. He collected money for improvements, spending £90 on the Chapel and recording it in a *Liber Donationum* (1630). Two tutors were maintained at £5 a year each; presumably they also benefited from their pupils' fees. But, as the country drifted into civil war, the Hall emptied of students. Dick Grenville was taken away by his father, Bevill, to join the invasion of Scotland in 1639. There, to his father's annoyance, he fell sick. He returned to the Hall and a bombardment of paternal letters, and died in Oxford in 1641.

Gloucester Hall was deserted after 1642, when the Royalist army made Oxford its headquarters. Some of its buildings were

ABOVE LEFT: *Benjamin Woodroffe, by Robert White.* ABOVE RIGHT: *The ruins of Beaumont Palace, converted by Benjamin Woodroffe for the Greek College, afterwards known as Woodroffe's Folly; the hostel was pulled down in 1804, but the ruins survived until the construction of Beaumont Street.* BELOW LEFT: *Small stone figure of St Michael and the dragon, found when building work was being carried out in 1824.* BELOW RIGHT: *Silver tankard presented to Gloucester Hall by Philip Harcourt in 1696.*

used as a forge for the repair and manufacture of sword blades under the supervision of William Legge, Master of the Armoury. Wheare died in 1647 and John Maplett was nominated by the Chancellor, the Marquis of Hertford. Within four months, they were both ejected and the Parliamentarian Visitors appointed Tobias Garbrand, a Calvinist. The Hall and Principal continued along exiguous lines; in 1649 there were three MAs, one BA, two readers and various officials, and Garbrand was given £50 to augment his income.

Maplett was reinstated in 1660, but withdrew two years later, and Byrom Eaton was appointed in his place. Eaton did not depend on profits from the Hall. He was vicar of Nuneham Courtenay and subsequently Archdeacon of Stowe and Archdeacon of Leicester. The Hall was a convenient place of residence for him. The Poll tax return of 1667 lists the Principal, his wife and two children and three servants, alongside three BAs, eight or nine undergraduates, two more servants, a family called Ford and a widow. By 1675, Anthony Wood could write of only one 'scholar' in residence, and he, with others, commented on the continuous decay of the buildings. It was the year that David Loggan published his engraving. At the same time, John Aubrey indulged his fancy: 'if I could be Principall of Gloucester Hall … I would undertake to make it an ingeniose Nest and would decoy thither several honest and ingeniose persons of either University and some from beyond Sea'.

Eaton resigned in 1692 and another Principal of independent means succeeded him. Benjamin Woodroffe accumulated an impressive collection of offices: Canon of Lichfield and Christ Church, Lecturer of the Temple, Chaplain to Charles II and James II and rector of St Bartholomew at the Royal Exchange. Much was expected; much was spent. At first he 'by his great interest among the gentry, made it flourish with hopeful sprouts'. But by 1700, student numbers had dwindled to nothing.

The Principal's interest was elsewhere. A year into office, with workmen around him putting the buildings in order, he had revived an idea that had been circulating in the University since 1677: to make Gloucester Hall a college for theological students of the Greek church. They would be drawn from Greece or Syria for a course of six years and supported by charitable societies or the

Opposite: *The backs of the cottages, watercolour by Bernard Gotch.*
Above: *The cottages today.*

Levant Company. The first batch of five arrived in 1699, wearing 'the gravest habit worn in their own country'. The Jesuits swiftly took note and promised superior accommodation and more appropriate teaching in Paris, where Louis XIV had endowed a college. Students absconded; scandals ensued. In 1705, the Greek church withdrew its approval and, two years later, the last student, Helladius, departed for the Continent. The experiment was over. For a century, its memorial was 'Woodroffe's Folly', the hostel built at the west end of what is now Beaumont Street. Woodroffe claimed to have lost some £2,500 over the scheme. He became bankrupt in 1709 and was imprisoned in the Fleet, a signal distinction. He died in 1711. The future of the Hall would be decided by his successor.

3. The Foundation of Worcester College

Emma Goodrum

In 1697 a Worcestershire baronet named Thomas Cookes signalled his intention to leave £10,000 for the establishment of a college at the University of Oxford. Sir Thomas had links with the University, having matriculated from Pembroke College in 1667, although he left without taking a degree. However, he proved reluctant to finalise the benefaction during his lifetime and his will, dated 19 February 1697, was so open in its wording that the new college became a battleground for different factions within the University. It was not until 17 years after Sir Thomas Cookes' intentions became known that Worcester College was finally established.

Sir Thomas married twice but both marriages were childless, and he therefore sought to preserve his name through educational foundations. Prior to his announcement in 1697, he had already endowed and refounded Bromsgrove School in 1693, and established a free grammar school at Feckenham in 1696; the final part of his educational scheme was the proposed foundation at Oxford, which would give preference to boys from his schools in Worcestershire. Aside from naming the College after the county of his birth, Sir Thomas Cookes made no decisions as to the details of his benefaction. The terms of his will stated that the money could be used to 'erect and build an ornamentall Pyle of Building' in which to establish a new college, or to 'raise or endow such other [existing] College or Hall in Oxford with … Fellowships and scholars places'. To settle the final destination of the £10,000, Cookes appointed a large and unwieldy body of trustees, consisting of the 25 heads of colleges and halls in the University, the Archbishop of Canterbury, and the bishops of Worcester, Oxford, Gloucester and Lichfield.

Left: *Sir Thomas Cookes (c.1648–1701), unknown artist,* c.*1672.* Right: *Lady Mary Cookes (1659–95), the first wife of Sir Thomas Cookes, unknown artist,* c.*1672.*

Deed declaring the intention of the Trustees to settle Sir Thomas Cookes' benefaction on Magdalen Hall, 22 November 1707.

When word of Sir Thomas Cookes' intentions reached Oxford, Benjamin Woodroffe, the Principal of Gloucester Hall, began a campaign to secure the benefaction to raise his Hall to the status of a college. It appears that Sir Thomas was initially attracted by Woodroffe's plans and the support for them he had obtained from the Archbishop of Canterbury and the Bishop of Worcester. Encouraged by this, and ignoring the fact that Sir Thomas was plainly reluctant to act during his lifetime, Woodroffe went so far as to have a charter of incorporation and set of statutes for the new college passed under the Great Seal in 1698. Both were rushed and later found to have been drawn up in a form invalid in law. More seriously in the short term, the provision the statutes contained for the appointment of future provosts to be made by the Chancellor of the University, rather than the benefactor and his heirs, so angered Sir Thomas Cookes that he broke off all negotiations with Woodroffe.

Gloucester Hall's chances of securing the benefaction had been seriously jeopardised by Benjamin Woodroffe's disregard for the wishes of the benefactor, and the rift that opened between them created space for a rival claim by Balliol College. Balliol proposed to engraft the Cookes Fellows onto its foundation and, by 1700, had reached the point of drawing up a set of statutes that were approved by its Visitor. The Archbishop of Canterbury, however, was still a firm supporter of Gloucester Hall and worked hard to reach a compromise with the Chancellor that would allow Sir Thomas Cookes and his heirs the right of nominating future provosts. Sir Thomas seems to have seriously considered the Balliol proposal but his desire to follow the guidance of the Archbishop, coupled with the concessions granted by the Chancellor, restored Gloucester Hall in his affections and, in August 1700, Cookes wrote to the Chancellor stating that he wished to 'compleat my Charity at Gloster Hall'. Yet, once again, Sir Thomas Cookes delayed making the final arrangements and when he died on 8 June 1701, his will was unchanged from that made in 1697 and, for all the machinations of Benjamin Woodroffe and the archbishop, made no reference to Gloucester Hall. The direction of the benefaction remained uncertain and, as control of the money passed to the group of trustees, mostly members of the University among whom Woodroffe was unpopular, the position of Gloucester Hall seemed worse than ever.

Benjamin Woodroffe had to act, and quickly. Once Sir Thomas Cookes' will had been proved, Woodroffe introduced a bill to the House of Lords with the purpose of reducing the number of trustees from 30 to four, eliminating the opposition factors from inside the University and leaving only the Archbishop of Canterbury, the Bishop of Worcester, Woodroffe himself and Sir Thomas Cookes Winford, Cookes' nephew, heir and executor. The bill passed its final reading in the House of Lords on 13 April 1702, despite the not disinterested evidence of Roger Mander, Vice-Chancellor of the University and Master of Balliol, who reported that Sir Thomas Cookes had declared he was 'off of Gloucester College [sic] and intended his charity for Balliol College'. Facing strong opposition from the University, led by Mander, the bill was defeated in its second reading in the House of Commons by 43 votes to 27.

Roger Mander had so far thwarted Benjamin Woodroffe's attempts to secure the benefaction for Gloucester Hall, but his hopes for Balliol fared little better as it soon became clear that it too could not attract sufficient support from the Cookes trustees. After William Delaune was appointed Vice-Chancellor of the University in October 1702, the matter lapsed and it was not until William Lancaster took office in 1707 that the settlement of the Cookes benefaction was raised again. By this point, the lack of action had provoked something of a scandal and Lancaster requested that the Archbishop of Canterbury call a meeting of the trustees. Three meetings were scheduled, for 21, 22 and 23 November 1707, and although the archbishop and the four bishops failed to attend, 19 of the 25 University representatives were present. The claims of Balliol College and Gloucester Hall were dealt a seemingly fatal blow: Balliol was rejected on the grounds that the money should go to a Hall, as they were poorer; Gloucester Hall, however, was deemed too poor, necessitating too much of the benefaction to be spent of the construction of the 'ornamentall Pyle' directed by Cookes' will. A third claim on the benefaction was now put forward as a compromise, and 16 of the trustees, forming the required majority, signed a declaration that the £10,000 should be settled on Magdalen Hall (then situated next to Magdalen College). This, of course, was not the end of the matter. Sir Thomas Cookes Winford, believing it to have been his uncle's intention to settle the money on Gloucester Hall, refused to release the £10,000 in his possession as executor, and in 1708 he petitioned the House of Commons for a private bill to settle the issue.

Lord Harcourt (1661–1727), by Godfrey Kneller.

Unfortunately, for Benjamin Woodroffe at least, he was no longer in a position to take advantage of the heir's support for Gloucester Hall. He had expended significant sums in the establishment of the Greek College, and had laid out £1,300 to purchase land near Gloucester Hall in anticipation of its foundation as a College. The delay in the settlement of the benefaction contributed to the financial problems he acquired on his second marriage, and in 1709 Woodroffe was committed to the Fleet Prison for debt; he died in London on 17 August 1711, aged 73.

The remaining trustees petitioned the Court of Chancery in an attempt to force Sir Thomas Cookes Winford to relinquish the

Anna Dei gratia Magnae Britanniae

Above: *The Foundation Charter, 29 July 1714.* **Right:** *The Great Seal of Queen Anne on the Foundation Charter.*

£10,000, plus the interest that had accrued since the will had been proved in 1701. However, the death of Benjamin Woodroffe had changed the dynamics of the situation, removing that opposition to Gloucester Hall that had been based purely on matters of personal unpopularity. In addition, the Keeper of the Great Seal, Lord Harcourt, now saw an opportunity to increase his influence in the University by placing his own man in the vacant seat at the head of a new college. In April 1712, Chancery began a full-scale investigation into the benefaction, taking depositions from a number of Sir Thomas Cookes' neighbours and servants, as well as from various members of the University. The records that survive in the College Archives indicate that, although a general consensus emerged that Sir Thomas had 'frequently expressed his thoughts of having the [money] settled at Gloucester Hall above any other place

Above: *The main quad from the Lodgings.* Right: *Mural from the Chapel of Sir Thomas Cookes holding a model of Worcester College.*

in the University', no clear evidence of a firm decision could be found, and according to his steward, 'Sir Thomas Cookes was of a very fickle and unsteady temper … and was not determined within himself at any time in his lifetime where the [benefaction] should be settled'. The Court sat on 31 October 1712 and the Lord Keeper, determined to bring the matter to a conclusion, ordered Sir Thomas Cookes Winford to hand over to the Court the £10,000 plus interest accrued. If the trustees saw this as a victory they were soon to be disappointed; Lord Harcourt subsequently decreed that, although Sir Thomas Cookes had not decided where to settle the benefaction in 1696 it was clear 'by undeniable Evidence' that he had later decided in favour of Gloucester Hall. The 1707 decision in favour of Magdalen Hall was set aside and the matter was referred back to the trustees. The subtext was more than clear: the trustees were to settle the benefaction on Gloucester Hall.

In ensuring that Gloucester Hall would be raised to the status of a college, Lord Harcourt was able to guarantee that he would have a voice in the University, for in November 1712, Harcourt's chaplain Richard Blechinden was appointed Principal of Gloucester Hall. The strong expectation was that he would become the first Provost of Worcester College. It was widely held at the time that, although the appointment of the principal was in the gift of the Chancellor of the University, Blechinden had secured the position by the efforts of his patron. William Stratford, a Canon of Christ Church, wrote at the time that 'His Lordship disowns his having had any hand in making Blechinden Principal, but nobody will believe'.

The trustees, led by the new Vice-Chancellor Bernard Gardiner, maintained their opposition to any intrusion on their right to determine the site of the benefaction and continued to promote the cause of Magdalen Hall for some time. Deliberations over the settlement moved at a slow pace and, in May 1713, Lord Harcourt issued another decree requesting a written update on their

progress. Another factor in the delay was the fact that Gloucester Hall could not be elevated to the status of a college as it did not own the freehold of its site; this was held by St John's College, having been purchased by its founder in 1560. Although the President and Fellows agreed to its alienation in principle in February 1713, it was not until November 1713 that the approval of their Visitor was given. The purchase of the site, which covered approximately the area of what is now the Main Quad, Pump Quad and the Provost's Rose Garden, was completed on 20 August 1714. Ultimately, the trustees based in the University were helpless to resist the combined patronage of the Lord Keeper and Francis Atterbury, appointed Dean of Christ Church in 1711, and they converted many of the trustees to the cause of Gloucester Hall throughout 1713. Finally, at a meeting of trustees on 28 November 1713, Gloucester Hall received the required majority of 16 votes and was awarded the benefaction.

As ever, things did not run smoothly. There was a further delay of nine months as the trustees were forced to devise new statutes for the College when those written by Benjamin Woodroffe in 1698 were found to be 'repugnant to the Statutes of the University ... [or] Sir Thomas Cookes' will'. The many delays had one happy outcome however, in that the initial benefaction of £10,000 had increased to £16,000 by the time it was settled. The letters patent from Queen Anne granting Worcester its status as a college, and approving the new statutes, were issued on 29 July 1714. The deliberations over Sir Thomas Cookes' benefaction had lasted the entirety of the Queen's reign, beginning in 1702 as she came to the throne and concluding only three days before her death.

Silver and silver-gilt bowl given to the College by Sir Henry Hoo Keate, one of the first undergraduates to matriculate at Worcester College.

Some Stipulations in the Statutes of 1714

No Fellow to have property of his own of more than double the value of his Fellowship, or hold a living rated at more than £10 per annum in the King's Book. Scholars to be elected on St. John the Baptist's Day. Dinner in Hall made compulsory by the statute *De mensis.* The clause *De exercitiis* providing for an arduous series of disputations in the public hall. On all public occasions and in Hall Latin to be the language employed, though an exception made for College meetings. The Provost to receive £80 a year, the six Fellows to receive £30 a year apiece, and the scholars £13 6s. 8d. The Fellows and Scholars also to receive fourpence a day for commons, and twopence a day for drink and bread. The Vice-Provost, the Dean, and the Bursar to receive £5 a year each, and the Chaplain £10 a year. The steward or seneschal to receive £5 a year. There are to be four college servants, the *promus* [butler], *coquus* [cook], *ianitor* [porter] and *tonsor* [barber]. The two first to receive £5 a year, the *ianitor* £8 a year, and the *tonsor* 20s. Bachelors to give a dinner on taking their degree, or pay 20s. to the Provost, and Masters of Arts not to spend more than 40s. over the public dinner they gave on taking this degree. The College gates to be closed before ten o'clock, and the keys given to the Provost. The Provost, Bursar and one of the Senior Fellows to visit the College estates annually, or at least once in seven years. If ever the revenues of the College went down, the salaries of all the officials to be curtailed; but any advantage that came of an increase in revenue to go to the common chest. The register to be kept in the Bursar's room, but the Provost might take it to his lodgings at his pleasure. Two iron chests to be kept in a convenient place, one to contain muniments, the other money and the rarer of the College silver and plate. Three keys to the two chests, to be kept by the Provost, Bursar and Dean. Two copies of the statutes to be made: one to be kept chained in the library, so that all who are interested in them might read; the other to be in the possession of the Provost. They are to be publicly read, at least once a year, by the Provost or Vice-Provost.

As summarised in* Worcester College *(1900)
by C. Henry Daniel and W.R. Barker

4. Dr George Clarke, Nicholas Hawksmoor and the Design of Worcester College

Eleonora Pistis

In 1714, after all those years of protracted legal wrangling, Gloucester Hall was transformed into Worcester College thanks to the £10,000 benefaction that Sir Thomas Cookes had originally designated for the construction of an 'ornamentall Pyle' at Oxford. One year later, Mrs Margaret Alcorne stated in her will that she would donate to the newly founded Worcester College a 'whole year's profitt' of her 'real estate … towards building a chapell, or other buildings, or repairs as the provost for the time being shal approuve of the best for the said College'.

Thus, on 8 June 1720, most likely before the proud eyes of Provost Richard Blechinden and some curious Fellows, the master mason and his workmen commenced the erection of the new building. As archival documents attest, with Alcorne's benefaction of £798 0s. 3d. the construction of the College began with the block intended to house the Hall, Chapel and Library. The College design that the master mason was working on is captured in a 1720 print by University engraver Michael Burghers **[fig 1].**

The design itself was the fruit of the long relationship between the amateur architect Dr George Clarke (1661–1736), Fellow of All Souls, and his friend Nicholas Hawksmoor (1661–1736). The first, besides having held numerous political offices, is commonly described as the unofficial architectural consultant at Oxford University at that time. The second, Nicholas Hawksmoor, was an expert architect trained by Sir Christopher Wren, who could boast an involvement with the most important new buildings in the kingdom. It is likely that Hawksmoor met Clarke, who from 1702 to 1705 was joint Secretary to the Admiralty, during the construction of the Naval Hospital at Greenwich in 1704. Hawksmoor was also familiar with Oxford through his collaboration with John Vanbrugh on the building of Blenheim Palace in Woodstock.

As early as 1708, Clarke had begun speaking with Hawksmoor about an ambitious plan of architectural and urban reform for the city of Oxford. In the years that followed, the two worked on new projects for All Souls, Queen's and Brasenose Colleges, for which they experimented with new layouts and architectural languages. Together they saw the rise of the new Printing House (the Clarendon Building) and paved the way for the realisation of a new '*forum universitatis*'. The latter, located between the Old Schools Quadrangle in the Bodleian and the Church of St Mary the Virgin, was conceived to accommodate the enlargement of the University Library (the future Camera) financed by one of their interlocutors, Dr John Radcliffe.

But Clarke and Hawksmoor had actually dreamt of something greater: a new '*forum civitatis*', a University church in the form of a majestic ancient temple, as well as other civic structures that, alas, were

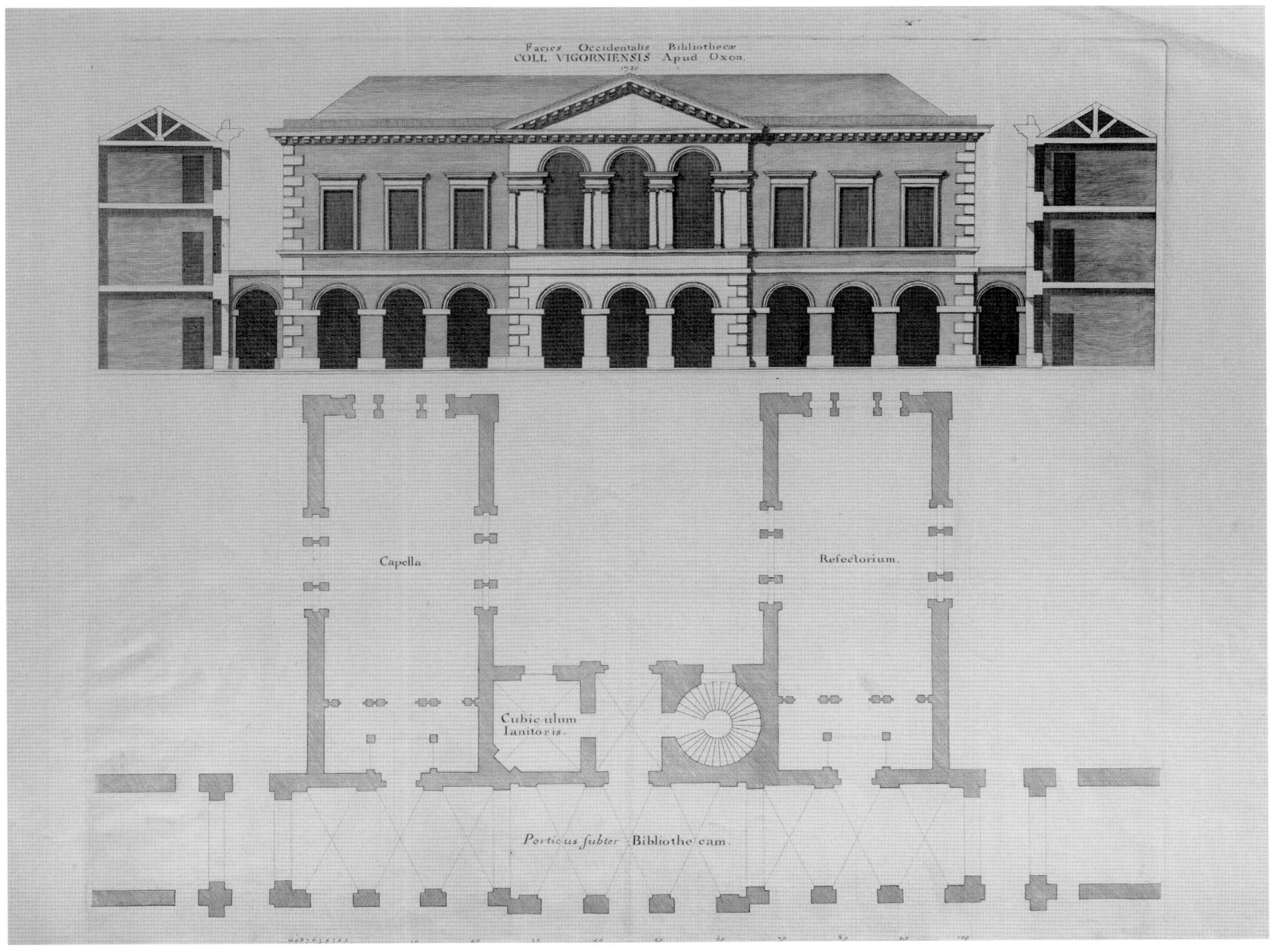

Engraving of the west side of the Library by Michael Burghers, 1720 [fig 1].

never built. According to their vision, city gates, obelisks, cupolas, temples and columns would have decorated a new Oxford. To escape the 'chaos' and 'tumult', as Hawksmoor had written to Clarke in 1715, the edifices and the institutions that these would have housed were to be rationally organised through 'Draughts and Designes for repairing the Old & Erecting New fabricks for the embelishment, and use of the University as may in time Come to perfection'.

When Clarke and Hawksmoor were discussing the Worcester College design, they not only had in common the same dreams and projects, but they also shared the same profound architectural culture. All this was mirrored in Clarke's extensive library, and partly in Hawksmoor's smaller one. Clarke's collections contained a surprising number of English and foreign treatises and manuals concerning architecture, as well as prints dedicated to ancient and modern buildings. It also included the important books and drawings that had once belonged to Inigo Jones, which Clarke in his will described as 'esteem'd to be very valuable'. There was more: Clarke also collected numerous designs by contemporary architects and artists. In this library-laboratory, books, prints and drawings converged with architectural practices, creating new ideas that were constantly tested through debate and comparison. Such a process undoubtedly characterised Clarke and Hawksmoor's approach to the design of Worcester College.

Today, the story of the College's design process can be deduced from the drawings preserved in the Library. Clarke and Hawksmoor's attention seems to have initially been concentrated on the building that would accommodate the most important and representative centres of the College's life: the Hall, Chapel and Library. Hawksmoor and Clarke began by studying the appropriate location for the edifice. The site on which the new college was to be erected was at the time in a peripheral zone, west of the city centre, surrounded mainly by extensive greenery. The solutions that had previously been adopted for the colleges located in the centre of Oxford, conceived with two quadrangles closed in on themselves, now had to be abandoned. For Worcester College they instead contrived an innovative U-shaped block that opened towards the city, while its back faced quiet areas suitable for meditation. The Hall and Chapel projecting eastward were connected by a central range that contained, on the first floor, a Library facing the west side of the building. Underneath, an open arcade was to connect and rationally organise the various parts of the College while offering protection from the rain.

We can imagine Clarke and Hawksmoor, once this basic layout was defined, weighing the possible architectural solutions to be adopted. It was perhaps Clarke who gave the first general and basic suggestion, and it was perhaps Hawksmoor who, as an architect, employed his imagination to transform the vague ideas of his amateur friend into real architecture. Perhaps in order to play with the architectural culture that he and Clarke shared, as well as to rouse attention and curiosity, Hawksmoor unusually annotated his drawings for Worcester College with the sources that, even down to small details, had inspired his projects. He used the books that lay open in piles on his worktable.

One of these was undoubtedly François Blondel's *Cours d'Architecture* (1698), open at page 599. In it, Hawksmoor could see the arch at the entrance to a bridge at Saintes, Charente. This was characterised by two archways framed by Venetian windows and surmounted by an attic. On the basis of this model Hawksmoor put together a scheme with a triple arch surmounted by a pediment, to be applied to the central bay of the first floor Library façade. To the side of the sheet containing a rapid sketch of the design, he carefully annotated: 'Arc sur le Pont du Xaintes' **[fig 2]**.

Top: *Sketch design for the west elevation of the Library by Nicholas Hawksmoor [fig 2].*
Above: *Alternative design for the west elevation of the Library by Nicholas Hawksmoor [fig 3].*

In another incomplete proposal Hawksmoor illustrated the same façade articulated by giant Doric pilasters on high pedestals – the first framing the Library's windows, the second the ground floor arcade. It was a solution reminiscent of 16th-century Rome, but Hawksmoor, on second thoughts, judged it to be 'Another way not so good as the Arc de Xaintes' **[fig 3]**. He thus continued working on this last theme, proposing, in an incomplete sketch, a variant with a façade without pediments and a low attic, which, as in ancient Rome, would have been covered in inscriptions. It is perhaps only after these attempts that Hawksmoor obtained larger and more expensive sheets in order to elaborate a complete project that included not only the definition of the Library, but also of the Hall and Chapel.

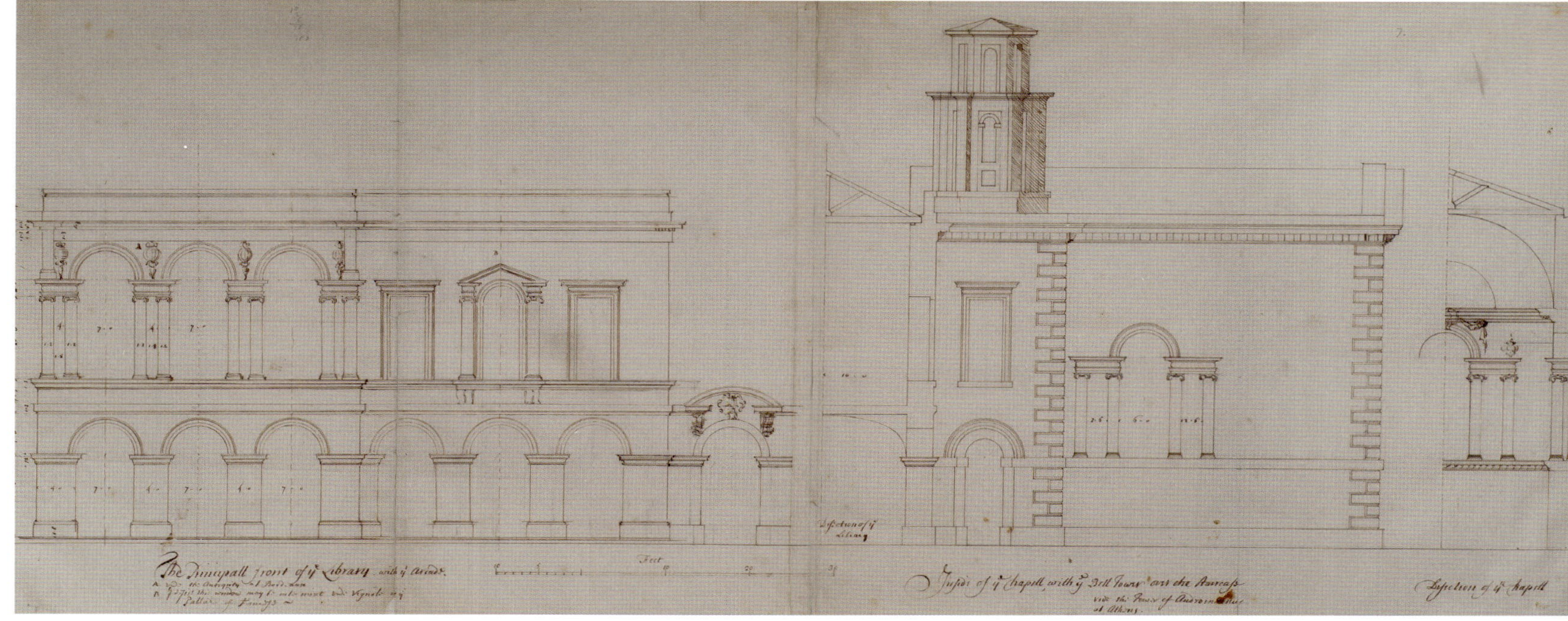

Above: *Design for the Library and Chapel by Nicholas Hawksmoor [fig 4].* Right: *West façade of the Library [fig 5].*

On one sheet **[fig 4]** he continued working on the previous idea for the central bay of the Library's façade. He returned to the layout with three Venetian windows without a pediment, but placed reliefs of ancient burial urns on the spandrels, noting that he was greatly influenced by 'the Antiquity at Bordeaux'. Once more it was a book that had served as inspiration for Hawksmoor, who, as far as we know, had never left England: Claude Perrault's edition of *Vitruvius* (1684), which illustrates a Roman structure with similar decorative elements.

In the flanking bays of the façade, characterised by three openings, the central window became another occasion for erudite quotation. The round-headed window framed by a broken-based pediment resting on volutes was taken from the second floor of the façade of the Farnese Palace in Rome, begun by A. da Sangallo the Younger and continued by Michelangelo. This time Hawksmoor was consulting the prints of the *Palazzi di Roma* drawn by Pietro Ferrerio and, misinterpreting their inscriptions, he wrote on the margin of his design: 'vide Vignole in the Palazo of Farnese'. Another sheet illustrates the Library's side façade, whose main feature is a window that recalls the central window of the Palazzo dei Conservatori in Rome, although this is not explicitly cited as a source.

Hawksmoor then concentrated on defining the Chapel façades, of which he showed the three visible sides and a north-south section. Here he was without doubt alluding to Inigo Jones' Queen's Chapel at St James Palace. Although Hawksmoor only noted: 'The Rusticks [i.e. quoins] according to Mr Jones, at St James Chapell', he borrowed much more from the celebrated model. In fact, the model inspired the entire idea of a simple rectangular pedimented block, with bracketed cornice, quoins and a Venetian window in its east end.

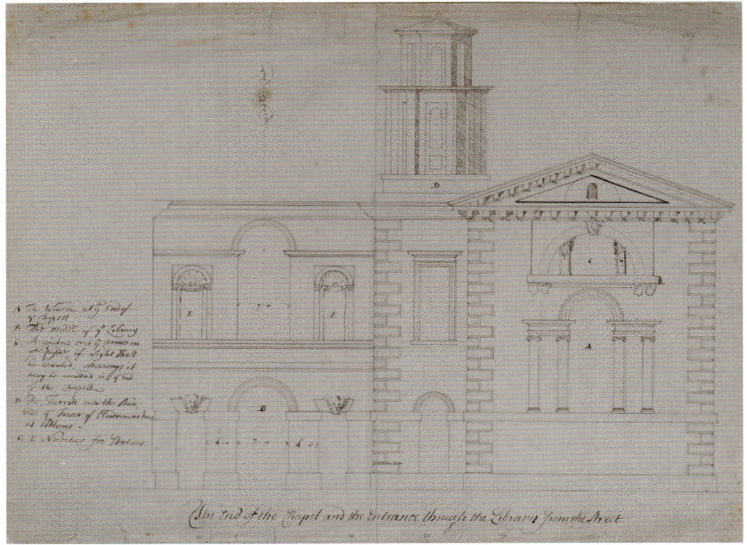

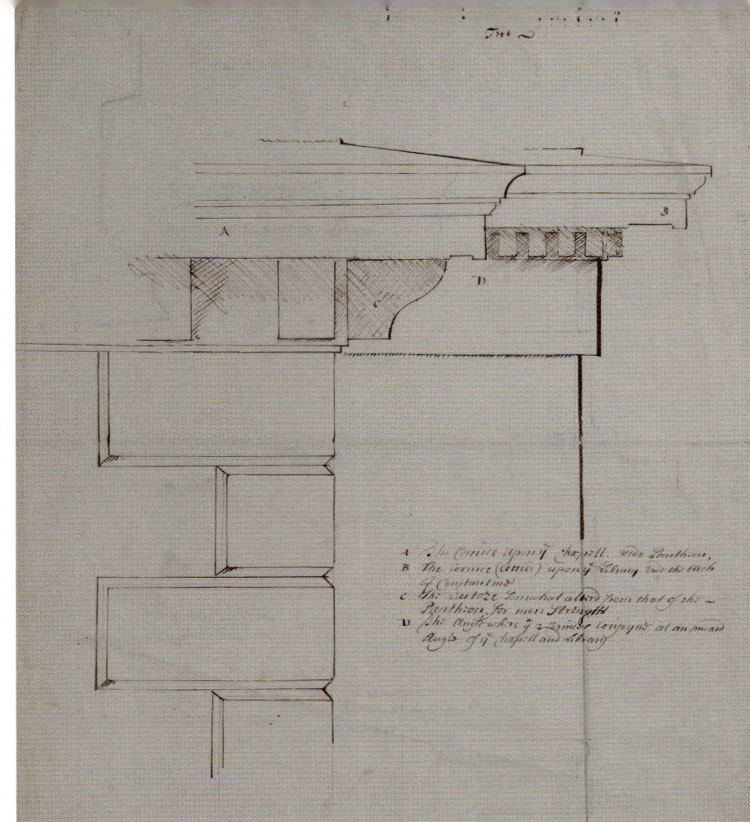

Top left: *Design for the east elevation of the College by Nicholas Hawksmoor [fig 6].* Above left: *Perspective drawing by Paul Draper based on Hawksmoor's drawings for the front of the College [fig 7].* Top right: *Design for some architectural details by Nicholas Hawksmoor [fig 8].* Above: *These architectural details as realised on the existing building [fig 9].*

On the sheet that illustrates the Chapel's north side, thanks to an ingeniously constructed flap of paper, the façade appears in two variants. With the flap down, it contains a single Venetian window placed high above a stringcourse. With the flap up, the Venetian window is placed in a lower position, surmounted by a roundel and flanked by windows surmounted by niches with statues. The south façade, shown on a different sheet of paper, has an isolated Diocletian window as in the first solution for the north façade, but, as in the second solution, it is in a lower position. A third sheet of paper then illustrates the north half of the College's east front, which today faces Beaumont Street **[fig 6]**. At the east end of the Chapel's façade Hawksmoor again placed a Venetian window, above which he proposed to locate a thermal window.

The façade's central section, which would have framed the entrance to the complex, is characterised by two round-headed openings one above the other, flanked on the ground floor by narrow openings, and on the upper floor by niches. Finally, at the corner between this façade and the Chapel's south side, Hawksmoor

Top Left: *George Clarke's design for the west elevation of the Library [fig 10].* Left: *Design for the west elevation of the Library, probably drawn to George Clarke's directions [fig 11].* Above: *Alternative design for the west elevation of the Library, probably drawn to George Clarke's directions [fig 12].*

drew a bell tower. This, with two-tier octagonal tops, emulates, as he himself explained, 'the Tower of Andromachus at Athens' – better known as the Tower of Winds.

Hawksmoor's drawings show only half of the entire design, but it would not be incorrect to suppose that the whole arrangement would have been symmetrical. Thanks to Paul Draper's drawing **[fig 7]** we can imagine how Worcester College would have faced Beaumont Street if Hawksmoor's project had been realised. It is not however clear whether there would have been two towers or only one, in order to indicate the presence of the Chapel.

On the final sheet of paper the architect worked on the details of the project **[figs 8–9]**. Besides the above-cited source for the quoins, he wrote: 'The Cornice upon the Chapell vide Pantheon'. Actually, this detail does not correspond with any of the Pantheon's cornices, not even with its depictions found in various treatises. However, it is an element that the architect had used widely in his famous London churches. In particular, it is similar to one cornice of St Mary Woolnoth Church in London, which in another drawing he defined as a 'Cornice Like that in the Temple of M[ars]. Vindicator'.

The free reinterpretation of ancient elements is, on the other hand, clearly admitted in another detailed annotation for the Worcester College project: 'The cartoze *somwhat* [sic] alterd from that of the Pantheon, for more strength' [emphasis mine]. Hawksmoor's task was to draw inspiration from the sources of the past, manipulating them in order to reconstruct a surprising new form of architecture. This is perhaps the reason why Hawksmoor focused Clarke's attention on his ability to connect various architectural elements, as in: 'The angle where the 2 cornices [of the Chapel and the Library] conjoyne.' A solution that is not different, for example, from one in Christ Church Spitalfields, London. Clarke, who was definitely more erudite, but less gifted with 'good fancy', seems to have appreciated his friend's work.

Indeed, two drawings attributed to Clarke show two similar variations on the designs proposed by Hawksmoor. For the Library façade's central part Clarke proposed a variation with a rustication, while in a second design he sketched in the central part of the first floor of the façade a temple-front recalling the lateral elevation of the Arch at Orange as drawn by Giuliano da Sangallo, or the loggia of the Pazzi Chapel in Florence **[fig 10]**.

Top Left: *Design for the east front of the College, perhaps by William Townesend [fig 13].* Above: *East façade of the College [fig 14].* Below: *Design for the College entrance by George Clarke [fig 15].*

The other surviving drawings, most likely drawn up by someone under Clarke's supervision, combine the preceding solutions with the superimposition of a Doric temple-front **[figs 11–12]**. In one solution the temple-front is juxtaposed with the façade's first level; in the other, it has a giant order supported by high pedestals and occupies the façade's entire height.

In summary, the design of the Library shown in the 1720 print mentioned above includes the definitive layout indicated by Hawksmoor, as well as some minor variations that were probably introduced by Clarke. It almost completely corresponds to what we see today **[fig 5]**.

The façade is supported by a powerful arcade. The central sector juts out and on the ground floor it is emphasised by the insertion of quoins in the side pilasters. On the first floor the scheme recalling the Arch of Saintes, surmounted by a triangular frontispiece, is of the Ionic order and its external bays, if compared to the previous designs, are elongated. A survey of the Library's façade has demonstrated that Hawksmoor's measurements, carefully noted in his drawings, were used in the final construction. The width of the arches below the Library is seven feet, the length of the base of the central pilasters is four feet, while their height is ten feet. The side bays, on the other hand, have three equal rectangular openings surmounted by a cornice. Finally, registered in the stone are some fragments from the erudite discussions between Clarke and Hawksmoor: the quoins 'according to Mr. Jones' – of the exact size that Hawksmoor indicated – and the cornice after the 'Pantheon' **[fig 9]**.

It is, though, more difficult to assess the façade facing Beaumont Street today, which was not illustrated in the 1720 print. Clarke's last dated proposal appears on the print published in *Oxonia depicta* (1733) by William Williams. But neither this nor any of the other surviving designs exactly corresponds to what was realised and registered for the first time in a survey by Charles Barry on 29 May 1837. The entrance of the College seems to be a combination of designs by Clarke and William Townesend **[figs 13–15]**. But there is no evidence for the dating and the authorship of the cornice and the roundels with festoons above Venetian windows of the Hall and Chapel.

Construction work, as already mentioned, began in 1720, but dragged on until about 1790, and the history of the building site

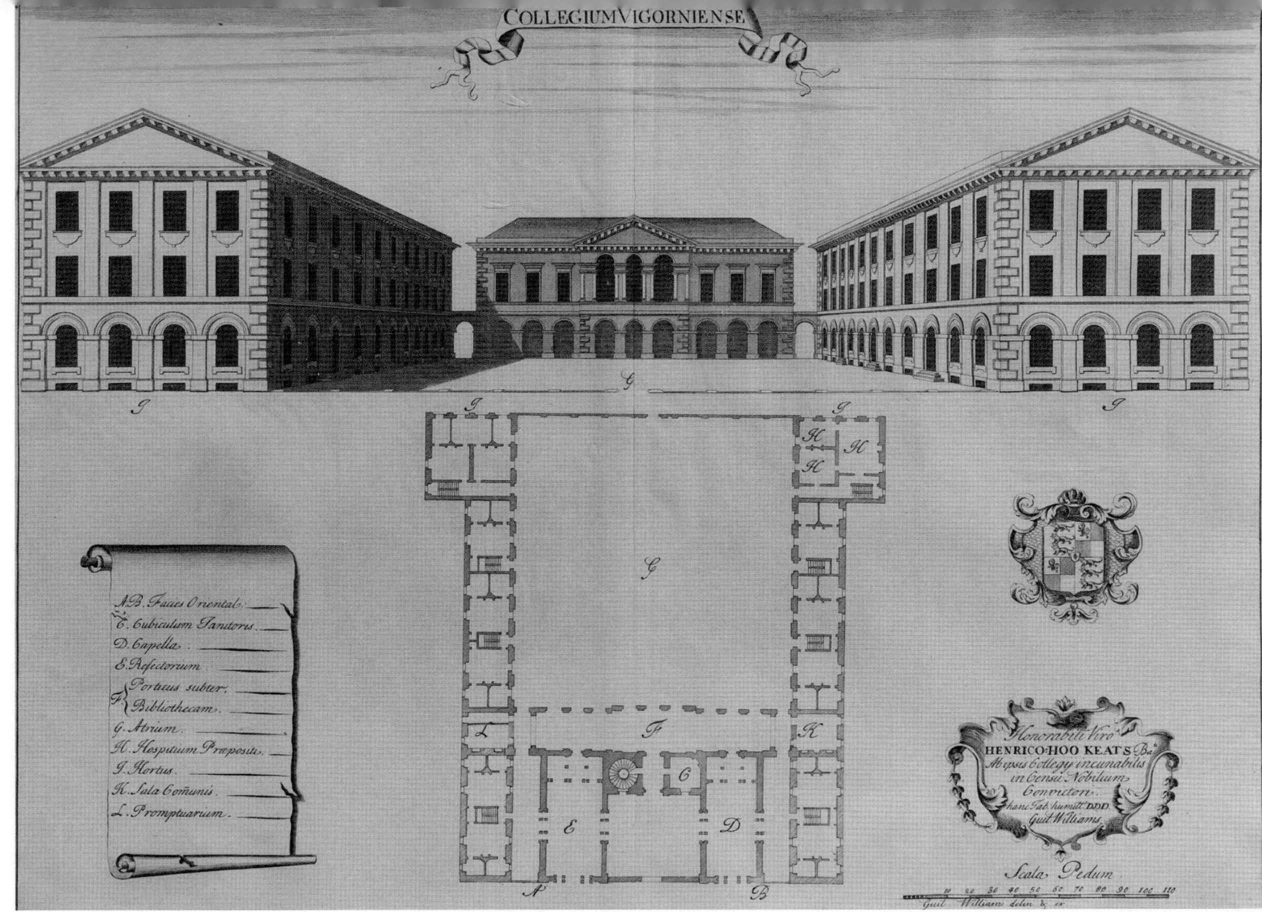

William Williams,
Oxonia Depicta, 1733,
plate LVIII [fig 16].

from 1720 to 1736 – the year of Clarke and Hawksmoor's deaths – is incomplete and barely documented. We know that in 1720 a carpenter was paid 'for boared and work covering the walls and making the centons for the mason' and that in 1722 work was being prepared for the 'floor and guttae for the Library', which in 1735 was still to be finished.

When Clarke wrote his will dated 12 November 1734, two years before his death, he left clear instructions for the completion of the College: £1,000 was destined 'towards finishing their Library'. He also left £3,000 'for building nine Chambers between the Library and Provost's Lodgings at *Worcester* College; and with the remaining Sum, for finishing the Chapel and Hall of that College'. As he himself declared, his intention was that 'the said nine Chambers be built according to the Plan and Elevation in the … Oxonia Depicta' **[fig 16]**.

The project presented in William Williams' volume shows a second wing, symmetrical to the one that Clarke designed, which would have allowed for the creation of another U-shaped arrangement that would have opened towards the west. Some of Clarke's drawings show the preliminary designs. They propose a façade whose ground floor recalls the arcade below the Library, while the upper floor façade is characterised by a regular sequence of simplified pilasters, which frames a double level of windows.

However, in a second codicil to his will, dated 8 January 1735, Clarke indicated that the chambers had to be 'built according to the Plan and Elevation mark'd on the back by me with the two first Letters of my Name, G.C. For I find there is not room enough between the Corner of the Library at Worcester College and the Provost's Lodgings, as they now are, for nine Chambers, according to the Design in the aforesaid Book'. The design has not survived, but a comparison with what was actually realised demonstrates that the residential range had been transformed from a 'single' to a 'double pile' in order to place smaller rooms in the rear.

A few months later, in March 1735, Hawksmoor responded to one of Clarke's letters asking for an 'estimate for finishing the Library, the Chapel and the Hall'. However, the interiors of the Hall and Chapel were only finished in the late 18th century, by James Wyatt, and transformed anew in the 1860s and 1870s by William Burges. But in 1738 Elizabeth Sheppard, under the name of 'Shepilinda,' observed that 'the Library is a fine room & handsomly built; & is now furnish'd with Books by the Donation of George Clarke'.

The two easternmost staircases on the north range of the Quadrangle were built by Clarke's trustees between 1753 and 1759. The rest of the range, including the Provost's Lodgings, was completed by 1776, following Henry Keene's modifications. The College's corresponding south range, however, has never been constructed. In its place stands, persistent through time, the original medieval building. Thus, when entering Worcester College quadrangle today we can admire a fascinating stratification of three centuries of memories.

5. Benefactors, Endowment and Finances

Provost Richard Smethurst

In 1864, halfway through the 300 years of Worcester College's history, William Burges was decorating the ceiling of the Chapel with paintings of the Garden of Eden and the expulsion from it. This might be taken as a metaphor for the College's finances, for this was the middle of its most prosperous period: the dreadful decline that followed began when work was in hand on the companion scheme to redecorate the Hall. As C.H. Daniel and W.R. Barker put it in the College History published in 1900, 'In the year 1878 began that fall of rents which has lowered the revenues of the College to a point probably below that of any other in Oxford.'

This is a curiously fatalistic remark, considering that C.H. Daniel had himself been the Bursar since 1877, and was only to demit office on being elected Provost in 1903. F.J. Lys, who became Bursar in 1908 (and continued to act as 'Senior Bursar' for nearly 20 years after he was elected Provost in 1919), stops short in his 'Account of a Stewardship' of outright criticism of his predecessor, though he does report that it was said that Daniel became Bursar 'because he found the work of a Tutor, which he spoke of [to Lys] as a "ploughing of sands", too uncongenial and because his light-hearted treatment of tutorial duties provoked the antagonism of T.W. Jackson [the Senior Tutor]'.

Lys does, however, trenchantly criticise the Fellows of a slightly earlier period for 'a shocking legacy of neglect or mismanagement', asserting that

> *For a considerable time before the great agricultural depression which began in the late 1870s the revenue had been ample in relation to the needs of the College, and if it had been used wisely the penury which followed need never have been so injurious. Internally it was prosperous, too. At that time when all undergraduates resided within its walls it had more rooms than most Colleges. In a list of members of Congregation and of numbers on the books … in the former category only six Colleges, and in the latter, seven, had a higher number.*

Lys was in a strong position to criticise, for he undoubtedly halted and reversed the steep decline, in which endowment income was halved over a 20-year period from 1878. Lys increased it by about £4,300 from the 'pitiably meagre' figure of about £2,250, 'out of which scholarships and exhibitions, as well as Fellowship emolument, had to be provided', adding, 'though it [i.e. an endowment income of £6,550] still remains undesirably small, and to a Bursar who has had in his hands the riches of another College might seem wholly insufficient'. The key to this success was his sale, in 1919, of almost all the College's farms, re-investing the proceeds in 'trustee securities yielding nearly 5%'. His timing was excellent: grain prices, for example, were 255% above their 1900 levels in 1920, but by 1928 were back to within 5% of the 1900 figure, and fell below it in the 1930s.

The estates Lys sold had been built up over the two centuries since Worcester College had been founded. Neither of the two predecessor institutions on the site had any endowment of their own to pass on. Sir John Giffard's initial gift of the site to Gloucester Abbey was most generous, but in the College's overall history it proved a mixed blessing. For it seems to have undermined the plans, dating from 1277, of the Presidents of the Chapters General of the Benedictine Order to create a St Benedict's College. Whether such an institution would have attracted endowment of its own (in a climate in which the development of the doctrine of purgatory was helpful to long-term benefactions), instead of remaining, as Gloucester College did, forever dependent on the prosperity and support of its parent monasteries; and whether, if it had gained such independence, it would have escaped being seized for the Crown at the Dissolution – all this is for counterfactual historians to debate. From a Bursarial point of view, it is appropriate simply to dream briefly what even a modest endowment would have been worth now, after over 700 years of compound interest.

Miniature of Sir Thomas Cookes and his first wife.

The only 'endowments' that Gloucester Hall brought to its transformation into Worcester College were its buildings, which as Loggan's print of 1675 pitilessly shows, were in a dilapidated state. Again, counterfactual historians might enjoy tracing the consequences if Sir Thomas White, in 1560, had decided to found St John's College here instead of apparently following a dream about a tree and finally siting it on St Giles'. Or if Dorothy Wadham had been willing, around 1608, to accede to the demands of the Principal of Gloucester Hall, Dr John Hawley, that he should become the first Warden of the College she was establishing in accordance with her late husband's wishes. Or if Dr Woodroffe's scheme for a Greek College had succeeded.

As it was, even this inheritance of decaying buildings was a help. For it was clear to those engaged in the protracted and often bitter wrangling over the destination of Sir Thomas Cookes' legacy that the money involved was insufficient to fund both the 'Ornamentall pyle' and the Fellows and Scholars to be housed within it. In November 1707, the majority of the Trustees voted that the funds should go to Magdalen Hall because it already had buildings capable of receiving the Fellows and Scholars, 'in which case the whole expense of building will be saved'. Five years later, the Bishops of Worcester and Oxford reported that (only) £1,000 would be sufficient to put the buildings of Gloucester Hall into the necessary order: they were mistaken.

Buildings apart, the other element of endowment which Worcester College received from Gloucester Hall, albeit indirectly and not for 25 years, was the benefaction of Sarah Eaton, daughter of Dr Byrom Eaton, Principal of Gloucester Hall 1662–92. Barker and Daniel remark that it is almost impossible to discover anything he did as Principal. But through his daughter's legacy, his purchases of estates in Northamptonshire in 1680 and 1681 came to Worcester College to endow seven Fellowships and five scholarships, to complete the building of the North range, including the splendid Provost's Lodgings, and, as we shall see, in the next century to provide a substantial supplement to the stipends of the Provost and Fellows.

Following Cookes' original legacy, Sarah Eaton's was one of two benefactions which augmented it by 'the incorporation in each case of additional Fellows and scholars, with a corresponding enlargement of the buildings for their accommodation'. The other major benefactor was the 'second founder', Dr George Clarke,

1714.

In Gratefull remembrance of such as do good to Worcester Colledge their names & their benefactions are here Registred. —

In Nov. 1714. The Reverend Mr Samuel Cooke of Worcestershire gave us in his life time a Study of books consisting of more than 400 Volumes. Our First & most kind Benefactor

April. 1717. Mr Edw: Dupper the first Steward of our College gave us a copy of our statutes writ by himselfe & very elegantly bound

June 16. 1717. Died — Mrs Margaret Alcorne a Widow Gentlewoman in St Giles Oxon. who by will bequeathed to this College one halfe of her Estate real & personal; After a long time at Law it was adjudgd, that the real estate was in another & yt she had no interest in it beyond her own life. So we have only one halfe of the personal estate, which is to us clear of all charges, Seven hundred ninety eight pounds & three pence. Which sum by Decree in Chancery in pursuance of Mrs Alcorns will is appointed to be layd out in buildings; wch buildings are accordingly begun. June 21. 1720. Namely, A Chappel, Hall & Library.

ABOVE: *Engraving for the Oxford Almanack of 1741, showing some of the College's benefactors.* LEFT: *Benefactors' book, kept by the first Provost, Richard Blechinden.*

who besides contributing designs for the new buildings and £5,000 towards them, and donating important collections to the new library, also endowed six Fellowships and three scholarships by transferring his estates in Wiltshire to the College.

Cookes' legacy, which had grown to £16,000 by the time it was received, had first been invested in stocks, but later was invested in estates. A lengthy letter to Richard Blechinden, the first Provost, from his patron Lord Harcourt, dated 31 December 1723 from Downing Street, records Harcourt's receipt on behalf of the College of the purchase deeds of an estate in Northamptonshire for £13,000. Harcourt continues: 'I would now congratulate you upon your being Provost of a wealthy College had I not some reason to fear your cares will increase with your wealth.' Harcourt then tells his protégé that someone from the Fellowship ought to go to see the estate and take possession of the Manor House 'which I hear lies in a most ruinous condition … so bad no one dares lye in it'. The extraordinary detail of Harcourt's instructions are a good indication not only of his support for and detailed interest in the new foundation (in which he had played a decisive role) but also of his fondness for Blechinden. This is reinforced by a charming postscript from his grandson, the childish writing contrasting with the handsome copperplate of the official secretary, asking Blechinden to visit him when he is in London and if he is at school 'beg a playday for us'. (Harcourt was said by a contemporary observer, Dr William Stratford, to have secured £600 from the King and three or four hundred pounds from the Prince for the College, but the archives have no record of this.)

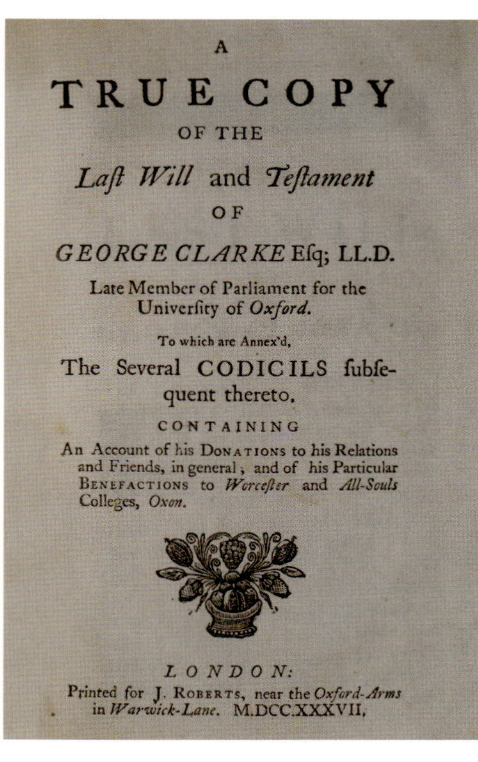

A

TRUE COPY

OF THE

Laſt Will and *Teſtament*

OF

GEORGE CLARKE Eſq; LL.D.

Late Member of Parliament for the Univerſity of *Oxford.*

To which are Annex'd,

The Several CODICILS ſubſequent thereto.

CONTAINING

An Account of his Donations to his Relations and Friends, in general; and of his Particular Benefactions to *Worceſter* and *All-Souls* Colleges, *Oxon.*

LONDON:

Printed for J. Roberts, near the *Oxford-Arms* in *Warwick-Lane.* M.DCC.XXXVII.

Far left: *George Clarke, Studio of Godfrey Kneller.* Left: *George Clarke's will, 1737.* Below: *Large silver-gilt cup and cover bequeathed by George Clarke, with receipted bill, 27 May 1737, for gilding and engraving the cup as requested in Clarke's will.*

Cookes' benefaction initially yielded £754 a year, of which just over £500 was earmarked for the stipends of the Provost, Fellows, College Officers, Scholars, and senior College staff such as the Porter, Butler and Cook. The total revenue, including Caution Money and battels, was £827 in 1715; total expenditure was £810, a surplus insufficient to begin the ambitious building programme. But a bequest from Margaret Alcorne (there are various spellings) in 1717 provided the impetus to make a start. Her first wish was to found Fellowships and scholarships. But her will was contested – despite containing penalties if her relatives did this – and was held to apply not to her estates but to her personal property alone, so the College eventually received £798 0s. 3d. There is no record of her connection with the College, but she lived in Oxford, and Blechinden clearly knew her well, for not only was he an executor, he was also capable of estimating, within weeks of her death, that only £600 would eventually come to the College, and that this would therefore be insufficient to found even one Fellowship, so it was put towards building work instead.

The next recorded contribution to construction is a loan of £1,000, against a bond signed by George Clarke in 1733 and duly repaid by his executors in 1736, made by Roger Bourchier, one of the Fellows. Roger Bourchier was unlikely to have been rich: he matriculated at Gloucester Hall in 1695, when Woodroffe, in his early years, was building up the numbers. He was a 'pauper puer' – that is, he undertook work in the Hall as a domestic servant – graduating in 1699, and taking his MA in 1702. He taught Woodroffe's Greek students and was a Fellow of Gloucester Hall, becoming one of the first Fellows, and Vice-Provost, of Worcester. His loan 'towards the finishing [of] the Library and rendering it fit to receive books' ensured that by the time of Clarke's death it was ready to house his collections. It remains puzzling how the Alcorne bequest and the Bourchier advance could alone have financed the new buildings over 16 years to the point where the Library was complete: perhaps the royal gifts did occur after all.

There were three solely 'academic' benefactions in the College's first half-century. In 1720 Lady Elizabeth Holford left money for two exhibitions, among benefactions to four colleges in all: as with Margaret Alcorne, her connection with Worcester is unknown, though more is known about her life. In the same year Dr James Fynney, Prebendary of Durham, left £2,500 to found two Fellowships and two scholarships for candidates from Staffordshire and Durham. Fynney was a Fellow of St John's, where he perhaps became a friend of Blechinden's – they were much the same age. In 1745 Thomas Chetle left £1,000 to the Fellows of the College, which was invested in property. His brother had been one of the first to matriculate at Worcester, in 1715.

Through its first 50 years the College thus made steady progress financially, and fitful progress in rebuilding. By 1764, its Cookes and Eaton estates were generating £1,470 a year. Fellows, Scholars and Exhibitioners cost £549 15s. 4d. 40 battels – including those of Fellows and Old Members (some of whom remained debtors for a considerable period) – were invoiced at £618 16s. 8d., giving a surplus of income over expenditure of £69 7s. 10. The freehold, which St John's had helpfully promised to alienate during the tense negotiations of February 1713, had been acquired for £200 in 1714, and in 1744, the original grounds of Gloucester College had been re-assembled by the purchase, from money provided for the purpose by Dr Clarke, of land to the north and west of the main quadrangle.

Above: *Sarah Eaton, by a follower of Michael Dahl.* Opposite: *Map of College estates in Hilmarton, Wiltshire 1790.*

By its centenary year, the College had received two further major benefactions. In 1777, Dr William Gower, the second Provost, who had been appointed from the Fellowship on Blechinden's death in 1736, left the reversion of his estate at Bransford (eventually sold for £3,690 in 1859) and £3,500 in old South Sea securities. In 1787, the Revd Thomas Kay unexpectedly left the large sum of £15,200 to endow an exhibition for a native of Yorkshire, and for the purchase of church livings. Seven were eventually purchased, the last in 1862.

The Clarke estates had also now come into the College's hands, and total estate gross revenues were over £6,000 (though food prices were particularly high at the end of the Napoleonic War). Roughly one third of that amount was attributable to the Cookes endowment, and a quarter each to the Eaton and Clarke benefactions. Battels were invoiced at over £3,700, but the internal accounts still registered a loss of £813: this was more than balanced by a surplus of £981 on the estates. A surplus was occurring on the Eaton estates, and in accordance with Sarah Eaton's will this was distributed between the Provost and Fellows, with the Provost receiving two Fellows' shares. Dr Whittington Landon was thus well compensated for his Provostship, receiving £340, over 50 times the remuneration of the College cook (who perhaps had more chance of gratuities): the present-day ratio is a little over 2:1.

As we have already noted, 50 years later, at the halfway point of its history so far, Worcester College was relatively prosperous. The principal reason for this was its buoyant numbers, with over 80 undergraduates in residence, producing a surplus of over £2,000 on room rents and the 'house account'. The increasing student numbers had resulted in a number of modifications to buildings. Three phases, beginning in 1821, added a total of 13 more sets, and in 1844 new kitchens were added, replacing the Benedictine

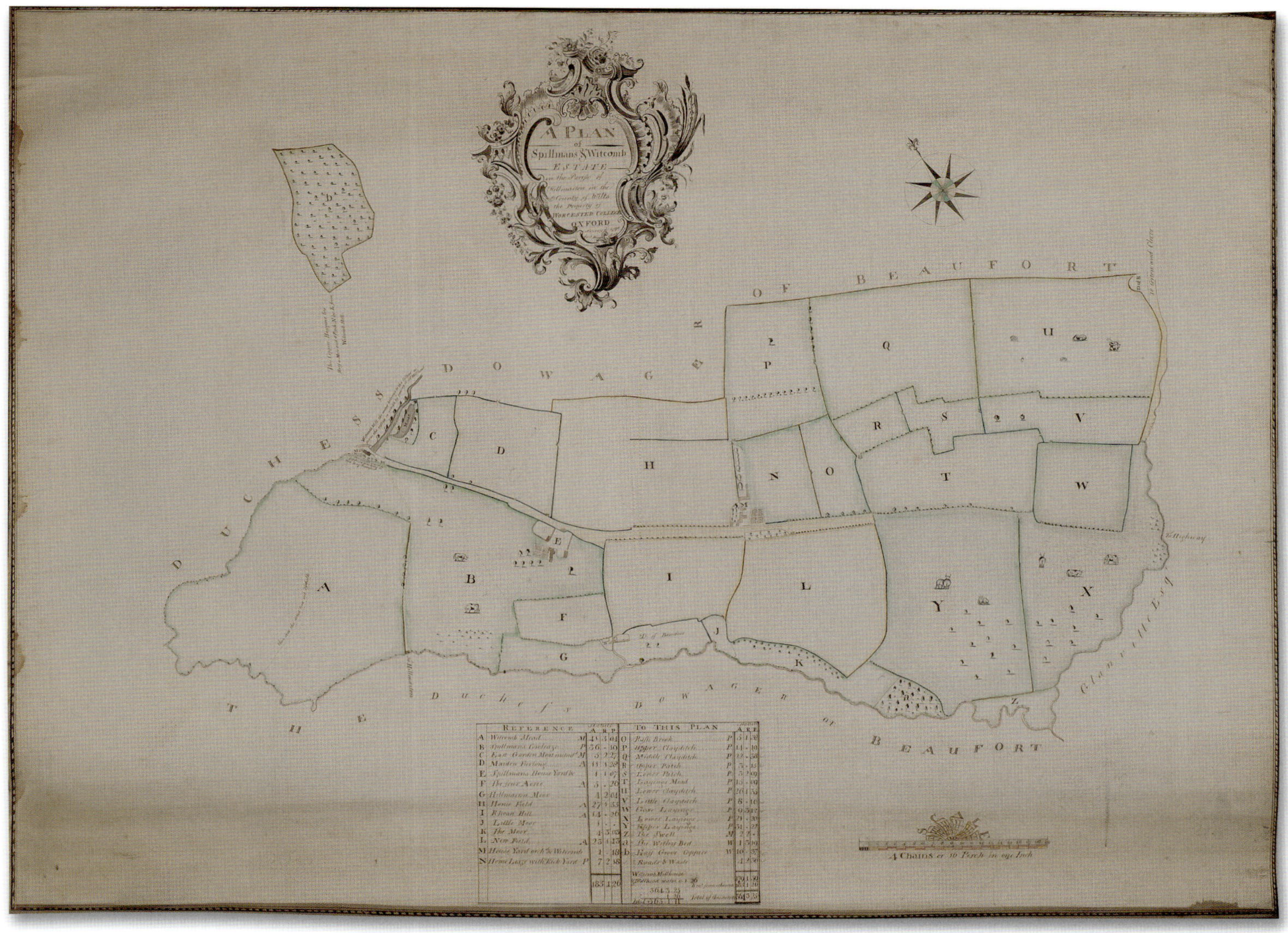

ones, which ran at right angles to what is now Staircase 12. The confidence of that era was perhaps best exemplified by the decision to use Burges, an exciting architect, new to Oxford, to redecorate the Chapel and Hall at a total cost of some £9,000, of which over £7,000 was contributed by members of the College, past and present.

We have already noted Lys' observations on this period, though it is not clear whether he was fair in quoting H.A. Pottinger as saying that in these years before the great agricultural depression the sole interest of the Fellows was to divide what was available 'up to the hilt': Sarah Eaton's will was clear that surpluses should be distributed. But an active policy of virement might have resulted in the surpluses occurring in accounts available for general College purposes. Agricultural prices fell after the end of the Napoleonic War (though less dramatically and regularly than after 1878), and the College did sell the former Gower estate at Bransford in Worcestershire in 1859 during a sequence of high prices. Later, when the agricultural depression deepened after 1878, it would have taken a very bold and confident Bursar to sell estates on a falling market: we have already noted that Lys' sales in 1919 were particularly well timed. There were some benefactions during this period of decline, but unfortunately none involving additions to general endowment: a scholarship in 1867 endowed by Mr Barnes in memory of his son who had died while an undergraduate, an exhibition funded in memory of Provost Cotton in 1883, and in 1899 the endowment by the widow of an Old Member of the Laycock Studentship in Egyptology. In 1898, a former Fellow, the

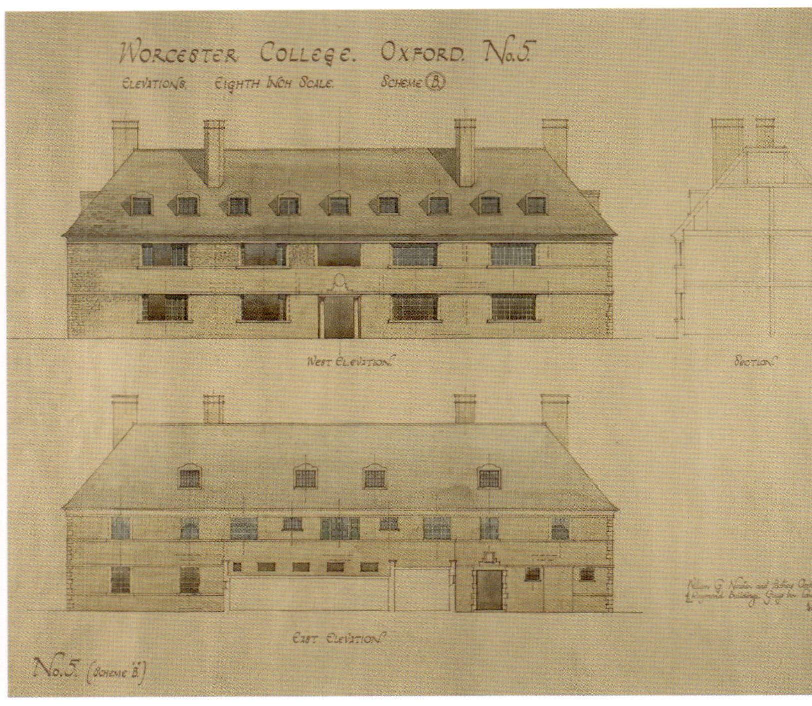

Left: *Francis John Lys, Provost 1919–46, by Henry Lamb RA, 1923.* **Above:** *Elevations for the Nuffield Building by William G. Newton, architect, 1938.*

Revd Rowland Muckleston, left money to provide pensions for College staff. Lys' reforms in due course supplemented this, at the same time providing pensions for Fellows, who for the 12 years after 1895 had been paid on average only just over a quarter of their statutory entitlement of £200.

Lys was indeed 'the model Bursar', even when Provost. Sir John Masterman recounts a telling incident when Lys had seemed rapt in attention at a sermon by the Chaplain, who afterwards expected some words of commendation. 'I have been thinking all this evening, Milburn', Lys remarked, 'whether we ought to have continuous or intermittent flushing in the New Building.'

This new building resulted from the biggest benefaction since the four 18th-century contributions of Cookes, Eaton, Clarke and Kay – £50,000 from Lord Nuffield in 1937, of which £20,000 provided the building which today bears his name and £30,000 strengthened the endowment. Two years earlier, Lys had asked for a contribution 'for the better endowment of a College bearing the name of the place of his birth' and found him 'sympathetic and impressed by the exiguity of the revenue on which the College was run'. But it was a Saturday walk around the gardens, with Lys explaining 'the various purposes for which money was urgently needed, including the new block of buildings of my dreams' which resulted in a cheque the following Monday morning. In 1945, Lord Nuffield gave a further £10,000 to found a medical scholarship, but though Lys' successor, Masterman, clearly became quite a close friend, enjoying golf with him at Huntercombe, his attempts to secure a further large benefaction were unsuccessful.

By now, with World War II over, student numbers were rising inexorably. At the turn of the century there had been 59; in 1925 Lys' addition of 13 sets with mansard windows in the roof of the Terrace building 'made it possible to take about 145', and the Nuffield Building was planned to take numbers over 150, with an appropriate increase in Fellows' sets. In 1948 M. Antonin Besse not only founded St Antony's College, but also gave a quarter of a million pounds to help the eight poorest colleges. Worcester undertook to

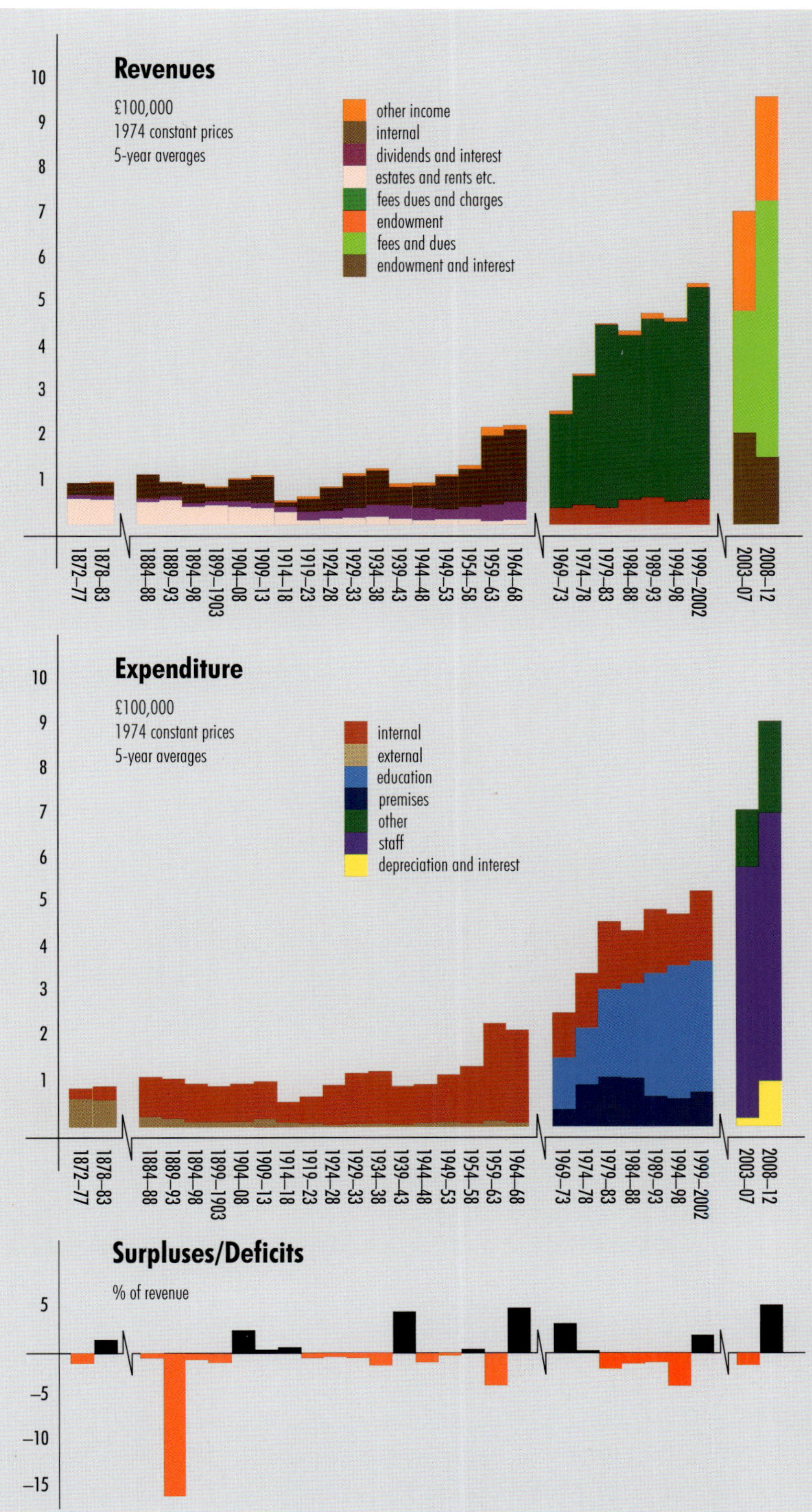

THE COLLEGE ACCOUNTS

These diagrams show the broad categories of revenues and expenditures as recorded in the College accounts. The totals have been adjusted to allow for changes in prices over the period using the RPI all items long run series 1800–the present (January 1974 = 100), published by the Office for National Statistics. There are obvious difficulties in adjusting prices from before the invention of electric light to the broadband present, but the figures give some idea of the 'real' growth of the College finances. No attempt has been made to adjust the figures, in particular to achieve consistency in the treatment of transfers to and from endowment and other funds. For example, in 1917 there was a recorded deficit of 3.9% of revenue, but the College had transferred £1,900 (almost 29% of total revenue) into 5% War Stock. Similar transfers continued throughout the inter-war period. In the late 1950s and early 1960s, receipts from the Historic Buildings Appeal accounted for 17% of income, to be disbursed later, while in the most recent period, a munificent donation has contributed 16% to recorded revenue.

As the diagrams indicate, the official format of College accounts has altered three times over the period: first in 1883–4, then again with the adoption of the 'Franks' accounts in 1969, following the recommendations of the Commission of Inquiry chaired by Provost Franks in 1966, and third from 2002, in preparation for Oxford colleges coming under the aegis of the Charity Commission: full compliance was achieved in 2011–12. This format is not easy to read across from Franks.

Nevertheless, some features of the College's finances over the last 140 years are clear. Income has risen almost ten times in real terms (student numbers have risen some sevenfold). Endowment income has doubled, yet now covers only about 14% of total expenditure, compared with almost 70% in the 1870s: charges to students for academic fees and accommodation, and 'other income' – principally from conferences and donations – have had to expand to compensate. Despite Provost Lys' attempt to offset the fall of more than 50% since the 1870s in the rents and other earnings from estates by switching the endowment into stocks and shares in 1919, that income did not exceed its 1878 peak in real terms for 100 years. Even total income from all sources did not get back to 1878 levels until 1930, falling again to the end of the Second World War, and recovering fully in real terms only after 1957.

Accounting changes make broad trends in expenditure less easy to follow. 'Internal' in the periods up to 1968 includes expenditure on board and lodging, education, and the maintenance of the College's functional property. These elements were helpfully separated out in the specially designed 'Franks' accounts (1969–2002), which show how premises expenditure was squeezed by the need to remain competitive in academic provision with other, better-endowed colleges. The more recent Charity-SORP accounts show the high proportion of staff costs in a residential, tutorially based institution; the rising interest and depreciation element results from extensive building over the last decade.

Over these 140 years as a whole, the unadjusted accounts show a tiny surplus, amounting to 0.18% of total income. After adjusting for special transfers, the last 25 years have seen an annual 'structural' deficit of around 5%. Clearly Sir Thomas Cookes' trustees were right in 1707 to be doubtful whether his legacy would prove sufficient for both the splendid buildings and the academic activity he envisaged for his new foundation: 300 years later, the overwhelming need is still to strengthen the endowment.

R.G.S.

ABOVE: *The Sainsbury Building, designed by MacCormac Jamieson Prichard, 1983.*
RIGHT: *Barrie and Deedee Wigmore with former Provost Dick Smethurst, signing the contract to fund three new posts.*

create a post in Modern Languages, establish a scholarship for a French undergraduate, and build a further 12 rooms. Despite this, Masterman records that, wishing to ensure that all undergraduates could spend two out of their (usually) three years in College 'or, at the worst, in a hostel closely adjacent to the College', he tried to keep numbers down to 240. But by the time he retired, in 1961, they had reached 315, necessitating another new building, the 'Casson' building, which was funded by an appeal to Old Members. Ten years later a further new building was funded by a generous gift from the Wolfson Foundation. Masterman had tried hard to gain the support of Isaac and Leonard Wolfson for the earlier building, but it was in recognition of the work of Oliver Franks (who in 1962 had succeeded Masterman) in helping to establish Wolfson College, Oxford, that the grant was made. Masterman (Vice-Chancellor at the time) and Franks, as one of the two trustees, had earlier worked closely together in raising £2.5 million for the Oxford Historic Buildings Fund, from which Worcester received nearly £124,000 for re-facing buildings between 1958 and 1965.

The tension between the need to strengthen the College's general endowment and its requirements to house its students, which has been evident since its foundation, now assumed a different form. Following the Robbins Report of 1963, all university students received maintenance grants, irrespective of their or their parents' income. At Oxford and Cambridge, the individual colleges' fees were paid (subject to annual negotiations with the Ministry of Education) by Local Authorities. Endowment was now required to cover those costs which the government would not meet (especially residential buildings), and to guard against the effects of fluctuating government 'block grants' paid to universities through the University Grants Committee. Such fluctuations were soon felt during the currency and oil price crises of the 1970s. One benefaction that had resembled an increase in general endowment when it was devised was the large legacy from John Amphlett in memory of his son John, who was killed on service with the RAF in 1942. The benefactor, not himself a member of the College but from a family with a history of ten members stretching back to 1735, died in 1949, and the correspondence shows that he was very concerned, after the general election of 1945, lest the government seize the assets of Oxford colleges. Evidently unconvinced by the College's reassurances, he entrusted the capital sum not to the College but to the Midland Bank, with the College entitled to claim the income for scholarships, exhibitions and bursaries – very necessary in 1949, but not so helpful as general endowment in the post-Robbins world of universal grants. (Though, of course, very helpful now, since the re-introduction of tuition fees in 2006.)

Endowment was becoming more important than ever. The very large increases in university and student numbers which followed Robbins led inevitably to financial pressures. First, research funding was concentrated in specific institutions as quality was assessed in a series of research assessment exercises (RAE). Secondly, the amount available to support teaching was spread more and more thinly: Oxford and Cambridge colleges were to some extent protected against this by the separate (though still publicly funded) college fees, but from 1997 this 'premium' was progressively reduced, so for all universities the taxpayer's contribution towards the teaching of any given subject was roughly the same (different subjects attracted different rates, for example if they required laboratory work). In Oxford, the wish to excel in successive RAEs meant that academics' teaching hours were reduced to leave more time for research, yet at the College level preserving the tutorial system was held to be vital, even when public funding for teaching was being reduced. So colleges drew on their endowment and appealed to their Old Members to fill the missing teaching posts and hours. colleges with smaller endowments depended proportionately more on publicly funded fee income, and so were under more pressure.

An Appeal launched under the Provostship of Lord Briggs (who succeeded Lord Franks in 1976), and led by David Mitchell, produced funding for part of the cost of six Tutorial Fellowships, and two major new buildings, both gifts from the immensely supportive Sainsbury family, while the Library was greatly enhanced by an ingenious new floor inserted into the roof, funded by Rupert Murdoch. A decade later, a second Appeal, under Provost Smethurst (who had succeeded Lord Briggs in 1991) also resulted in the funding of six posts, three through the great generosity of Barrie and Deedee Wigmore. A new graduate building, the gift of Kotaro and Minoru Ono, supplemented one first built in the 1970s, paid for out of revenue and now bearing the name of David Mitchell, who had agitated for it as the first Tutor for Graduates. The increasing

Top: *HRH Raja Nazrin Shah, Crown Prince of Perak in Malaysia, with the Provost, on the occasion of his donation of funds for the new lecture theatre.*
Above: *Competition-winning design for the Nazrin Shah Building and Lecture Theatre by Niall McLaughlin Architects.*

Above: *The first garden party for College benefactors, 2013.* Opposite: *The staircase leading to the Library, one of the major legacies of Worcester's 'second founder', Dr George Clarke.*

numbers of graduate students had earlier led to the construction of a large building at the far end of the sportsfield, shrouded by the trees along the canal: this was funded by contributions from Old Members under the Business Expansion Scheme. Since the completion of the Ono-funded building, named in honour of Lord Franks, this 'Canal Building' has housed third- and fourth-year undergraduates.

In 2002, the Governing Body decided that it had to respond to the competition of better-endowed colleges, some of which were able to house many more of their students than Worcester was, by setting itself the target of building enough rooms to house all undergraduates for the whole of their course, three or four years (40% are now on four-year courses), by the end of the decade. The initial impetus was supplied by a gift from Peter Earl, and the rest of the project was funded by a loan backed by the funds to be raised from the development of a site at Wolvercote (which had been withdrawn by Lys from the 1919 sale because it 'may acquire a higher value for building'). Unfortunately planning enquiries, followed by the global financial crisis that began in 2007, seriously delayed this counterpart financing. Given the incomparable setting of the gardens and grounds, these new buildings should help the College to raise its revenue from vacation conferences to meet its endowment income shortfall. An important requirement if this great potential is to be fulfilled is the construction of a large lecture theatre, for which funds have recently been provided by a magnificent donation from HRH Raja Nazrin Shah, Crown Prince of Perak in Malaysia, who read PPE at the College in the late 1970s.

Throughout the last 40 years the College has benefitted greatly from very many smaller benefactions, from which it is difficult to select examples. But mention must be made of the many contributions by the trustees of the legacy of C.H. Wilkinson, especially to the Library, of the many projects supported by the Worcester College Society, and of the legacies from Dr J.M. Walker, Professor R. Martin, and Richmond Douglas, which have made possible the restoration of the Chapel and organ. The affection in which the College is held by its staff as well as its Fellows and Old Members is well illustrated by the gift of his life savings by James Smith, who worked in the Hall and then as a Scout, with his wife Dorothy as a hostel-keeper in Beaumont Street, for 20 years from the late 1950s. He was very keen on sport, as was appropriate for someone who looked after Sir John Masterman in his latter years, And his legacy of £100,000 has contributed to refurbishing the Pavilion, restoring the tennis courts and equipping the new gym. We owe so much to so many contributors.

Yet in spite of all this support, the College's finances remain precarious. Sir Thomas Cookes' legacy was indeed too small an endowment for his 'Ornamentall pyle' and the academic life he wished to promote within it. But the beauty of the site, the original benefaction to Gloucester College by Sir John Giffard, and the charm of the medieval buildings which Gloucester Hall passed on, continue to inspire the affection which has ensured that the College has survived – just – and flourished over the centuries.

The Tercentenary Appeal, launched in 2014, has the bold ambition of fully re-endowing the College for the next 300 years. Together with Nazrin Shah, Barrie and Deedee Wigmore are once again taking the lead, along with the Sainsbury family. A Worcester College Endowment Trust has been established and among the first benefactions to the Campaign have been support for the rebuilding of the ancient kitchens from Sir Timothy Sainsbury and the Headley Trust, the funds to endow in perpetuity an Asa Briggs Fellowship in the Humanities from Lord John Sainsbury, and gifts for general endowment from the Wigmores.

NB: I am greatly indebted to the Worcester College Archivist, Emma Goodrum, for her indefatigable assistance in the preparation of this article. RS

6. Worcester and the Oxford Movement

Peter Nockles

The Oxford or Tractarian movement, whose birth is commonly symbolised by John Keble's Assize sermon on 'National Apostasy' delivered on 14 July 1833, and which is associated with the names of John Henry Newman, John Keble, Richard Hurrell Froude, and (later) Edward Bouverie Pusey, was partly a response to the crisis in church and state triggered by the constitutional changes of 1828–33 and the Whig government's decision to suppress Irish bishoprics. However, its deeper roots lay within the broader cultural, literary and spiritual reaction against the Age of Reason and Revolution. It was also nurtured within the academic milieu of the University of Oxford and its collegiate life and polity.

Richard Church, Dean of St Paul's, and originally one of the younger members of the Tractarian firmament, in his 'master narrative' *The Oxford Movement. Twelve Years 1883–1845* (1891), evocatively compared the atmosphere of Tractarian Oxford with that of 15th-century Florence – in both cases a quaint and unwieldy polity was rent asunder by intense and passionately factious rivalry and animosity, the conflict being the more intense for being so parochial. As Dean Church put it, these theological contests, 'for a time turned Oxford into a kind of image of what Florence was in the days of Savanarola, with its nicknames, Puseyites and Neomaniacs, and High and Dry, counterparts to the Piagnoni and Arrabbiati, of the older strife'.

Many of its participants later recalled that it was the *genius loci* and *ethos* of the University of Oxford that helped shape and configure the Oxford Movement, itself a product of the home of, in Matthew Arnold's famous phrase, 'lost causes and ... impossible loyalties'. Within the University individual colleges were divided by the theological struggle, some gaining a reputation as Tractarian strongholds. Worcester was certainly not at the forefront of what Mark Pattison, a disillusioned former acolyte, famously described as the 'collective madness' or 'nightmare' engendered by what he called 'the whirlpool of Tractarianism'. The index to David Newsome's masterly study of the Oxford Movement, *The Parting of Friends* (1966) lists as many as 26 entries for Oriel College and only one for Worcester. Yet the College was by no means untouched by this movement.

In his *Lives of Twelve Good Men* (1888), John William Burgon (1813–88), undergraduate at Worcester, 1841–6, included the memorials of two prominent Worcester figures caught up in the turmoil of the Oxford Movement: Richard Lynch Cotton, Provost from 1839 until his death, and Richard Greswell. Two other notable figures in its history, John Miller and William Palmer, were also accorded honourable mention. Provost Cotton, a moderate Evangelical, was no friend of the Oxford Movement but as Dr

The construction of Beaumont Street, from a watercolour by George Hollis, c.*1828.*

Pusey's brother-in-law he played a conciliatory role. Unlike other college heads, he did not change the dinner hour at Worcester in order to prevent undergraduates hearing Newman preach in the evening at St Mary's. On the other hand, William Law Pope, Vice-Provost during much of the period 1842 to 1851, was less sympathetic. He was a staunch supporter of Newman's theological opponent and *bête noire* Renn Dickson Hampden. As the brother of Elizabeth Pope, wife of Richard Whately, one-time Fellow of Oriel, with whom Newman notoriously fell out, Pope's anti-Tractarian credentials were in little doubt.

Worcester's relative detachment from the Oxford Movement was partly the product of a physical detachment, its relative geographical isolation. Burgon, albeit half humorously and prior to the building of Beaumont Street, related the aged President of Magdalen, Martin Joseph Routh's verdict: 'The way to Worcester College lay through a network of narrow passages, and was pronounced undiscoverable'. Nonetheless, new trends in university life such as the growth of college reading parties and university debating societies meant that an apparently quiet 'backwater' and small society such as Worcester College was much less likely to be immune or shielded from the wider religious controversy and cross-fertilisation of ideas that was then engulfing other colleges and the University at large, than might have been the case in earlier eras. The young Henry Tripp (born 1817) became imbued with Tractarian principles while an undergraduate at Exeter College, 1836–8. However, in 1838 Tripp transferred to a Scholarship at Worcester College and carried over his Tractarianism with him to Worcester, reminiscing 50 years later that he had attended Newman's sermons at St Mary's while an undergraduate at the College. Tripp went on to act as a tutor at William Sewell's high church collegiate foundation of St Columba's, Rathfarnham, near Dublin in the 1840s. Thomas Hugo (1820–76) who as Vicar of Haliwell, Lancashire (1850–1) antagonised both his patron and bishop because of his 'zealous propagation of extreme high-church views' and later became a prominent Ritualist, also appears to have come under Tractarian influence during his time as an undergraduate, 1839–42.

Cotton's predecessor as Provost, the mercurial Dr Whittington Landon, who matriculated at Worcester in 1775, was elected Fellow in 1782. His tenure as Provost lasted from 1796 until his death in December 1838. He was a fine specimen of a 'high and dry Tory' or 'two Bottle orthodox' of the old school who would fiercely oppose even the Chancellor the Duke of Wellington's modest suggestions for university reform in the 1830s. For the stiffly orthodox Provost Landon, religious 'enthusiasm', fanaticism (or what he would have regarded as 'cant') of any complexion, was anathema as a potentially

Worcester College from the north, c.*1835.*

subversive, destabilising and divisive force in a close-knit academic society. It was consequently unfortunate that some years prior to the rise of Tractarianism, Provost Landon was forced to confront among one of his Fellows, Joseph Charles Philpot, a particularly virulent form of religious enthusiasm, characterised by extreme hyper-Calvinistic evangelicalism, bordering on Antinomianism, opposition to infant baptism, and a disdain for academic learning. This colourful episode culminated in Philpot's jeremiad against the Provost and the spiritual state of the College, splendidly titled *A Letter to the Provost of Worcester College, on Resigning his Fellowship, and Seceding from the Church of England* (1835). Philpot adopted an unappealing stance of isolation and religious superiority within the Common Room, leaving it upon record, how, 'soon after he first felt the weight of eternal things, oftentimes seated after dinner in the Common Room with the other Fellows, amidst all the drinking of wine and the hum and buzz of conversation in which he took no part, he has been secretly lifting up his heart to God'.

Philpot's strictures on the everyday convivial ways of collegiate life hardly seemed designed to endear him to his colleagues, not least the Provost. He asked Provost Landon, 'where in all the practice of the University, do I see the marks of Christ, or the "footsteps of his flock"? Can they be traced in the drawing and dining-rooms of the Heads of Houses? In the Common-rooms of the Fellows?'. Few Provosts could have had a ready answer to such a question. The College must have breathed a collective sigh of relief at Philpot's departure.

John Miller, lithograph by J.H. Lynch after a painting by Turnham Barton.

Richard Greswell, by John Bridges, 1837.

A feature of the Oxford Movement was its attempt to breathe life and reality back into decayed institutions, whether they were those of Church or University, and to rekindle the medieval spirit and ideals of their foundations. Places became invested with romanticised historical significance, so that even the buildings of Oxford truly 'spoke'. Burgon's first response to his sight of Worcester College, rapturously captured in a letter to his sisters in January 1841, conveys something of the Tractarian delight in Oxford's ecclesiastical, monastic past: 'I was extremely anxious to see Worcester College, as you may readily suppose, a place that is to become my home and I was not disappointed'. Although 'the most recent collegiate foundation in Oxford', for Burgon, the most noteworthy thing was that the College 'occupies the site of the most ancient establishment for religious instruction in Oxford' with the exception of St Frideswide's Abbey: a high claim indeed for Gloucester College (and one that would probably be disputed by the three other 13th-century colleges, University, Merton and Balliol).

One of the more obscure figures who prepared the ground for the Oxford Movement was John Miller (1787–1855), Fellow, 1810–23. A friend of John Keble, one of the Movememt's acknowledged leaders, Miller had early academic achievements (scholar of Worcester 1806, Fellow 1810, winner of the Chancellor's First Prize for Latin Prose 1810, Select Preacher 1814, Bampton Lecturer 1817) but his later career was shrouded in quiet self-effacement and retirement. Miller, however, left an indelible impression on the Worcester undergraduates whom he taught, notably Richard Greswell. Moreover, his sermons were as formative on the succeeding Tractarian generation as were Keble's *Christian Year* (1827). Miller's Bampton Lectures were particularly influential, while a sermon preached before the University in 1829, *Truth's Resting-Place amidst the strife of Tongues*, perhaps with the example of Philpot in mind, warned against 'religious adventurers' running into extremes and going 'out of the pale of church communion'. Moreover, the Preface to Miller's *Sermons*, published in 1830,

Provost's Lodgings from across the Lake, by Joseph Murray Ince (1806–59).

struck an almost prophetic note in regard to the future Tractarian movement and its later course. Miller criticised the restless spirit of religious enthusiasm, but also took aim at the doctrinal aridity and spiritual coldness of rational religion and complacent defenders of the imperfections of the contemporary Church of England. He warned of the dangers of a likely reaction in the direction of Rome among those 'many minds of quality that can least be spared from the communion of our own Church' who sought more devotional fervour and yet were repelled by the excesses of enthusiasm.

Better known than Miller in the annals of the Oxford Movement, was William Patrick Palmer (1802–85). Palmer had been educated at Trinity College, Dublin (graduating in 1824), and after studying for ordination under that acknowledged precursor of the Tractarians, John Jebb, Bishop of Limerick, he migrated to Oxford in 1828 when he was incorporated at Magdalen Hall, proceeding to MA in January 1829. In 1831 Palmer transferred to Worcester College, though he never became formally part of the Fellowship. He resided in the newly constructed Beaumont Street, looking after an aged mother, until his marriage to a daughter of Admiral Beaufort in 1839 following the death of his mother.

The reason for Palmer's move to Oxford was to pursue scholarly studies into the primitive origins of the English liturgy. Palmer's pioneering liturgical scholarship, partly based on the earlier research of Bishop Charles Lloyd, found expression in his highly influential *Origines Liturgicae, or Antiquities of the English Ritual* (1832), in which he sought to demonstrate that the Book of Common Prayer was a product of 1,500 years' development. The dry and technical character of the work did not lessen its impact, and it left an indelible mark on future Tractarian liturgical studies. To 'most Oxford men', Thomas Mozley later recalled, 'it was like an accident of continental travel before railways – the sudden view of a vast plain full of picturesque objects and historical associations'.

By 1831/2, Palmer's liturgical scholarship had brought him into contact with the future Tractarian leaders, notably Newman, Froude, and Keble. He seems to have had a hand in Newman's own education in high churchmanship, in that Newman consulted Palmer when preparing his *Arians of the Fourth Century* (1833). By the summer of 1833, Palmer and Newman had become close friends, with a mutual respect for each other's learning and abilities. As an Irish high churchman Palmer was particularly troubled by the Erastian challenge to the Church of Ireland represented by the Whig ministry's suppression of ten Episcopal sees and confiscation of revenues. Palmer's initial enthusiasm for the Movement can be explained by the apparent readiness of his Oxford friends to take up the cause of the embattled Irish church. However, a parting of the ways in due course was to take place.

Newman's encomiums on Palmer's work might seem to place Palmer, with his Worcester College connection, at the very heart of

the Oxford Movement. However, Newman immediately proceeded to explain why this was not so. In Newman's eyes, Palmer lacked certain necessary key qualities which rendered him defective in terms of a correct *ethos:*

> *He was deficient in depth; and besides, coming from a distance, he never had really grown into an Oxford man, nor was he generally received as such; nor had he any insight into the force of personal influence and congeniality of thought in carrying out a religious theory, – a condition which Froude and I considered essential to any success in the stand which had to be made against Liberalism.*

Notwithstanding this lofty dismissal, there were some who considered Palmer the most accomplished theologian in the Church of England.

John William Burgon came up to Worcester at the mature age of 28 in 1841. It was Dr Pusey, as Provost Cotton's brother-in-law, who guided Burgon in his choice of Worcester College. In a jocular and vividly descriptive letter to his sisters, Burgon described his visit to Oxford on 19 October 1841 in the company of Henry Rose ('the bear and his keeper') to present himself for admission as a commoner at Worcester College, through the intermediary good offices of Pusey. After visiting Parker's bookshop, which Burgon described as 'a kind of lounge for young men who love books', he described his and Rose's meeting, by arrangement, with Pusey at the 'Angel' Hotel. Pusey 'immediately entered on the subject of our visit with Rose, and very kindly proposed to conduct him (and me) to Worcester College, where he said he would introduce us to the Provost of the College, having first distinctly declared it to be his opinion that Worcester College, was the best I could go to'.

Burgon proceeded to describe the walk in Pusey's company to the College along Beaumont Street, but regretted that he could not convey in writing Pusey's conversation because 'it was very slight' and 'because I heard him imperfectly'. The walk ended with Pusey's knocking at the Provost's door and ushering Burgon and his companion Rose into the Lodgings.

Another figure worthy of notice in the galaxy of characters associated with Worcester College and the Oxford Movement, was one of its most accomplished 19th-century Fellows, Richard Greswell (1800–81). For his friend Burgon, who included him in his panoply of *Lives of Twelve Good Men,* Greswell was the 'faithful steward'. Emanating from Lancashire, he was elected in 1818 to a scholarship restricted to sons of clergy at Worcester College, being tutored by John Miller, and gaining a double first before being appointed a tutor and elected Fellow of the College at the age of 24. By 1826 he was the College Bursar. Ordained in 1828, he became one of the most eminent mathematicians in the University. In the history of the College, Greswell's main claim to fame was supposedly, during his time as Bursar, his having laid out the College Gardens at his own expense, although doubt was cast on this claim by Provost Lys. Later, he helped drain Port Meadow and laid out walks there. Greswell was an assiduous college tutor, and after another stint as Bursar in

1833/4 he married in 1836 and moved into a house in the newly built Beaumont Street (in the construction of which he took an interest).

Greswell became a life-long friend of William Palmer, and was of a similarly retiring and self-effacing disposition, and assisted Palmer with his *Origines Liturgicae*. We are left in no doubt about Greswell's commitment to the principles of the Oxford Movement by a letter from his daughter Julia to Burgon after her father's death in 1881: 'You are doubtless aware that in his early manhood he joined the "Oxford Movement" and decidedly belonged to what was called the Tractarian school, being very intimate with such men as Dr Pusey, Mr Keble (who examined him for his degree), Mr William Palmer & Mr Newman, but he has not advanced with the times.'

On the national stage, Greswell put his Tractarian principles regarding the primacy of church education into practice by his strenuous advocacy of the work of the National Society for the Education of the Poor in the Principles of the Established Church (founded 1811). Greswell was a friend of Gladstone and there is substantial extant correspondence between them in the British Library. In his capacity as a supporter of the Tractarians, Greswell acted as chairman of Gladstone's election committee for the Oxford University parliamentary seat from 1847 until Gladstone's defeat in 1865. Gladstone even stayed with Greswell in Beaumont Street rather than his own college when he came to Oxford after the election.

Another Worcester figure associated with the Oxford Movement and the only one in this earlier phase of its history to go over to the Church of Rome was Charles Seager, a somewhat eccentric Oriental scholar. Seagar was Pusey's assistant lecturer in Hebrew. He was the author of a work promoting the use of auricular confession and was instrumental in introducing Mark Pattison, Fellow of Lincoln College, before his recoil from Tractarianism, to wider Roman Catholic circles and to the work of Kenelm Digby and Count de Montalembert. Seager's conversion to Rome in the autumn of 1843 was an acute embarrassment to Pusey and Newman; Newman complained that Seager of Worcester was going round Oxford preaching like 'Peter the Hermit' (the fiery preacher of the First Crusade), stirring up trouble and 'unsettling people'. Newman sometimes left him in charge of the University Church and often returned to find that Seager had caused problems. Thomas Mozley has left a vivid description of the man as he appeared in that famous pulpit: 'He was a man of sad aspect, with a deep hollow voice, and he preached so continually on hell and all its horrors that the Principal of Brasenose, whose family attended the church, was obliged to protest and threaten withdrawal. He could not answer for the consequences on the weaker members of his household.'

Effect of the passing of Mr Bouverie's bill for the Abolition of Tests on the Fellows of a College in Oxford, *satirical cartoon* c.*1866*.

The Oxford annalist, G.V. Cox, gave a graphic account of Seagar's conversion to Rome, in his diary recollection for November 1843: 'one of the earliest "perverts" was Mr Seagar of Worcester College. It was said that he went to Oscott "for a literary enquiry", that, after dinner, controversy was started by Dr Wiseman, and was kept till four o'clock next morning, when Mr Seagar "cried for quarter"... at 8 a.m. of the same morning he was baptised.'

A survey of Worcester College and the Oxford Movement would not be complete without notice of a younger brother of John Henry Newman, Francis Newman, who became an undergraduate at Worcester in 1824. Francis never shared in or approved of his brother's abandonment of Evangelicalism for high churchmanship and Tractarianism and was mortified by what he regarded as his brother's eventual apostasy to the Church of Rome. For his part, John Henry Newman was horrified by what he regarded as his brother's drift away from orthodox Christianity into a form of Unitarianism. The rift was illustrated by John Henry telling his brother bluntly in 1833: 'St Paul bids us to avoid those who cause divisions: you cause divisions, therefore I must avoid you.' Francis Newman was responsible for an interesting counter-history to that set out by his elder brother in his famous *Apologia pro vita sua*. After his elder brother's death in 1890, he set out to lay down for posterity his own very different version of events. In his *Contributions to the Early History of the late Cardinal Newman* (1891), Francis Newman claimed that his brother's Romanising leanings were evident from a very early date. In October 1890 Francis Newman sent Provost Daniel the manuscript of what he called 'my little book'. In the accompanying letter dated 8 October 1890, he informed the Provost:

> *In 1824 when I first took permanent rooms in Worcester College he in my judgment at that time, just after he was ordained Deacon, attempted to fill me with doctrine that I thought Papist ... Until his funeral I expected to carry all this to my grave. Now I see I cannot tell half a story. I must tell the whole. It will seem quite unbrotherly: but since 1824 to be in a relation really brotherly was impossible. In 1844 when he joined the Romish church, I thought he had become an honest man, and in many senses he did, but never would we find any point of common interest or common desire.*

all ye fowls of the air.
O ye children of men
COCK ATOO
DODO
CRANES
UNDER GRAD
PETER
O all ye beasts & cattle.
O all ye Seas
SALMON
MATTHEW
WHITE BAIT.
KANGAROO
KORAN.
Effect of the Passing of Mr Bouverie's Bill for the Abolition of Tests
on the Fellows of a College in Oxford.

Above: *Bible covers made by Barkentin & Krall to William Burges' designs, incorporating 17th-century panels.* Opposite: *William Burges' design for the Chapel, painted by Axel Haig, 1863.*

Francis Newman did not succeed in drawing out Provost Daniel on this sensitive subject, and the general consensus was that Francis had committed an act of fratricide which even opponents of the Movement found distasteful. Perhaps sensing that he was getting nowhere, Francis Newman wrote again to the Provost in February 1891, simply stating that 'I did not send to the Library a little book concerning my brother the late Cardinal, because it revives ecclesiastical differences'. Here was a sad reminder of that 'parting of family' as well as 'parting of friends' which characterised the Tractarian debates that dominated the intellectual life of Oxford in the high Victorian period.

It cannot be maintained that Worcester College was in the vortex or at the forefront of the Oxford Movement. Worcester was not a 'Tractarian college' in the (admittedly qualified) sense in which Oriel, Exeter, Merton, and Magdalen, arguably were. For example, in an albeit biased survey of the tutorial body of Oxford colleges as to their predominant religious party affiliation or inclination, the Anglican Evangelical newspaper *The Record,* in its issue of 27 February 1845, classed Worcester College as 'mixed', lying mid-way between those colleges such as Oriel, Magdalen, and Exeter, who were without 'Protestant tutors' and those such as Wadham, Pembroke, and St Edmund Hall, which it deemed to be 'free from Puseyism'. Perhaps the closest association between the two has come down to us through the diffused and indirect architectural and aesthetic legacy of the movement discussed elsewhere in this volume – the decoration of the Chapel in the 1860s to the designs of William Burges.

A revived religious spirit which cannot be confined to the label 'Oxford Movement' left its mark within Worcester College by mid-century. In his rather solemn and long-winded address in the College Hall in front of an audience of over 200 in Trinity Term 1839, the newly installed Provost, Richard Cotton, on being presented with his portrait, 'complimented the present generation of Worcester men' very much at the expense of their predecessors, whom, he said, were 'remarkable neither for talent nor piety'. There would still be echoes in the College of more boisterous and rowdy times, as in the account in a letter of one Fellow, J.D. Collis, of a great Irish dinner held in Worcester on St Patrick's Day 1841, with '34 Paddies altogether'. After 'diverse depredations' had been committed by the company on their way home, Collis wistfully commented that there 'are to be no more Irish dinners' at Worcester. An era was passing away.

7. Worcester at War

Jessica Goodman

We shall pass in summer weather,
We shall come at eventide,
When the fells stand up together
And all quiet things abide;
Mixed with cloud and wind and river,
Sun-distilled in dew and rain,
One with Cumberland forever
We shall not go forth again.

Nowell Oxland, 'Outward Bound' (1915)

On board a ship bound for Gallipoli, Nowell Oxland of the 6th Battalion Border Regiment might well have wondered how 12 short months had wrought so much change. Just a year earlier, he had been a history student at Worcester College, secretary of the Lovelace Club and Captain of the Rugby Team. Now, he was a Second Lieutenant, on his way to fight for his country. Oxland, whose poem 'Outward Bound' was published in the *Times* in 1915, was killed at the Battle of Sulva Bay in August of that year. He was one of 89 Worcester undergraduates who lost their lives in the conflict. Twelve of these were young men who did not even have the chance to begin their studies, called up to fight before they had set foot in Oxford.

William 'Willie' Elmhirst, a contemporary of Oxland, recorded the events of his first year at Worcester in *A Freshman's Diary*. In the introduction to the published journal, Sir John Masterman, a third year when Elmhirst arrived in 1911, notes that over half of the young men mentioned in the slim 96-page volume lost their lives in the First World War. Elmhirst himself was killed at Serre in 1916, and just a week before his death he wrote to his mother:

> *Out here one becomes so used to the idea of death, and that in most unpleasant forms, that it comes to seem a very small thing indeed. I have seen some far from pleasant sights during the last few days, but it is astonishing how little it affects one, though it takes people in very different ways.*

The *College Records* for 1916–18 give citations for military awards made to Worcester men for their brave service. Among them was Captain David Hirsch, awarded a Victoria Cross for his steadfast bravery in establishing lines of defence even when he was severely injured, and encouraging his men by example until the moment of his death.

James Percy Wetenhall was one of the lucky Worcester soldiers who did make it back home. Born in 1895, he came up to Oxford

Nowell Oxland.

William Elmhirst.

in 1914 to read Greats, having been excused from service because of a back injury. His first year was spent playing sport and enjoying College life just like any undergraduate. However, thoughts of his friends out in France played on his mind, and after just a year in Oxford he talked his way into the army, joining a secret tank corps. He was to have an eventful war.

The tanks were not called into service until 1917, at the Battle of Cambrai. *The War History of the 6th Tank Battalion* records how on 26 November his tank, Mac II, was seen to be knocked over in the melee. His mother received a letter some months later reporting that her son was missing, along with the rest of his crew. However, James and his colleagues were in fact prisoners of war in Germany, as an official card sent home to his sweetheart would soon reveal. James' letters from that period, under the censor's watchful eye, tell little of the hardships he endured, but instead recount whimsical anecdotes, like the prison orchestra they had managed to form, in which he played the violin.

In this way, James survived the war, and returned home. The thought of taking up his studies again after such an experience did not appeal to him; he was keen to marry and start a family, which he did, in 1920. That family was to become a Worcester dynasty: his son, another James, came up Worcester to read PPE in 1949, while five of the second James' own children would eventually pass through the College. James Percy himself went on to have a long and successful career in hospital administration, eventually founding the National League of Hospital Friends in 1949.

Cadets on the steps of the Main Quad during the First World War.

As James whiled away the time in the German camp, Oxford was experiencing its own version of the war. Emptied of undergraduates, many of the colleges were requisitioned for official use. Worcester, reduced to fewer than a dozen students, was used as quarters first for an Officer Training School, and then for a Company of an Officers' Cadet Battalion. The sports pitches served as a drill ground, and up to 170 cadets at any one time lived in College and ate in Hall. A 1917 War Office memorandum to all colleges providing quarters states that for a daily fee of between 4s. 9d. and 5s. 3d. per cadet, the College was required to meet all outgoings, including fuel and light, baths, rates, taxes, insurance '(fire, air, bombardment) … in precisely the same way that a hotel furnishes board and lodging at an inclusive charge per day'. The College was entitled to compensation for any damage caused by the military forces quartered there, and received £341 19s. in January 1919 for necessary repairs to individual and common rooms.

Under the University and Colleges (Emergency Powers) Act, 1915, all colleges of Oxford and Cambridge were given permission to pass emergency statutes. In practice this meant excusing serving Fellows and students from residency requirements, suspending Fellowships and scholarships for the duration of the war, using money from specialised funds to supplement reduced income from student fees, and taking service into account during admissions after the war. The University put special arrangements in place for students whose studies had been interrupted by the conflict, allowing them to count time spent in service as residency (up to four terms), and excusing them from certain sets of examinations, according to the point at which they suspended their student status. It was thus that James

Above: *First World War Memorial in 1919.* Right: *Worcester College gardens during the Second World War, photographed in 1943.*

Wetenhall, like many of his contemporaries whose studies were interrupted by war, was awarded a BA degree with the note '*aegrotat*'. The word refers to a medical certificate of illness, and denoted that the student had been excused from certain requirements of the degree. Men who matriculated immediately after the war were given permission to enter for Final Honours Schools any time from one year after matriculating, thus allowing them to take a shortened degree, and move on into the world of work.

A commemorative service for all those killed in the War was held in the Chapel on 25 June 1919, and the memorial to lost College members was paid for by subscription from Old Members and the families of those killed. College life gradually returned to normal: the *College Record* for 1919–20 noted with surprise just how quickly drama, sport and music had been taken up again. However, the gaps left by students and staff who never returned were palpable. Admissions were restricted for some time to avoid the numbers of students outstripping staff availability and building capacity.

During the Second World War, the change in Oxford was less noticeable, particularly as the University provided a shortened five-term 'War Degree' for those in the services. From 1940 to 1945 a total of 217 men applied for these courses at Worcester, 14 of them from the US Army. A series of photographs taken in 1943 shows a peaceful College, apparently completely unchanged by the war. While undergraduate numbers were diminished, the College was not requisitioned for war use, and the odd sandbag or gas mask were, according to the *Record* for 1938–9, the only signs of conflict. In 1940 the *Record* notes the contrast with the previous war, when at one stage only two undergraduates were in residence: 'Today the rooms given up to the Army are occupied by clerical departments whose members live outside the College and although thirty-two of the sixty-three men in residence are Service cadets, they are all matriculated members of the University who pursue some academic studies.'

Charles Crichton was just such a cadet, and in letters home to his mother in 1941 he recounts the strange life of luxury he was leading, rowing and playing tennis as the war raged elsewhere. He also provides a none-too-flattering portrait of the non-cadet undergraduates, whom he describes as 'floppy': 'Decadent isn't the

Left: *Air Vice-Marshal Sir Keith Rodney Park, by William Rothenstein, 1941. Earlier, as Commander of the Oxford University Air Squadron from 1932 to 1934, Park was a member of Worcester SCR.* Below: Diversions, *1940, and* More Diversions, *1943, edited by C.H. Wilkinson.*

word for this place. The undergraduates even steal our respirators. One signaller tracked his. Perhaps it was only borrowed but he removed it and we are awaiting results. The culprit has till Monday to confess before he goes into the lake!'

In between warnings about the falsity of propaganda and breathlessly excited accounts of his flight training, Crichton recounts the academic studies they were required to pursue alongside their military classes: 'The Proffessors [sic] have a silly habit of trying to prove every little statement … by colossal proofs involving trigonometry and differential calculus. Everyone begins to yawn and for the rest of the hour they might be lecturing brick walls.' These classes resulted in some 'v. tiresome University exams', before the men were finally let loose on the RAF, their six months in a strange haven over, and keen to enter the real world and 'help with bashing [Hitler]'.

This was not, of course, the full story. The College still had to contribute to the war effort: the railings on College land opposite the entrance were removed for scrap metal, and a firefighting corps was trained up to collaborate with members of Somerville, Ruskin and the Oxford University Press in case of emergency. Preparations began even before the outbreak of war. The room under the Hall (at the time used to store servants' bicycles) and Lecture Room A were designated refuge rooms, and provided with firefighting equipment, though a letter of June 1938 indicates the Bursar did not yet feel it necessary to provide tinned food beyond what was already stocked in the kitchens. In March of that year the Provost received a reminder to nominate staff members to train as Air Raid Wardens. The three blank application forms that remain in the archive suggest no-one ever came forward. Further documents preparing the University for warfare instruct colleges to estimate the space required to store historical treasures and paintings, should this be necessary. When war did arrive, the Provost's Lodgings were used as a depot for the Red Cross and Order of St John, and received a state visit from the Duchess of Kent in 1941. In April 1945 a Lancaster bomber crashed on a farm site owned by the College in Wantage,

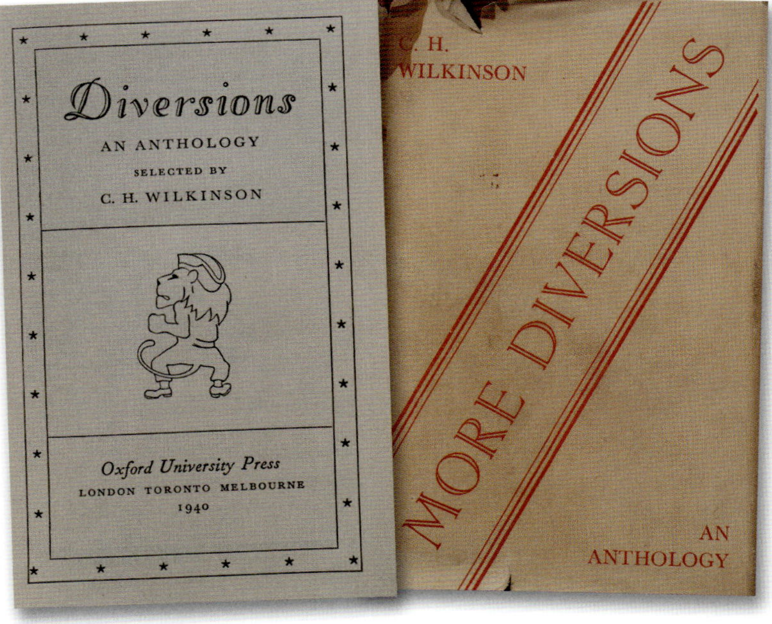

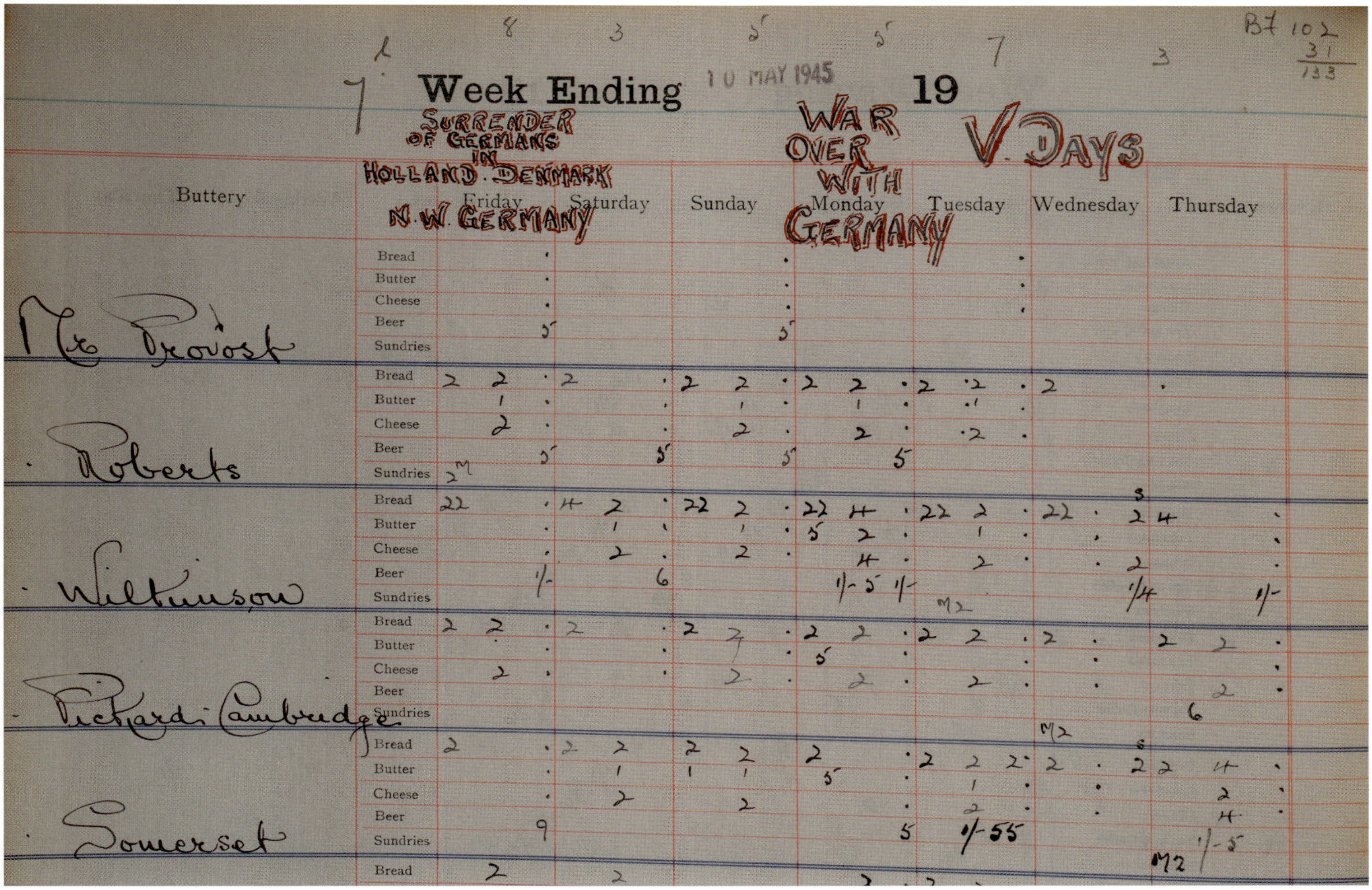

Celebration of the end of the Second World War by College servants in the Buttery book, 1945.

its ten-ton bomb resulting in a crater 57ft deep and 160ft wide, and £1,137 of repairs to the farmhouse and surrounding buildings.

Across the world, College members were playing their part. Ed Lewis had read Classics and Modern Greats at Worcester from 1934. During his undergraduate years in the University Officer Training Corps he was aware of the rumblings of war from mainland Europe, and immediately after graduating he accepted a University Commission and a post in the Navy Gunners at Woolwich. Just two years later Britain was at war, and over the next six years Ed was to fight in Belgium, Dunkirk, the Middle East, Algeria and Sicily. He describes his time in Worcester as the perfect preparation for his army career, which continued long after the end of war, taking him all around the world: 'It couldn't have been better in terms of personal development. I've always been so conscious of how much Worcester has done for me. People like me who were at Worcester in the pre-war period are some of the luckiest people in the world.'

Surprisingly, he suggests that the most useful legacy of his Worcester days was the Latin over which he had slaved as a first year. Sent out on reconnaissance in the Italian countryside, he was unable to find any useful observation points:

> *To see if I could get a general view of the country across the river I went some of the way up Mount Massico, about a mile behind the battle position. As I sat studying the ground through my field glasses, I suddenly found that a priest had come to join me! After a friendly 'Buon giorno' we were lost for conversation as he knew no English*

and I no Italian. I then had the bright idea of trying my Latin on him, so I said 'Parlate Latinum?', he nodded, and in no time we were getting on famously and he helped me to identify on the map all the features that I could see. I was glad to have put Classical Honour Moderations to good use!

Another Worcester alumnus who put skills gained at Oxford to good use was Oliver Philpot. He was among those who escaped from the prison camp at Sagan, Silesia, in 1943, by placing a wooden vaulting horse near the wires. In his account of the escape, *Stolen Journey*, he recalls the final leg of his long, dramatic journey from Stalag Luft III to a neutral Swedish ship at Weichselmünde:

I bent down and scrambled along the horizontal fenders with which the dock front was faced, and kept above the water but below the level of the surface of the dock. In seconds I reached the fence where it jutted out. It was child's play. I swung out on the projection of it over the water. It took my weight. I went slowly in order to avoid catching on the barbed wire. The exercise was extraordinarily similar to climbing after midnight round the railings which jut out into the lake of Worcester College Oxford.

It is good to know that the training provided by flight from the Dean or the Proctors' Bulldogs proved useful preparation for this more serious escape.

English tutor, Dean and Librarian, Cyril Wilkinson, who had received the Military Cross, the *Croix de Guerre* and the Italian *Croce di Guerra* in the First World War, and was Defence Commander of Oxford City from 1940, produced two anthologies for servicemen, *Diversions* and *More Diversions*. These pocket-sized collections contained extracts ranging from Shakespeare and Homer, to Worcester alumnus De Quincey, to modern comic reflections and nursery rhymes. Intended to 'provide relaxation in these days of stress and strain', as the cover of *More Diversions* put it, the books not only received newspaper plaudits, but also inspired personal letters to Wilkinson, notably from the relatives of Anthony Lyttleton, killed at Anzio in 1944, who spoke to his mother just days before his death of his delight at reading his old favourites so far away from home.

Annual volumes of the *College Record* during the second conflict contain long lists of men killed in action or held as prisoners of war. Of those who did return, the *Record* for 1945 notes that they had little trouble taking up the course of their studies, even if many arrived with wife and children in tow. The shortened War Degrees were continued to allow men to enter into a career more quickly.

Second World War Memorial in 1946 – every Remembrance Day the Provost reads out a list of those lost in the two wars.

Due to wartime restrictions, vital College equipment was in short supply: the *Record* invites Old Members to send any textbooks, gowns or sports clothing in College colours to help out the post-war undergraduates. The Second World War memorial was also paid for by subscription, and inscribed with a quotation from Milton's *Tractate of Education*: 'Brave men and worthy patriots, dear to God, and famous to all ages.'

1939: A Memory of Worcester

It was part of the post-Munich precautionary plan that major centres of administration such as Ministries would be evacuated to provincial cities, whose contribution to hosting them increased towards the safer west. Oxford had a good share, which dictated the twinning of many colleges – Worcester with St John's – to make room for the civil servants' offices from London.

This in turn – together with other factors like conscription – demanded rapid and radical change in the University itself and all its colleges. The three-year degree course was reduced to two, with pass degrees but no honours degrees being awarded. The longer legal course was shortened, but Medicine, the longest one for obvious reasons, remained unchanged. Tutors were lent and borrowed from one College to another, as required by the departure of so many to war service roles elsewhere (later including Bletchley).

The main convulsions took place in Michaelmas Term 1939, and left a very different University in place. Some students worked extra hard to gain maximum benefit from the reduced number of terms. Others gave up, believing they would forget anything they learnt even if they survived the war. Many concentrated on sports, where the calling-up of better players gave unforeseen chances to less good ones. The JCR was shared with St John's (there was no MCR in those days).

Others tried to cram everything into a five-term stay, because those who had won Scholarships or Exhibitions were allowed by their schools and colleges to come up immediately for the Hilary term. With the dates of call-up and the list of 'reserved occupations' constantly changing, it was worth doing this as a last resort. It sometimes also meant changing one's degree course from a serial one like Modern History to a more modular one like PPE.

It could certainly not be said that Oxford during the 'Phoney War' of 1939–40 was a place of gloom. The University adjusted well to the new situation, and everyone made the best they could of it. But it did of course become gloomier after the German attack on the Low Countries and the subsequent fall of France. Call-ups were brought forward, and two afternoons a week were spent at the University OTC (commanded by our Dean, Colonel Wilkinson) obtaining 'Cert A' and 'Cert B' to entitle one to direct entry to the Services. In my case, as a presumed future foot-soldier (though that later changed to armour) the process in August 1941 took me to Sandhurst, after only one cheerful and four gloomier terms at College.

Among my best friends were Peter Viney (later distinguished in the RAF, and whose brother perfected airborne radar for it); Peter Vansittart, later a good novelist; Colin Powell and James Sharpe, neither of whom survived the war. The Senior Scholar in the year before myself was the amiable Richard Adams, future author of *Watership Down*. My tutorial environment during those five terms consisted of Mr Bryan-Brown (the Public Orator) as my Moral Tutor; Mr Alan Brown of Queen's (later an MP for Oxford) as my Study Tutor; Mr Rodzianko of St John's as my Economics Tutor; and Mr Pickard-Cambridge as my Tutor in Moral Philosophy. My best friend among the Fellows was the History Tutor Dr Vere Somerset, whose comic opera *The Imbroglio* we put on at the Playhouse under the direction of a youthful Peter Ustinov.

Gowns were worn on all appropriate and some inappropriate occasions. Dinner in Hall was taken seriously, with sconcing for any solecism and keen competition among Scholars for the quickest faultless reading of the Worcester Grace. (My personal best was 17 seconds, but Mr Bryan-Brown said I marred it with false quantities.) Behaviour in the JCR and drinking in the Buttery were reasonably decorous. The only rules I recall being regularly flouted were those on return before midnight (the actual climbing-in being easy but hard to do without being spotted by Bryant, the formidable Head Porter) and on having young ladies in one's rooms beyond the appointed hour (which sometimes entailed helping them to climb out).

Hugo Jones

Place

8. The Hall

Jessica Goodman

The Hall is a central part of College life, and each generation of students feels protective of the particular incarnation in which they know it. Yet the Worcester Hall is not the timeless space it appears in the candlelight of a formal dinner. In the 300 years since the foundation of the College, it has undergone a series of renovations and alterations, not all of which have met with universal acceptance.

Although the Hall was included in the first central College building planned by Clarke and Hawksmoor, its interior was not completed until 1783–4, according to a design by James Wyatt (who also designed the original décor for the Chapel). With large false doors, an elegant chimneypiece, and a simple strip of decorative plasterwork at shoulder height, it would have been recognisable to modern Vigornians. Just under a century later, William Burges was commissioned to revitalise both Chapel and Hall, and the contrast with Wyatt's original simplicity could not have been greater. Burges' plans were typical of his rather exotic, gothic style, which was most famously demonstrated in designs for Cardiff Castle and Castell Coch. In Worcester's Hall, Burges complemented dark oak panelling in the lower section with a lavishly painted ceiling decorated with lines, key-patterns and other designs in a variety of colours. Into the panels were inlaid the arms of Old Members, and of some of

Opposite: *James Wyatt's design for the east end of the Hall* c.1783.
Above: *William Burges' design for the Hall, painted by Axel Haig, 1873.*

the original monastic orders from Gloucester College. Nonetheless, the outcome was not entirely what Burges has intended, but rather represented a compromise forced by budgetary restrictions: his original designs, inspired by the Italian cinquecento, had included marble cladding, a full-height chimneypiece, and a gilded ceiling, but they were rejected as too ornate and costly.

Even Burges' compromise was not to last longer than two decades: in 1909, under instructions from the architect Edward Warren, the colourful painting was replaced by a simple two-tone colour scheme. The large wooden door, which had been preserved by Burges, was plastered over, and in the 1920s the screen dividing the Hall from the serving area was removed. What remained was a curious hybrid, between Burges' sumptuous panelling below, and something akin to Wyatt's light simplicity above.

The Hall was to undergo one final renovation before it reached its modern incarnation, but it was a renovation that would be the subject of a passionate and fiercely fought dispute between the College and some of its former members. In 1965, plans were announced to restore the Hall according to the 18th-century plans of Wyatt. The proposal sparked outrage among some alumni, who saw the change as a desecration of their memories of Worcester, and a slight on those commemorated in the wooden panelling.

R. Morley-Fletcher exemplified the feelings of many when he wrote to Provost Franks in June 1965:

Left: *The Hall in 1893.* Opposite right: *The Hall in 1966.* Far right: *The Hall after the removal of the panelling.*

Instead of the dark floor-to-ceiling panelling which makes some College Halls so gloomy, we have the effect of a solid dining room below, lightened by what one might call a drawing-room appearance above. This may be scoffed at as a hybrid, but if so I think it is a very successful hybrid, which has stood the test of time and become a period piece worth preserving. I have not seen the Wyatt drawings which I understand it is proposed to follow, but I have the impression that the result would be all drawing room and no dining room.

A particularly vehement opponent of the change was former Provost Sir John Masterman, who argued that the College has always been a hybrid of different generations, and that it was the duty of each new generation to add to, and not destroy, the creations of its forbears. It is thanks to Masterman that we have such splendid images of the Burges Hall today, for he requested that a colour record be made at his own expense. In a letter to Provost Franks, he recalled the impact the Hall had made on him as a young man up in Oxford for interview: 'The names and coats of arms made me feel … that I belonged … to a community, and a community with a long and honourable past as well as a traditional and bright future. … You will get a fine chamber if you reconstruct, but I think you will lose the atmosphere of a traditional college Hall.'

A number of letters in opposition to the renovation were presented to a College meeting in the summer of 1965, but no change was made to the decision. In early 1966, F.J. Chapman asked the College Society to petition the College to halt the plan, on the basis that Old Members might be less likely to contribute to future works if they felt the changes bought by their contributions could be removed on a whim.

History Fellow James Campbell wrote to Masterman in defence of the project. He acknowledged the difficulty the Governing Body had faced in coming to its decision, particularly in the light of the reaction of Old Members. However, while he recognised the importance of preserving the memory of those who had contributed to the Burges project, he argued that the 1870s renovation itself had been a controversial change, while the new plans represented a restoration of the past, rather than a disrespectful attack. He saw this as the best way to resolve the 'mish-mash' the Hall then represented.

Further attempts to halt the renovation plans were unsuccessful. In a resigned letter to those who had signed his petition, Chapman described the plan as an 'unforgiveable breach of trust' on the part of the Provost and Fellows. The College Society was asked officially to 'deplore' the alteration in June 1966, although by this stage work had already begun. Morley-Fletcher wrote in the Oxford Mail of the 'vandalism' being perpetuated by the Fellows and cut the College out of his will. In August he wrote to Masterman: 'To eat in Wyatt's corner house restaurant would be an insult to the memory of many of my friends now dead, and would be turning the knife in the wound.'

Such strength of feeling has been dissipated by time; the furore over the refurbishment has been relegated to a historical footnote. Modern students are unaware that the Hall was ever any different, and proudly describe it as the only 18th-century hall in Oxford. The panelling from the Burges design was largely placed in storage. Only the panels commemorating a few notable members are preserved on the staircase leading to the Upper SCR: the rest of the names commemorated on the Burges panelling are recorded on a plaque above the servery. They, and Masterman's scrapbook of photographs and cuttings, are the only surviving evidence of the dispute, and of the rift that tore through Worcester alumni nearly five decades ago.

The College Grace

Nos miseri homines et egeni, pro cibis quos nobis ad corporis subsidium benigne es largitus, tibi, Deus omnipotens, Pater cælestis, gratias reverenter agimus; simul obsecrantes, ut iis sobrie, modeste atque grate utamur. Insuper petimus, ut cibum angelorum, verum panem cælestem, verbum Dei æternum, Dominum nostrum Iesum Christum, nobis impertiaris; utque illo mens nostra pascatur et per carnem et sanguinem eius foveamur, alamur, et corroboremur. Amen.

We unhappy and unworthy men do give thee most reverent thanks, Almighty God, our heavenly Father, for the victuals which thou hast bestowed on us for the sustenance of the body, at the same time beseeching thee that we may use them soberly, modestly and gratefully. And above all we beseech thee to impart to us the food of angels, the true bread of heaven, the eternal Word of God, Jesus Christ our Lord, so that the mind of each of us may feed on him and that through his flesh and blood we may be sustained, nourished and strengthened. Amen.

9. Worcester Chapel, William Burges and the Art of Illumination

Susan Gillingham

Although work on the Chapel, Hall and Library began in the 1720s, following Margaret Alcorne's bequest of £798, legal wrangles and other demands on funding meant that the Chapel was not completed until over 70 years later. Throughout this period, the Chapel was located by Staircase 12, appropriately on the site of the medieval camera used by the Benedictines from Malmesbury Abbey from about 1298, as the red griffin over the door bears witness. James Wyatt was eventually responsible for the neo-classical designs of both Hall and Chapel; the latter was consecrated in 1791, on almost the same site as Whethamstede's Chapel of 1424. Since then little has changed in its structure: the domed ceiling, the pillars and pilasters, the corner niches, the antechamber, and even the false West Door, set offside centre, remain. In fact, the only significant difference is the addition of three windows on its north side.

What has changed, of course, is the decoration. By the 1850s, Fellows and Scholars deemed the Chapel rather drab for daily worship, with its faceless woodwork and its 'stone-coloured paint now begrimed with dust and gas'. The Governing Body considered William Burges' designs on 9 December 1863. Their choice of Burges – who was already gaining a reputation as an exotic and exuberant art-architect with medieval Gothic predilections – demonstrates their hope for a dramatic transformation. Burges' designs certainly exuded a remarkably eclectic synthesis of artistic tastes. His commissions and sketches show he not only had an affinity with French Gothic art and architecture, but also with classical Byzantium; and not only with Italianate architecture, but with classical archaeology and the architecture of Greece. He was also drawn to 19th-century Pre-Raphaelite art: his friends included Dante Gabriel Rosetti (who like Burges had been educated at King's College School) and the upcoming pre-Raphaelite glazier, Henry Holiday. He was also a fairly prominent Freemason. His churchmanship was neither Catholic nor evangelical, neither broad church nor liberal. So on 9 December 1863, Burges' plans were approved by the equally eclectic Governing Body (comprising 18 clergy and just two laymen). The only change they asked for was, predictably, 'a more distinctly ecclesiastical character'.

Burges' fascination was with the Middle Ages. 'I have been brought up in the 13th-century belief, and in that belief I intend to die', he once said. It is hard to know what drew him to this 18th-century chapel: maybe its medieval origins. Yet, other than the three windows, it lacked the challenge of architectural change, and Burges, trained also as a civil engineer, usually relished redesigning the outside as well as the inside of a commission. Maybe it was simply the challenge of working with so many different

Carvings of a dodo and a unicorn on the finials of the Chapel pews.

surfaces, such as plaster, glass, walnut wood, alabaster, marble and stone. Maybe – and this is a theory that no commentator on Burges has yet expanded – it enabled him to decorate the Chapel so that it resembled an illuminated medieval manuscript. There are instances of this in his other works – the Hebrew calligraphy and iconography on the walls of the Roof Garden at Cardiff Castle, for example. His two periods in Constantinople would have introduced him to Byzantine medieval artefacts and his fascination with Gothic France would have surely included Carolingian and Anglo-Norman decorated manuscripts from, for example, workshops in Paris and Rheims. So it is not impossible that, as well as other obvious influences, Burges would also have imitated this medium. Burges frequently used the number seven throughout the Chapel, and there are seven features in the refurbishment that suggest it.

One of the first impressions is the overwhelming number of animals, birds and plants dominating the walls and pews, giving the Chapel the appearance of a medieval bestiary. Three of the six arabesques on each side of the windows, each illustrating the words of the *Benedicite* above them, are rich in illustrations of birds, beasts and sea-creatures. The walnut-wood carvings on the finials of the pews depict over 30 animals, some mythical and symbolic, for example, the unicorn and pelican by the Chaplain's stall; some biblical, as cockerel, lion and lamb; some simply whimsical, as the dodo and the pangolin (by the Provost's stall) and the tortoise (by the Vice-Provost's). On one side of the east window, an ox and bullock symbolise Jewish sacrifice, and on the other a lamb and (again) a pelican symbolise Christian sacrifice.

Another prominent feature is the group of six gilded friezes running horizontally around the Chapel, just above the dado. The rich colours and the naturalistic figures displaying medieval drapery are reminscent of the gilded illuminations of saints and martyrs in, for example, Byzantine Psalters. Furthermore, the geometric and

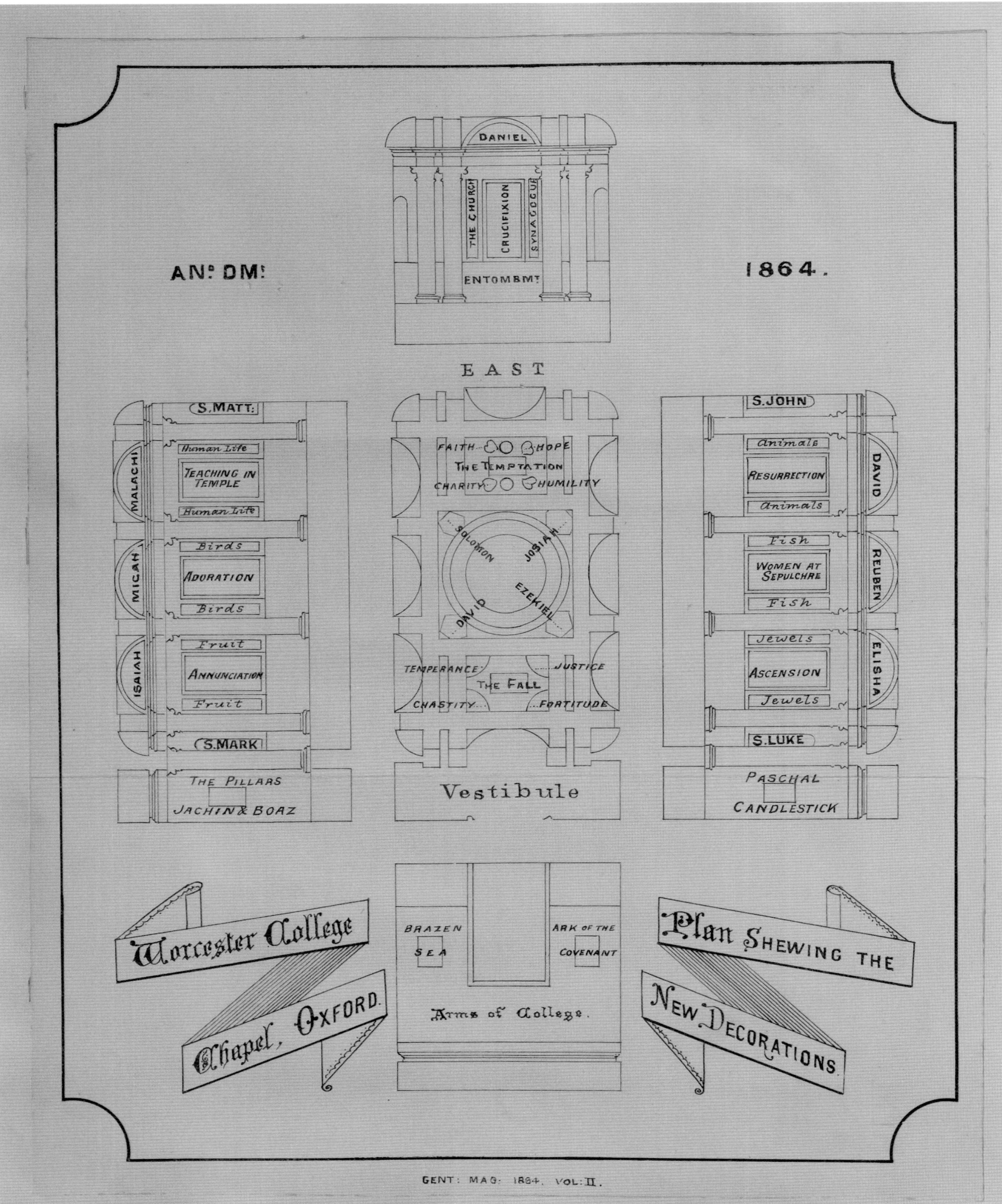
DANIEL
THE CHURCH
CRUCIFIXION
SYNAGOGUE
ENTOMBMT
ANo DMI
1864.
EAST
S.MATT:
Human Life
TEACHING IN TEMPLE
Human Life
MALACHI
Birds
ADORATION
Birds
MICAH
Fruit
ANNUNCIATION
Fruit
ISAIAH
S.MARK
THE PILLARS
JACHIN & BOAZ
FAITH
HOPE
THE TEMPTATION
CHARITY
HUMILITY
SOLOMON
JOSIAH
DAVID
EZEKIEL
TEMPERANCE
JUSTICE
THE FALL
CHASTITY
FORTITUDE
Vestibule
S.JOHN
Animals
RESURRECTION
Animals
DAVID
Fish
WOMEN AT SEPULCHRE
Fish
REUBEN
Jewels
ASCENSION
Jewels
ELISHA
S.LUKE
PASCHAL
CANDLESTICK
BRAZEN
SEA
ARK OF THE
COVENANT
Arms of College.
Worcester College
Chapel, Oxford.
Plan Shewing the
New Decorations.
GENT: MAG: 1864. VOL: II.

Opposite: *The Chapel design from* The Gentleman's Magazine, *1864.*
Above left: *Statue of St Mark.* Above right: *Statue of St Matthew.*

floral decoration in the antechapel – what has sometimes been called 'Pompeian ornament' – reminds one of Greek-inspired flourishes in Byzantine manuscripts.

One of the most popular types of medieval manuscripts was the illuminated Gospel Book. Here Burges' medium is stained glass rather than a smaller vellum canvas, but in the Middle Ages the two forms were closely related. The arrangement of seven scenes from the life of Christ also has many associations with coloured miniatures depicting Christ's life in medieval Psalters; such scenes are also found in *Bibles Historiales,* whose 'narrative' was simply scenes from the life of Christ.

Both medieval Psalters and Gospel Books display a fascination with the personae of the four evangelists. Burges' addition of the evangelists in the four niches caused a reaction from a few Fellows, who thought this was close to popery. Alongside and above each statue are representations of the lives of each evangelist: these were hardly objects of veneration, but rather, as in medieval manuscripts, they served simply to teach the origins of the Christian faith.

One key motif of both western and eastern illuminated Psalters, as well as in the *Biblia Pauperum,* is to use Jewish and Christian symbols to illustrate the superiority of the New Testament over the Old. One obvious example in the Chapel is the seven prophetic figures in the lunettes high above the seven windows, where what is written on the scroll is seen as fulfilled in the window below it. Another instance is on the wall panels on each side of the East window, which depict a classical trope in medieval manuscripts and

Left: *Painted panels showing the figures of the Blind Synagogue and Seeing Church.* Opposite: *The prophet Daniel over the east window.* Opposite below: *St Olaf and St Benedict.*

architecture of the 'blind synagogue' and the 'seeing church'. By the entrance, the ante-chapel is full of Jewish symbols (the Ark, the scrolls of Law, the Menorah) but, as one moves through this 'Tent of Meeting' into the Chapel itself, one makes a journey from the 'shadows of Judaism' into the 'Christian light'.

Lavishly illuminated manuscripts have a patron, whether ecclesiastical (an abbot or prior) or secular (a wealthy landlord). The Chapel reveals a similar practice: Charles Henry Olive Daniel, who had also been educated at King's College School, was in 1863 a Fellow (later to become Provost) and he was a key supporter of Burges' commission. He is commemorated two, possibly three, times. 'Olive' Daniel's red beard and hair are immortalised on the frieze to the left of the Vice-Provost's stall, where he has become the Norwegian warrior-saint 'Olaf'. Daniel is also found in the adjacent gilded frieze of the 12 prophets. And most prominently of all, he leans over his scroll, from the book of Daniel, above the east window.

Finally, an unusual feature of Worcester Chapel is its 'wordiness'. It has almost as many words as illustrations, and many of these are from canticles and psalms. This again echoes illuminated Psalters, Books of Hours and Breviaries, where words and illustrations play off each other to facilitate prayer. In the 1860s Matins was compulsory: hence Burges' choice of two morning canticles: the *Benedicite*,

Above: *Frieze of angels.* Right: *St Cecilia and her pipes, from the frieze of martyrs.*

which runs in a sevenfold schema around the cornice, and the *Te Deum,* which runs in gold inlay around the dado at the backs of the pews. Burges also used antiphons from psalms used at Matins: Psalm 95, the *Venite,* is inscribed above the main door ('Today if you will hear his voice, harden not your hearts ...') and below it is Psalm 100 ('Enter into his gates with thanksgiving'). The seven prophets also offer words as they hold up their scrolls in the lunettes above in the windows. And on the floor of both the chancel and nave are further words in Latin. This is clearly a chapel to be 'read' as well as viewed.

In addition to words, there is music. For example, in the frieze on the north side, the angels (Uriel, with a psalms scroll, Raphael, Gabriel and Michael) sing the words 'to thee all Angels cry aloud', accompanied by a choir of eight others who respond with 'Holy Holy, Holy, Lord God of Hosts'. The same psalm chant is found on the organ bench. On the frieze of martyrs by the Provost's stall, with its witty inscription 'God', St Cecilia is commemorated with her pipes; on the mosaic floor, St Wilfred also holds a (as yet unidentified) scroll of music; and on the alabaster candlestick, choir boys sing the *Te Deum.*

Since the 1860s, the Chapel has twice been cleaned (1949 and 1981) but the major restoration work took place in 2002, bringing Burges' designs to life in all their vivid detail. At this time, the organ was also restored, and the Chapel now promotes two highly competent choirs. So this is a place where what is seen (in decoration and word) is integrally related to what is heard (in organ and song). Even if Burges really did not intend the Chapel to be used like a medieval Prayer Book, unwittingly, he seems to have achieved this result.

Left: *Choirboys singing the* Te Deum *around the alabaster candlestick.* Below: *Cleaning the frescoes.*

10. The Library

Joanna Parker

Worcester's magnificent library contains one of the richest collections among Oxbridge colleges, and continues to make a major contribution to scholarship, especially in the areas of architectural history and of 17th-century history and literature.

As a result of the College's unusual history, the Library's strengths do not lie in its holdings of medieval manuscripts. Unfortunately, the library of Gloucester College was dispersed at the Dissolution of the Monasteries, when 'manuscripts flew about like butterflies', as John Aubrey wrote. One manuscript, a collection of anti-Lollard tracts given to the Library by John Whethamstede, Abbot of St Albans, passed into the hands of a former Fellow of Merton, Robert Serlys, who presented it to his college; it was generously returned to the Library by Merton in 1938. It contains Whethamstede's verse injunction to the students:

Fratribus Oxonie datur in munus liber iste
Johannem Whethamstede
Per patrem pecorum prothomartiris Angligenarum •
Quem si quis rapiat • raptim titulumve retractet •
Vel Jude laqueum • vel furcas sensiat Amon •

To the brothers of Oxford this book is given as a gift
John Whethamstede
through the father of the sheep of the protomartyr of England-born men [ie. St Alban],
which if anyone should take, or, taken, should retract the entitlement,
may he feel either the noose of Judas or the gallows of Haman.
[translation by David Howlett]

More books have survived from the Gloucester Hall period. A donations book from the period with entries by Degory Wheare for 1630–39 gives some titles, and a surviving catalogue dating from the early 18th century provides more. John Aubrey gave an interesting collection of books and manuscripts, chiefly mathematical. One, by Thomas Hobbes, is inscribed 'For my noble frend Mr Aubrie. From his servant Tho: Hobbes'; another is Aubrey's own copy of Euclid acquired in 1648 when he was an undergraduate at Oxford at Trinity College.

But it is to the period after the re-foundation that the wealth of the Library derives, with the munificent bequest of George Clarke in 1736 and the less celebrated but also sizeable bequest of books from Provost Gower in 1777. These collections together make it a treasure-house of 17th- and early 18th-century material.

Top: *Whethamstede's verse injunction to the students.* Above: *Inscription by Thomas Hobbes in one of the books given to Gloucester Hall by John Aubrey.* Right: *George Clarke's bookplate.* Far right: *Miniature of George Clarke.*

George Clarke (1661–1736) was a collector on a grand scale. He was not especially interested in early printed books, and he had only one medieval manuscript (of the *Life of the Black Prince* by the herald of Sir John Chandos), but he bought in all areas of the learning and culture of his day: theology, law and science; classical literature and antiquities; history, maps and travels; art, architecture and literature, including many items by Dryden, Pope and Prior. His collection of architectural treatises was 'one of the best of his time', according to the architectural historian Howard Colvin. It included 50 books from Inigo Jones' library, many with annotations, the most famous of which is the copy of Palladio that Jones took with him on his tour of Italy in 1613–14. Clarke bought mostly in England. He did twice go to the Continent, once to the Low Countries in 1706 and once to France in 1715 but, to his regret, he never got to Italy. Friends and agents also bought for him from abroad. Clarke's remarkable collections of prints and drawings are described in more detail in the chapter on 'Treasures'.

Clarke's collection is more than the sum of its parts, remarkable though these are: it is of considerable interest as a well-preserved example of an early 18th-century library, from which we can learn much about the culture of the period – for example, the dominance of French culture, shown in the many French books and the prints of French buildings and interior decoration. It illustrates the interconnections between an individual and his tastes and pursuits and his times.

Clarke's library was not just for show or assembled for the pleasure of acquisition: he read his books (in his brief autobiography he speaks of 'the satisfaction and amusement' which reading had afforded him before the failure of his eyesight) and annotated them, often writing out passages from other

The DEVISES MOTTO'S &c used by the Parliament Officers on STANDARDS, BANNERS, &c in the late CIVIL WARS; taken from an Original Manuscript done at ye time now in ye hands of Benja. Cole of Oxford. Publish'd at ye Desire of divers Gentlemen to be Bound up with ye Lord Clarendon's Histy.

Ora et Pugna Iuvet et Iuvabit JEHOVAH	Lex Suprema Salus Patriæ	Only in Heaven	One of These	My Oath and Sword Maintain this Word.	Pro Rege Lege Grege
Majr. Skippon one of the Comittie for the Militia and Capt. of a Troop of Horse 1642	Capt. Harvie Capt. of the City Trainbands and Capt. of a Troop of Horse 1642	Capt. Manwaring one of ye City Capt. and Capt. of a Troop of Horse 1642	Capt. Brown one of ye City Capt. and Capt. of a Troop of Horse & Coll. of a Regt. of Dragoons 1642	Captain Wasberne Capt. of a Troop of Horse 1642	Capt. Withers
	Ut Rex Noster Sit Noster Rex	Deus … Sic Pacem Quærimus	Pro Protestantibus	Non est Lex Iunior Vita	Rex Persona Pugnans Potestate sua; Verbum Dei; Lex Populi
Capt. Brown a Draper by St. Austins Gate London	Capt. Gold	Capt. Massingberd	Capt. Graves	Capt. Robinson Capt. of a Troop of Horse & Comp. of Foot	Coll. Maleverer Coll. of a Regt. of Horse 1642
Propter Deum Conventum Evangelium	Dissipantur Inimici	Fructus Virtutis	Neque Video Neque Timeo	Coram Zerubbabel	Agitata Virescit
Capt. Creed Capt. of a Troop of Horse 1643	Coll. Ridgely	Sr. William Waller	Capt. Ayloffe	Capt. Norwood Capt. of a Troop of Horse Lond. 1643	Sr. Nich. Buron on his Expedition 1640 to ye North
Fides Temerata Cogit	Only in Heaven	If God be wth us who shall be against us	Bella Beatorum Bella	Pro Deo Principe et Patria	Eripiendo Malos a rege Stabilitur Iustitia Solium
Capt. Trenchard on his Expedition to Ireland 1642	Sr. Arth. Haslerig	Capt. Duglas 1642	Capt. Long 1642	Capt. Neal 1642	Capt. Lilcott 1642 taken at Edge Hill after 6 Months Imprison. Died 1643
For Religion King & Country Ama Puissance	Pro Divinis … Humanis …	Ut Servet Incolumem	God we shall do Through Valiantly	In Extremis Apparet Deus	
Earl of Stamford 1642	Capt. Hen. Ireton 1642	Coll. Lambert 1642	Capt. Russell 1642	Coll. Doding	Capt. Roper 1642
Verbum Dei	Deo Duce Nil Desperandum	Soyes Ferme	Tam Gladio Quam Trula; Sanguis Cæmentum Facit	Muto Quadrata Rotundis	Lacerata Pro Patria Pugna
Majr. Ludlow 1642	Capt. Sheffield	Sr. Willm. Constable Kt. & Bart. Coll. 1642	Capt. Reeve 1642	Coll. Cook of Gloc. sh.	Capt. Moulson 1643
Magna Charta; Preserva Legem Domine	Patriæ Poscente Paratum	Per Bellum ad Pacem	Cave adsum	Conantia Frangere Frango	Stat Cadit Huc
Capt. Hooker	Capt. Barnard	Lord Grey	Majr. Guntier	Capt. Mason	Majr. Weldon
Pro Deo et Patria	Gladius Jehovæ et Gideonis	Contra Impios	For Reformation	Oramus Pro Rege Pugnamus Pro Deo Morimur Pro Patria	For ye Cause of ye Lord I draw my Sword
Sr. Willm. Sanders	Capt. Aylworth	Capt. Noke	Capt. Copley	Majr. Whitby	Capt. Markham

Sold by Benj. Cole in Bear Lane

Opposite: *Devices and mottoes used on the Parliamentary army standards, engraved and published by Benjamin Cole, 1726. From Clarke's print collection.* Above and below right: *Set of engraved playing cards satirising the South Sea Bubble, published by Thomas Bowles and Emanuel Bowen, 1720, from Clarke's print collection.*

books and manuscripts. In one of his copies of Serlio's treatise on architecture (Venice, 1569) he made notes on the different editions and transcribed Inigo Jones' annotations from the copy in Queen's Library whose shelfmark he notes. In his copy of the Ben Jonson folio of 1640, he wrote out a passage about Jonson from Clarendon's *Life*, then in manuscript, and an unpublished poem to Jonson by his stepfather Samuel Barrow. He noted in his copy of 'An Elegy upon the Death of My Lord Francis Villiers' (a small eight-page pamphlet, of which only one other copy survives) that it was 'by Andrew Marvell', and this is how the poem got into modern editions of Marvell's poetry. He used his collections as working collections. From his prints he learnt about foreign buildings; they provided sources for the Oxford Almanack designs, which he was involved in producing, and his drawings, prints and books gave ideas for Oxford buildings. He shared his library with others. In a letter to Charles Jervas dated 29 November 1716, Alexander Pope writes:

> *That you have not heard from me of late, ascribe not to the usual laziness of your correspondent, but to a ramble to Oxford, where your name is mentioned with honour, even in a land flowing with tories. I had the good fortune there to be often in the conversation of Dr Clarke. He entertained me with several drawings, and particularly with the original designs of Inigo Jones' Whitehall.*

Clarke's library would also have been available to Nicholas Hawksmoor. Links can be traced, for example, between some of John Webb's drawings for churches in Clarke's collection and some of Hawksmoor's church designs.

Clarke was interested not just in his own collection but in libraries in general. He made regular recommendations of foreign purchases for the Bodleian Library, and donated gifts of books and pictures. He also made two unsuccessful attempts to secure the Thomason Tracts (the huge collection of Civil War pamphlets assembled by the bookseller George Thomason, now in the British Library) for the Bodleian, which suggests a particular interest in the recent past. He was very aware of the value of his library. In his will, he left careful instructions about how it was to be cared for. For example, £50 was to be laid out each year for new purchases. One of the first Fellows to be appointed from his foundation was to be Library-

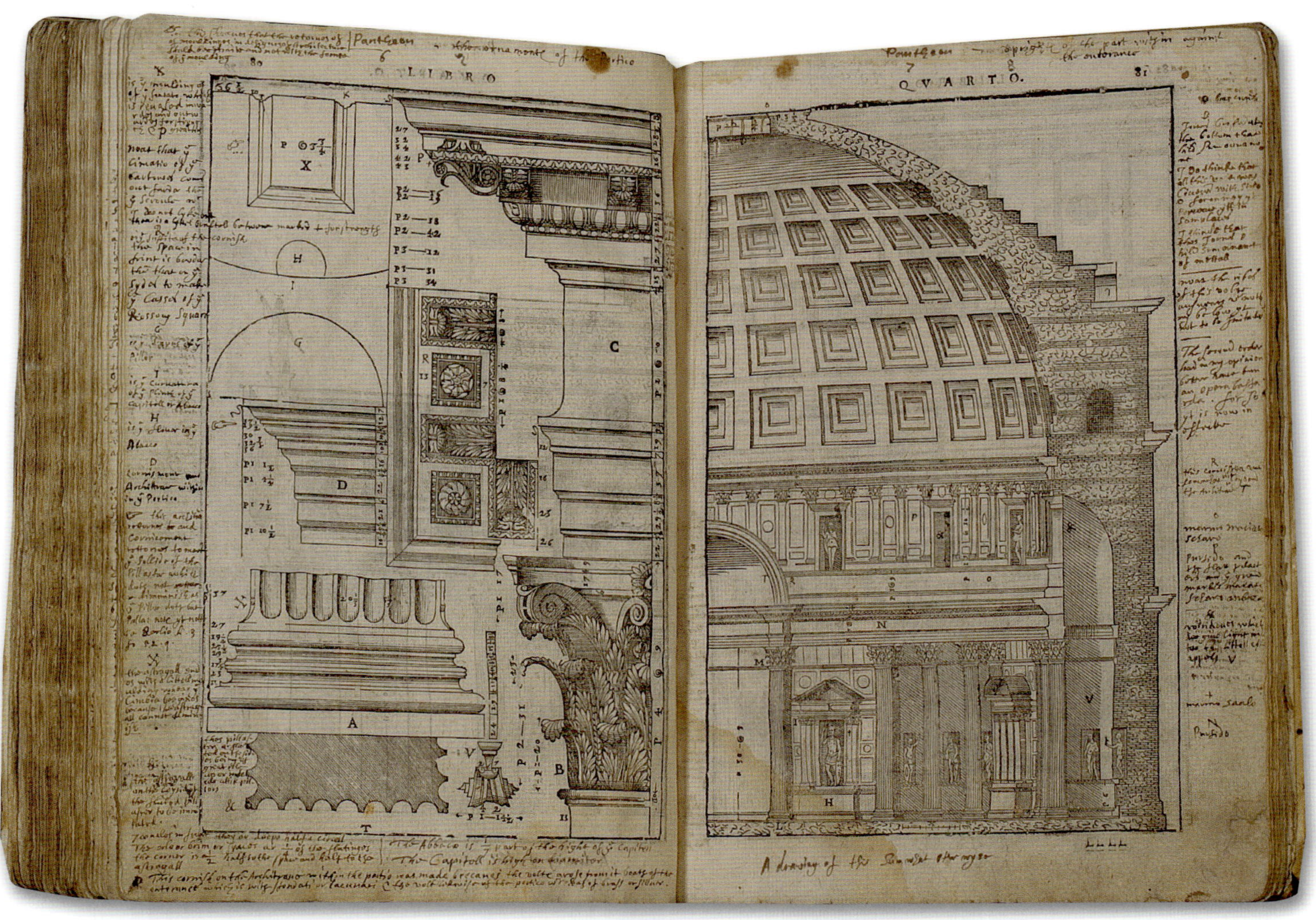

Pages from Book IV of Andrea Palladio's I quattro libri dell'architettura *with Inigo Jones' annotations.*

Keeper, and to aid him 'there should be some young Gownsman to attend constantly in the said Library, to reach down Books, and other Services there', to be paid £5 per annum. The Library was to be inspected once a year to make sure the books were all present, and the Library-Keeper was to be removed from his post by the Provost and Fellows if he neglected his duties, without appeal to the Visitor. Clarke also took trouble to make sure his books would be housed in appropriate conditions. Two letters that he wrote to Richard Blechinden in 1734 show him taking a keen interest in the fittings. At the end of the first letter, written from London on 16 January, he asks a question about the bookcases: 'I am sorry to hear your Library windows have sufferd so much by the late winds. Don't you intend to have shelves for books, between the Windows? Francklin says he has no orders about them'. In the second letter, written on 23 January, he returns to the subject:

> *Mr Francklyn's son told me the shelves were up on the East side, and ends of your Library, but that none were ordered between the Windows: I told him, that I thought it was designd, to have some there, and bid him speak to Mr Bourchier. Should not the doores that are to stand before the books, be wyred? I did not understand that any directions were given for the doeing it.*

He wanted his legacy to the College to be preserved for future use.

It was presumably because of this perspective that he did not dispose of the papers of his father, even though he was of a different

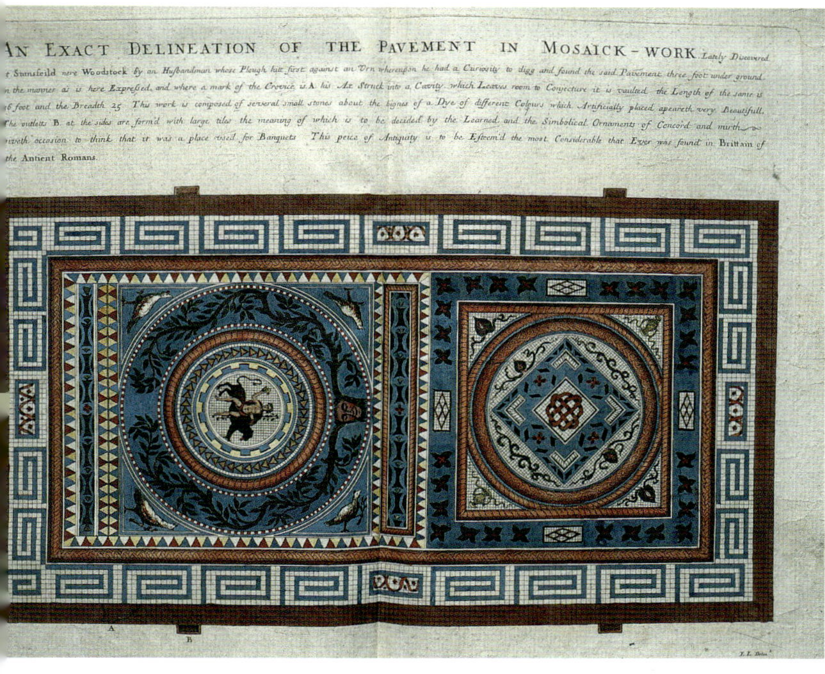

ABOVE: *Print of the Stonesfield Mosaic, 1712, from Clarke's print collection.* BELOW RIGHT: *John Webb, theatre drawings: plan and elevation, from Clarke's drawings collection.*

political persuasion. George Clarke was a moderate Tory, who survived the Glorious Revolution, holding office under Charles II, James II, William and Mary, and Anne. He had a picture of Charles I by Edward Bower in his rooms at All Souls which John Faber, probably at Clarke's instigation, made into a mezzotint entitled 'The royal martyr'. Thomas Tickell wrote a poem about it, in which he hailed Clarke in the following lines:

O Clarke, to whom a STUART trusts her Reign
O'er Albion's Fleets, and Delegates the Main;
Dear, as the Faith thy loyal Heart hath sworn,
Transmit this Piece to Ages yet unborn.
This Sight shall damp the raging Ruffian's Breast,
The Poison spill, and half-drawn Sword arrest;
To soft Compassion stubborn Traitors bend,
And One destroy'd a Thousand Kings defend.

Another collection of prints owned by Clarke and published by Thomas and John Bowles (*c.*1727) describes 'The reign of Charles I', and ends with Charles I's apotheosis, with flights of angels and cherubs. In contrast, William Clarke had been a member of the parliamentary army secretariat and took notes for the General Council of the Army at the radical army debates in 1647. In 1650 he went to Scotland with Cromwell, and stayed behind as secretary to successive commanders in chief, including General Monck. As a trusted agent of Monck's he flourished after the Restoration; he became Secretary at War to Charles II, was granted the Great Lodge and 60 acres in Marylebone Park and was knighted in 1661. He had, however, been present at the trial and execution of Charles I, taking notes on the scaffold, something he presumably kept well hidden after the Restoration. It is not known how much George knew about his father's history, but it is a fair surmise that he understood the significance of the papers as historical documents.

William Clarke's library adds immensely to the scholarly value of the collection. Like his son, he was an assiduous book collector from his youth, and was clearly a man of considerable general culture. Little is known about his early life, but he must have come from an educated family, as he started collecting books in his boyhood, and by the time he died he had a good general collection of theology and religious controversy, law and literature, including poetry and plays. In addition he assembled a huge collection of 7,000 contemporary pamphlets and newsbooks, second only in size to the Thomason collection, and containing many rare and some unique items, often with a Scottish interest, because he was based in Scotland for so long. William Clarke must have pursued book

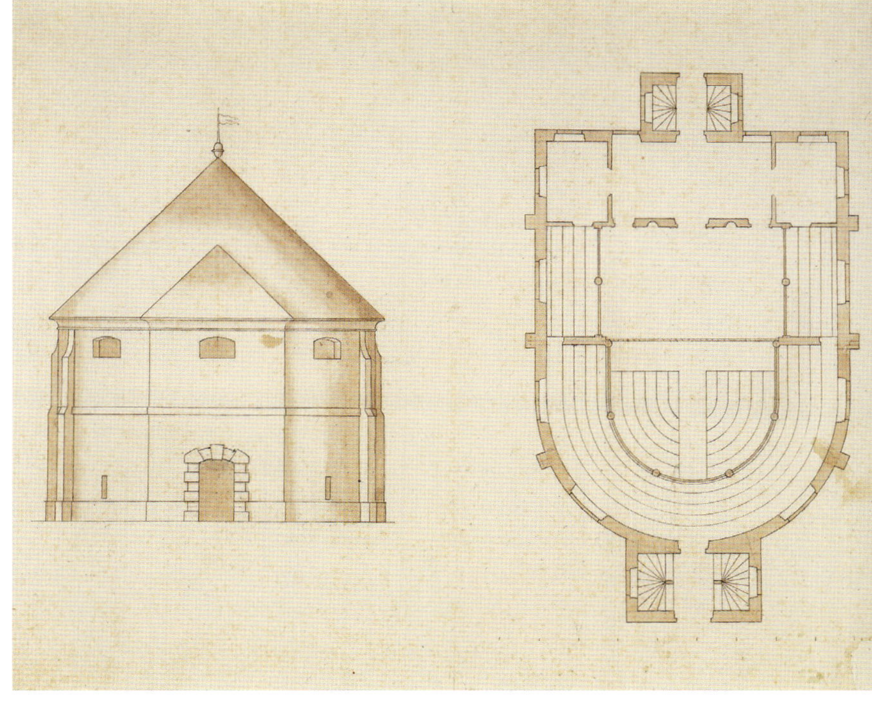

Medley prints, c.1706, by George Bickham the Elder. From Clarke's print collection.

collecting with a certain passion; among items he acquired were some books from the royal library when it was dispersed – at the Restoration, he had to pay a fine of £20 for books, paintings and furniture which had belonged to the King, which he claimed he had disposed of when in Scotland, although several books from the royal library with Clarke's signature in them are still in the Library, including Charles Butler's *Principles of Music* (1636), beautifully bound in vellum for Charles II when Prince of Wales.

The Clarke papers, William Clarke's record of his work for the Parliamentary army, are a key source for understanding several aspects of the English Revolution. They consist of some 47 quarto and folio volumes, partly in shorthand and partly in longhand. Clarke was transcribing his shorthand notes into longhand before his death in 1666 in the Second Dutch War. By the time of his death, he had reached 1651 and so had made a transcript of the Putney Debates, destroying the original shorthand notes. The Clarke papers sat on the shelves in the Library probably unread until the end of the 19th century when the Librarian, H.A. Pottinger, brought them to the attention of Sir Charles Firth, who edited substantial parts of them for the Camden Society. In 1973, Eric Sams identified the shorthand as being Thomas Shelton's *Tachygraphy*, the same system that was used by Pepys; subsequently Dr Frances Henderson made a complete transcript of all the shorthand parts of the papers, some of which has been published by the Camden Society. This is a great example of the important role libraries can play in preserving things that will be of interest to future generations.

George Clarke would surely have been pleased that his collections continued to be studied in later times. The architect and landscape designer Sanderson Miller records in his diaries that he

Above: *Charles Butler,* The Principles of Music, *1636, bound in vellum for Charles II when he was Prince of Wales.* **Right:** *'His Highness Hoo Hoo Hoo, Protector of Lubberland': satirical woodcut of Richard Cromwell, 1659, from William Clarke's library.*

visited Worcester to look at the drawings and books. On 6 January 1750, he records that he was in Oxford and 'At Worcester to see Jones' designs', and again on 6 November 1756 he notes: 'Went to Worcester library. Made catalogue of books on architecture.' Some later reactions due to changing tastes might have disappointed: Dean Burgon writes in his account of the College in Shaw's *Arms of the Colleges of Oxford* (1850):

> *In the presses is a large collection of engravings, and a few drawings, bequeathed by Dr Clarke. Among these, are discoverable some of the monstrous designs of Hawkesmoor and others, for modernising All Souls', Brasenose, Magdalen, and other colleges, – designs which it is evident were at one time gravely entertained, and which it ought to be a matter of sincere rejoicing to reflect were eventually set aside.*

Clarke's books were significantly enriched by the bequest of Provost Gower's books, and Gower's signature is almost as common as Clarke's monogram. Gower's interests were mostly literary. His collection of plays may well have been larger than Clarke's; together they make up over 1,000 volumes. Both owned Spanish books, but Gower's collection was again somewhat larger. He also contributed books in Portuguese, Arabic and Hebrew.

Two Librarians and book-lovers of a later period further enriched the Library's holdings: Henry Allison Pottinger, Librarian, 1884–1911, and Cyril Hackett Wilkinson, Librarian, 1919–58. Pottinger, who gave all his books to the College, was an omnivorous collector; he is said to have had a special coat made with pockets to hold books, and he bought up contemporary pamphlets and books on every conceivable topic, as well as older 16th-century material.

Wilkinson was a bibliophile in a different mode from Pottinger, a member of the Roxburghe Club and a lover of first editions

Above: *Portrait of Cyril Hackett Wilkinson by Allan Gwynne-Jones RA, 1959.*
Right: *Window in memory of Richard Sayce, engraved by Simon Whistler, showing Montaigne's tower.*

and bibliographic rarities. His knowledge of the Library was unrivalled and he wrote an excellent account of it for the Oxford Bibliographical Society. He made extensive notes of provenances and ownership inscriptions. He brought off a great coup in acquiring for the Library some of the Clarke papers that had not come to Worcester but had ended up in the collection of F.W. Leyborne-Popham at Littlecote House in Wiltshire; those he did not manage to acquire were subsequently lost, including George Clarke's autobiography. He also purchased a good collection of newsbooks to add to William Clarke's. He used decanal fines to buy more plays for the theatre collection. He assembled the collection of Daniel Press items and other private press books. His personal collection contained many 16th- and 17th-century items, and he left a careful selection to the Library to fill gaps in the collection, for example a first edition of Spenser's *Faerie Queene* (1590 and 1596); the rest were auctioned at Sotheby's and the proceeds went into a trust for the College. On the debit side, to modern eyes, his fondness for taking rare pamphlets out of bound volumes, trimming the edges and re-binding them in morocco or cloth was mistaken. The 'special preparation' for applying to leather bindings that he describes in his article had the unfortunate effect of leaving white smears on many of the leather books. But we are all the prisoners of our own time. It was Wilkinson who had T.J. Wise made an Honorary Fellow; he is said to have justified this after Wise's exposure as a forger and thief by remarking that it had stopped Wise from stealing from the collection!

The modern library has been built up more recently. The Worcester alphabet of the 1920s (of which at the moment we only know the one couplet) says:

L is for Library – no use for Schools
'First Editions Only' is one of the rules.

But in 1928–9, the room above the Hall was converted into an undergraduate reading room: the floor was strengthened by rods

Above: *The Lower Library.* Right: *Detail of the books.*

carrying it from the roof, a new ceiling, lighting and heating put in, and access to it provided by continuing the staircase upwards (total cost £937). In 1981, the undergraduate library was extended into the roof space over the Lower Library through the generosity of Rupert Murdoch and other donors. The attitude of some of earlier generations to the Library is summed up in the Worcester anecdote in which two undergraduates are conversing at the foot of the Library staircase. One says to the other, 'Do you know what is up those steps?' When told that it is the Library, he exclaims, 'Thanks for the warning!' Today, the College has a much-used, up-to-date library, whose range has been significantly improved by gifts and bequests from Fellows and Old Members. The important bequest in 1995 by an alumnus of Magdalen College, Cyril Eland, has added a modern architectural library to complement that of George Clarke.

11. The Gardens and Grounds: Green Thoughts in a Green Shade

Edward Wilson

A garden is not made in a year; indeed it is never made in the sense of finality. It grows, and with the labour of love should go on growing.

There are old gardens that one might fear to touch, and yet I suppose that the most devout and respectful worshipper and worker in one who really loved it would leave some impress on it.

F. Eden, *A Garden in Venice* (1903)

The inheritance into which Worcester entered was, of course, that of Gloucester Hall, and there is a general view of all the colleges by Ralph Agas, 1578, re-engraved in 1732, in William Williams' *Oxonia Depicta* ([1733]; Plate IV). This, with the label 'Glocester Haule', shows trees in the Provost's garden and trees to the north ('Part of Glocester haule') in what we term the Orchard, but this is not much help, since the gardens of all the colleges are shown as serried ranks of trees. In Plate V, a general view of Oxford dated 1733, the Provost's garden has four rectangular beds, an enclosing west wall, with to the south and north a number of elaborately patterned beds. Plate LVIII, the design for the never-completed 18th-century re-building, simply has a narrow strip at the west end marked *Hortus.*

Our other source for the gardens of Gloucester Hall is David Loggan's *Oxonia Illustrata* (1675) in which Plate II, a general view of Oxford, shows what look like two rectangular beds with some trees in the Provost's garden, but in plate XL there are clearly four beds with trees, low hedges round them, paths around and between, and four enclosing walls. The front quadrangle is grassed with two intersecting paths forming an X (also shown in Plate II), but these have gone by the time of Williams' Plate V (1733).

Recently, a new piece of evidence concerning the gardens in the 18th century has come to light: an unpublished manuscript (Bod. Lib. MS. Top.Oxon.d.287) entitled 'Shepilinda's Memoirs of the City and University of Oxford Janry 7th 1737–8', and written by Elizabeth Sheppard, 'daughter of William Sheppard, Gentleman Commoner of Hart Hall and now Principal of Frog Hall'. It is written in a lively, gossipy and occasionally skittish style (she says at the very end of the manuscript, 'Dedications are generaly at the Beginning of a Book which made me chuse mine at the latter End'). The account begins with a description of Worcester, and she writes of the gardens: 'the Provost has one Garden, & the Fellows another; & in the Midle of the great Quadrangle (which is most Beautifully laid out, in fine Gravell Walks,) Stands a fine Rustick Tempietto which is look'd upon, as a very great piece of Antiquity'.

There are two puzzles: first, nothing in the perimeter path (the X pattern of paths on the lawn had gone by 1733) would seem to merit

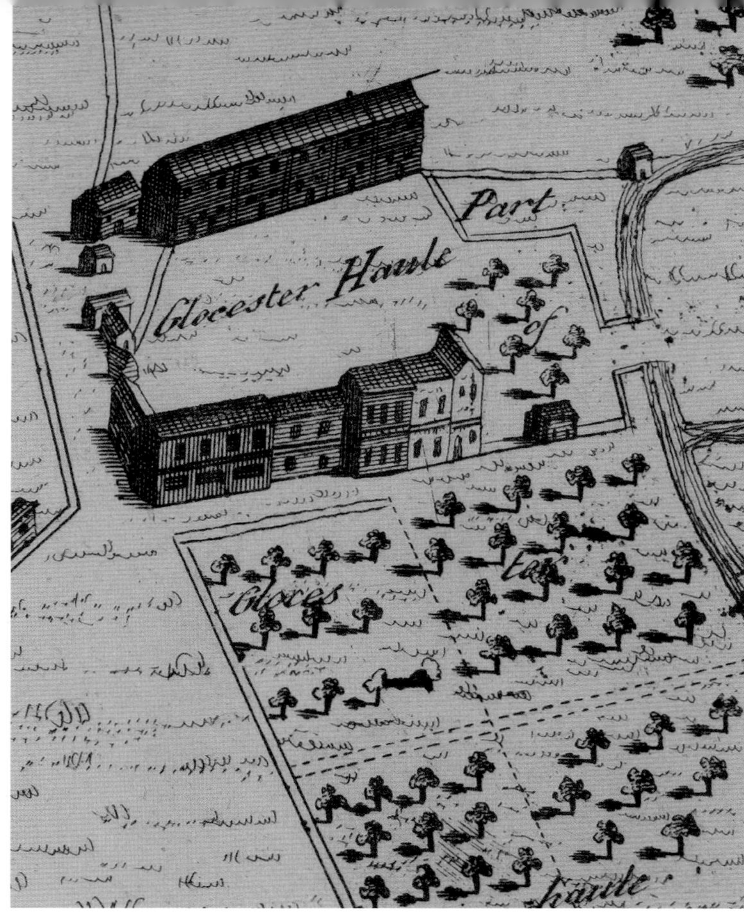

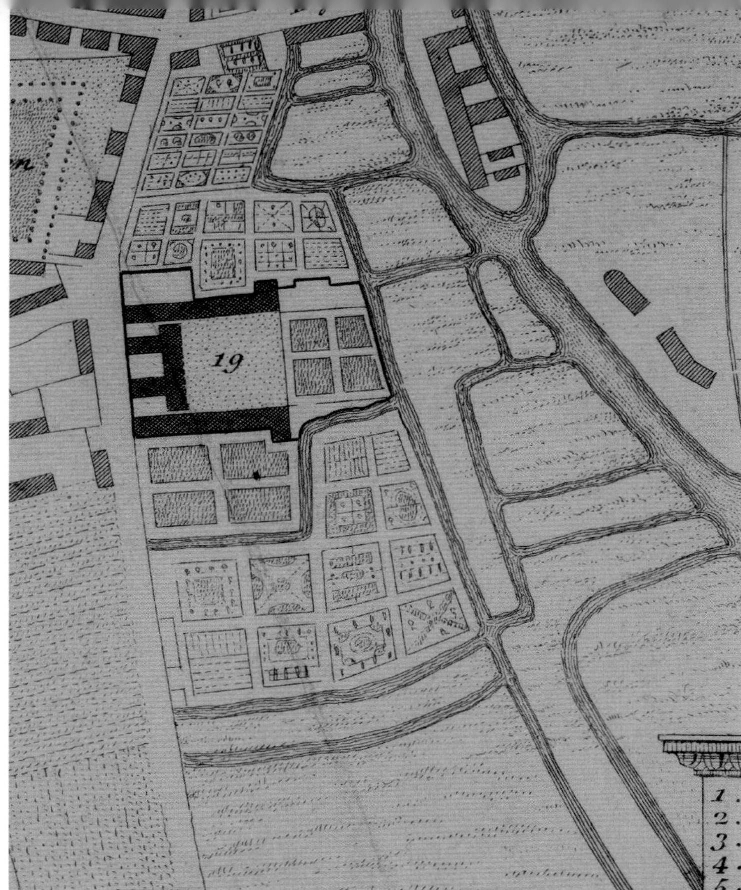

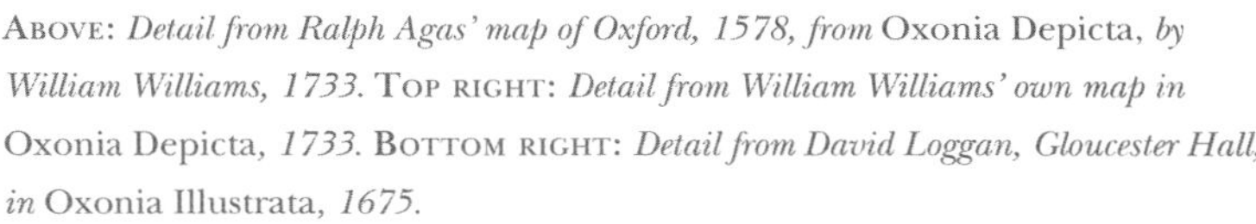
ABOVE: *Detail from Ralph Agas' map of Oxford, 1578, from* Oxonia Depicta, *by William Williams, 1733.* TOP RIGHT: *Detail from William Williams' own map in* Oxonia Depicta, *1733.* BOTTOM RIGHT: *Detail from David Loggan, Gloucester Hall, in* Oxonia Illustrata, *1675.*

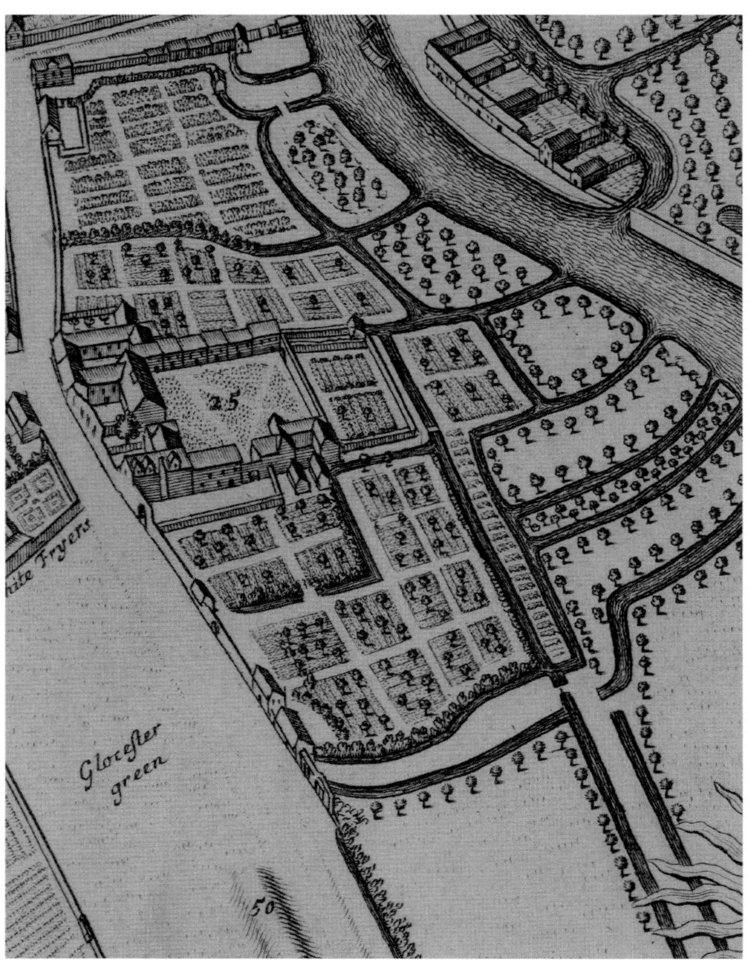

Sheppard's 'fine Gravell Walks', and secondly, what is the 'Tempietto' (the ending '-ietto' is heavily written over other letters)? The *OED* has no record earlier than 1896 for *tempietto*, Italian, literally a 'little temple', meaning 'A colonnaded building, frequently of circular form, surmounted by a dome'. At first, we might be inclined to think of a typical Claude-like Arcadian structure like the temples at Rousham or Stowe, perhaps brought back in pieces for re-assembly from a Vigornian's Grand Tour. But Sheppard's 'Rustick' and 'Antiquity' remind us that classical loggias, grottoes and pagan statuary are found as early as late Elizabethan gardens. A grotto in Lord Burghley's garden at Theobalds in Hertfordshire was thatched with grass and its columns covered with the bark of trees to look like oaks and pines, and might well merit the word 'rustic'. There is no other reference to the *tempietto* in either engraving or writing. However, our Librarian, Dr J. Parker, has pointed out to me that in the right-hand corner of the Provost's garden in Plate XL of Loggan is a small barrel-vaulted building with a domed door (see front endpaper) not present in Williams Plate V. Had this been taken down by 1733 and then re-erected by 1737–8? If so, it was perhaps quickly demolished as not grand enough for the cloister and north terrace. In any event,

W. A. Delamotte Delt.
Garden Scene. Worcester College
Garden Oxford.

Miss Sheppard was, reasonably, more bowled over by a four-walled *hortus conclusus* than by the Front Quad (Williams Plate V).

There was in the late 18th century a knowledgeable and keen botanical awareness among the Fellowship. William Sheffield (Fellow 1758–77 and Provost 1777–95) was described by the naturalist vicar Gilbert White of Selborne with whom he corresponded as an 'excellent Botanist', and Stephen Long Jacob (Fellow 1788–99), whose father Edward had published in 1777 *Plantæ Favershamienses*, is said to have inspired the horticultural interests of Thomas Garnier (1776–1873), a keen botanist and gardener, when at Worcester.

The 18th century saw extensive purchases of land: grounds to the south, now the Nuffield Lawn, up to Hythe Bridge Street (1741); and to the north and west, including the present Sports Field (1744). They were the subject of the planting of numerous trees. In the House Account for 1787, 15 kinds of tree are mentioned but normally only in general terms (lime, spruce firs, Scotch firs, silver firs, etc.), but a notable exception is the Weymouth Pine (*Pinus strobus*: 17 in all); this, discovered in North America in the Jacobean period, was given some patrician cachet by its being planted at Longleat by the first Viscount Weymouth (1640–1714), and its inclusion at Worcester shows a horticultural sensibility to the College as the setting of a grand house.

This high Georgian glamour continued into the 19th century. The listing of *Accuba* [*sic*] twice in the House account of 1813, and again as *Accuba japonica* in 1814 is remarkable, for this is *Aucuba japonica*, introduced to England in 1783, and, wonderfully, these original plants survive in the shrubbery near the canal-side garden sheds. As exciting, are the four 'evergreen Honeysuckles' listed (also in 1813), as these are almost certainly *Lonicera japonica*, introduced into England in 1806, though I have not found it in the gardens today. The College was planting extraordinarily new plants and beginning its flirtation with Japan which was to continue with the influence of Alfred Parsons in the early 20th century. And to look up at the ancient, towering *Taxodium distichum* 'Nutans', introduced into England *c.*1789, probably the 'Virginian Cedar' listed in 1813, is to be humbly aware of the debt owed to our forefathers.

With the 19th century we are into the horticultural aesthetic of the picturesque, a movement in which one of the major thinkers and exponents was Richard Payne Knight (1751–1824). Four of his works are in the College Library, including *The Landscape, a Didactic Poem in Three Books* (London, 1794), and *An Analytical Inquiry into the Principles of Taste* (London, 1805); no accession dates are recorded, but from the hands in the catalogues we can say that they were here in the early 19th century. As we also know that the College purchased from Knight the advowson of the living of Neen Sollars in 1799, then seeing a connection between Knight's idea that a constructed landscape should be like a painting (especially Claude) and the College's development of the grounds in picturesque terms will not seem far-fetched.

Opposite: *Garden scene by William Delamotte, drawn in 1836 for Ingram's* Memorials of Oxford, *1837.* Above: *Arched gateway leading to the playing field, restored in memory of H.V.F. Somerset in 1971.*

The credit for this transformation is given by College tradition to Richard Greswell when he was Bursar (1826–7, 1833–5), but this was doubted by Provost Lys. Indeed, the Lake is mentioned first in 1817 when Francis Brickenden was Bursar: on 12 July is the item 'Pd Pumpers at Lake' (Account Book for 'Improvement Fund', no. 1), and the first of a number of references to the purchase of 'Fish for Lake' is on 7 November. In Knight's words, the rationale for a lake is:

Not to attract th'unskilful gazer's sight,
But to concentrate, and disperse the light;
To shew the clear reflection of the day,
And dart through hanging trees the refluent ray; ➤

Where semi-lights with semi-shadows join,
And quiv'ring play in harmony divine.
Motion and life the thicket seems to take,
And then reflect them back upon the lake:
Soft flick'ring tints in every part appear,
Bright without glare, without distinction clear;
While the strong lights that in the centre play,
As more diverged spread a fainter ray,
Till lost in thick'ning shades they die away.
(The Landscape, ii.103–14)

The lake, with its riparian trees and shrubs, still marvellously realises this watery vision.

Towards the end of the century there was a major development of the grounds. On 23 June 1892 the undergraduates asked that the practicability of converting the College Meadow (used for pasturing the Provost's cows) into a cricket field be considered. Work began in 1897 and was finished in 1900; the pavilion was designed by Thomas Tyrwhitt, an architect and Fellow-Commoner 1898–1901, though Provost Lys, acutely sensitive to the faults he found in others, called it 'unsuitable' and too expensive. Others have thought it just right.

Opposite: *The herbaceous border.* Top: *Climbing roses on the terrace.* Above: *The Provost's Rose Garden, replanted in 2007.* Right: *Wisteria round the entrance to the tunnel through to the front quad created in 1856.*

The history of the gardens in the 20th century is an illustration, in George Eliot's words, of 'the stealthy convergence of human lots'. C.H. Daniel (1836–1919) became Provost in 1903, and according to Lys had no knowledge of plants or any interest in them; however, in 1878, he had married his cousin, Emily Crabb Olive (1852–1933), herself gifted in the arts of embroidery, painting, bookbinding and penmanship, and who was also the cousin of Alfred Parsons (1847–1920), one of the very great garden designers in the Arts and Crafts movement. Doubtless, it was Mrs Daniel who was behind Parsons being given the commission to design the Provost's Rose Garden in 1903. When Daniel was elected Provost the garden passed into Lys' hands and after the First World War when the Rose Garden had got 'sadly out of hand' it was restored and replanted by Lys. Over the years it once more got out of hand, and was again restored in 2006–7.

Parsons had illustrated *The Genus Rosa* (1910–14) by Ellen Ann Willmott (1858–1934), and it was perhaps this connection which led to Lys becoming acquainted with her. She was one of the outstanding gardeners and patrons of botany of the late 19th and early 20th centuries, and Lys visited her garden at Warley Place near Brentwood in Essex and from which she sent him seeds of several plants; in turn, she visited the College offering suggestions and recommendations. Probably both Parsons, who spent two years

Left: *The new bridge to the Provost's garden, 2005.* **Above:** *The herbaceous border.*

in Japan about which he wrote in his *Notes in Japan* (1896), and Willmott, who partly financed the 1907–8 plant-hunting expedition to China of E.H. Wilson, are responsible for a number of Japanese and Chinese plants still in the garden, thus continuing a taste for the daringly oriental which began with the Aucubas and Loniceras from Japan in the early 19th century.

Each generation has left 'some impress' on the gardens and grounds. The College has been blessed with Provosts, notably William Sheffield and F.J. Lys, and some informed and supportive Fellows, who really knew their plants; the thoughtful and aesthetically aware use of Richard Payne Knight's theories is remarkable. It is an impress not only of those within the College, but of movements and people outside it – the Picturesque and Arts and Crafts movements, *japonisme*, and the great Miss Willmott. There has been from the beginning an adventurous policy of plant acquisition, echoed in our own time, for example, by the purchase of two first generation Wollemi pines (*Wollemia nobilis*) at the Sotheby's auction in Sydney in 2005. It is a garden which, as Frederic Eden said, 'with the labour of love should go on growing'.

NB: I am indebted to Mark Griffiths for walking round the gardens with me, and by his plant identifications making the dry bones of the archives live. EW

PEOPLE

12. The Provosts

The Provost

In 1283, John Giffard founded an Oxford cell for the 13 monks of St Peter's Benedictine college in Gloucester. So began the story of the place that in the early 18th century became Worcester College. Over the 300 years between 1714 and 2014, there would be 13 Provosts. None of them has been a monk, but all in their distinctive ways have sought 'to afford an example of piety, honest conversation, prudence, labour, and study, so that his life might be a mirror to which the whole house should conform': that was how the role of Provost was defined in the original College Statutes.

Dr Benjamin Woodroffe, the penultimate Principal of Gloucester, had long dreamed of turning his Hall into a College. As we have seen, first there was his scheme for the Greek College. Then there was his plan to cash in on the goodwill of the Worcestershire baronet Thomas Cookes – a project that, as we have also seen, began even before the Greek scheme collapsed to leave only a rickety building on the corner of Beaumont Street and Walton Street, which became known as Woodroffe's Folly and stood unoccupied until it too collapsed in 1806. When the charter for the proposed Worcester College obtained the Privy Seal in 1698 it was decreed that 'the said Benjamin Woodroffe shall be the first and only Governor thereof, under the title of Provost'.

Opposite: *Richard Blechinden, by Thomas Gibson, 1728.* **Above:** *The Provost's Lodgings, watercolour by Bernard Gotch (1876–1964).*

What did the title mean? Oxford has an abundance of names for Heads of House – Masters and Principals, Wardens and Rectors – but there are only two other Provosts, those of Oriel and Queen's (both established in the 14th century). Provost is also the title of the heads of the two sister foundations of King Henry VI, Eton and King's College Cambridge. Trinity College Dublin had a Provost, as did St Leonard's, a 'college of poor clerks' that had formed part of the University of St Andrews since the 16th century. In later days, Provost would become a favoured name for the senior *academic* administrator (second in line to the President) in many major American universities.

One suspects that Woodroffe chose the title for two reasons. By joining the company of two other Oxford colleges from the days before the dissolution of the monasteries, he was implying an element of continuity with Gloucester College, something consistent with the highly monastic spirit of the Statutes he drafted for his new college. And by putting himself into the same bracket as the Provosts of King's and Eton, two of the highest academic offices in the land, he was engaging in just a little self-aggrandisement. Provost: from Latin *propositus*, a person who is set or placed over others, its earliest usage being monastic, denoting the head or president of an ecclesiastical chapter or religious community; in secular contexts, an officer or official in charge of some establishment, undertaking, or body of people. The Provost in Shakespeare's *Measure for Measure* is Governor of a prison, and such were the restrictions on the lives of the Fellows and Scholars of Worcester College at its foundation that the analogy is not inapt.

Together with the Fellows, the Provost had control of the endowments. This remains the case. His job was to elect the Scholars and to hold examinations. All the way down to the time of Masterman in the 1950s, the Provost had control of what we now call Admissions. Peter Palumbo (Lord Palumbo) recalls how, despite being the son of an East End immigrant, he got to Eton and won the 100 metres on sports day. A small but distinguished-looking man was sitting on a shooting stick, watching the race. Afterwards, he came up to the breathless youth and said, 'Boy, I understand your name is Palumbo?' 'Yes, sir.' 'Well, my name is J.C. Masterman and I am the Provost of Worcester and I would like you to do me the honour of coming to my College – we could do with a good runner.'

The Provost received a stipend of £80 a year (paid quarterly). He also collected and kept for himself the rents on the rooms of the Scholars and some of the Fellows.This handsome privilege has, alas, long passed away.

The legal wrangling over the control and whereabouts of Cookes' new college having lasted for some 15 years, poor old Woodroffe died before realising his dream of becoming a Provost. So it was that when Worcester finally came into being in the summer of 1714 the first Provost was not the eccentric and egotistical visionary who

W. Gower

Silex Scintillans:
or
SACRED POEMS
and
Priuate Eiaculations
By
Henry Vaughan Silurist
LONDON Printed by T.W. for H.Blunden
at ye Castle in Cornhill. 1650

Inset: *Henry Vaughan,* Silex Scintillans, *1650, with Gower's signature.* Right: *William Gower, by Thomas Gainsborough.* Opposite: *Samuel Foote, mezzotint by Thomas Blackmore after Joshua Reynolds.* Opposite right: *Whittington Landon, by John Bridges.*

had devoted his latter years to achieving our foundation, but a run-of-the-mill cleric from St John's, Richard Blechinden. According to his contemporary, the eminent antiquarian Thomas Hearne, he was 'good for nothing but drinking and keeping jolly company'. As Provost Daniel and his student W.R. Barker put it in the College history they published in 1900, Blechinden may thus be seen as 'a man after Oxford's own heart'. To be fair, though, he was also a close friend of Dr George Clarke. They died within five days of each other, in October 1736. Blechinden was first to go, but secure in the knowledge that the great reward for his loyalty to Clarke, who had fallen out with his colleagues at All Souls, was that his friend's unparalleled collection of books, pamphlets and engravings would come to Worcester and allow the College to rise from *parvenu* to custodian of one of Oxford's greatest libraries.

Blechinden was succeeded by William Gower, who had been one of the first Scholars of Worcester and who thus remained on the books for 63 years, inaugurating a tradition that extends all the way to Provost Smethurst (on the books for more than 50, and counting). Some described him as 'the most lumbering of pedants', while others considered him one of the most eloquent speakers in the land. His every phrase, it was said, could be written down and judged perfect in English style, a distinction shared with a most select few, most notably Dr Samuel Johnson.

Gower had the distinction of being painted by his friend Thomas Gainsborough, but had a less happy relationship with one of the most famous men of the age: Worcester student and one-legged bisexual stand-up comedian, Samuel Foote. He had two legs while he was here – the amputation of the left one followed his being thrown from the Duke of York's stallion which he was riding in response to a challenge at an occasion hosted by the Earl of Mexborough (one of whose descendants was a Worcester man in the 1950s, sent down by Masterman for trashing a room on a visit back to Eton). In *Mr Foote's Other Leg* (2012), the biographer Ian Kelly has told the whole story of this extraordinary life, which comes complete with aristocratic sex scandal, celebrity actors and some of the most brilliant writing the English comic theatre has ever seen. Kelly has

some lively pages about Foote's undergraduate career, in which debt played a larger part than study. He was well known for his imitation of the pompous Provost. The story goes that on one occasion he was summoned before Gower for a dressing down. Knowing the Provost's predilection for long words, he brought along a dictionary, and periodically asked Gower to pause while he looked up the meaning of what was being said to him. Foote was eventually deprived of his Scholarship, charged with, as Gower put it in a notice posted at the College entrance, 'a long course of ill-behaviour [that] has rendered himself obnoxious to frequent censures of the society publick and private' and with 'lying out of College' and refusing 'to answer to several heinous crimes objected to him'.

In 1777 Provost Gower died and Vice-Provost William Sheffield succeeded him. A College man all his career – Scholar, Fellow, Bursar, Dean, Vice-Provost and finally Provost – his only claim to fame is a correspondence with the great naturalist Gilbert White, author of the pioneering *Natural History of Selborne* (1789). Four letters from Sheffield to White survive, and they show considerable knowledge of the natural world. He once spent a happy fortnight at Selborne, walking in the woods, identifying a rare bird, proving himself an excellent botanist and, as White recorded in his journal, making 'a very rapid Progress in Entomology'. The visit sounds as if it provided very welcome relief from the internecine disputes among the small band of Worcester Fellows which characterised Sheffield's quotidian life.

Sheffield's successor was Dr Whittington Landon, the first Provost of Worcester to become Vice-Chancellor of the University. He suffered from gout and was borne to Chapel in a Bath chair. He was also Dean of Exeter, so he divided his time between College and Cathedral. His greatest moment of glory came in the summer of 1814 when he hosted on behalf of the University a visit from the allied Sovereigns of the anti-Napoleonic alliance, in celebration of Bonaparte's abdication. The Provosts of Worcester have hosted many distinguished visitors: Briggs invited Harold Macmillan on the occasion of the 700th anniversary of Gloucester College and Bate welcomed Aung San Suu Kyi to the Encaenia garden party on

LEFT: *Richard Lynch Cotton, portrait by Sir William Boxall.* ABOVE LEFT: *Richard Lynch Cotton in procession as Vice-Chancellor in 1852, by Thomas Woollen Smith (matriculated 1851): Cotton is the small figure.* ABOVE: *Richard Lynch Cotton as an old woman 'dressed for a Tea-fight', drawn for the series of Oxford caricatures published by Thomas Shrimpton & Son, booksellers of 23–24 The Broad.*

a glorious summer's day in 2012, with the Provost's Rose Garden in full bloom and a receiving line on the bridge across the lake weir. But Landon takes the palm for presiding over the simultaneous visit of the Prince Regent, the Duke of York, Tsar Alexander of Russia, King Frederick of Prussia, Metternich the Chancellor of the Austrian Empire, the Chancellor of Prussia, Field Marshall Blücher and General von Bulow. They did a typical Oxford grand tour – Christ Church, the Bodleian, the Clarendon building of the Oxford University Press, the Radcliffe Observatory, honorary degrees in the Sheldonian, lunch in the Radcliffe Camera. The front of Worcester was lit up by fireworks at the end of the day and Landon said the grace before and after the formal dinner in the Codrington Library at All Souls, but he did not manage to entice the royal party into the grounds of the College itself.

Landon died in December 1838. In June that year news came of the marriage of his niece Laetitia Landon, who under the initials 'L.E.L.' had become one of the most admired poets in the land. Laetitia and her husband sailed immediately for the Ivory Coast of Africa. In October, she was found dead in mysterious circumstances,

Revd William Inge, Provost 1880–1903.

poisoned with an overdose of prussic acid (suicide, accident or murder?). One is tempted to suppose that the shock of the news was what did for the Provost.

Next came Revd Dr Richard Cotton, the longest-serving Provost, who held office from 1839 to 1880. As discussed in another chapter, he was much involved with the theological disputes that dominated Oxford in the high Victorian period – though he married a sister of Pusey, he was a vigorous anti-Tractarian. An admired preacher, he was a gentle, generous, much-loved soul. After an end-of-day conversation in the Common Room he would retire to the Lodgings rather than stay with the Fellows for supper and card games.

Shortly before his death he presided over what was believed to have been the only infant baptism ever celebrated in the College Chapel. This was Rachel, daughter of one of the Fellows, Charles Henry Olive Daniel. His turn as Provost was to come later. In the interim, Dr William Inge served from 1880 to 1903. Though he had been a Scholar of the College and, briefly, a Fellow, he was not an internal candidate. The fact that he was imposed on the College by the Chancellor, Lord Salisbury, led to a change in the Statutes whereby future Provosts would be elected by the Fellows rather than appointed from on high. 'Appointed to preside over a college in which he was practically a stranger,' wrote Inge's *Times* obituarist, 'he won before long by simpleness and genuineness of character, by sterling goodness, and a certain magnanimity of disposition the deep affection of many and the respect of all' – which is all that a Provost may hope for. He was much involved in both Church and University affairs, not to mention missionary activities and the education of lay readers at Keble. Self-effacing and self-deprecating, he kept quiet about the fact that as an undergraduate he had been a member of the University cricket XI. He suffered from severe ill-health in his later years and died in the Lodgings in the middle of Eights Week. His son, William Ralph Inge, became a famous (and allegedly Gloomy) Dean of St Paul's.

Henry Daniel, who held office from 1903 until his death in 1919 a few weeks short of his 83rd birthday, was not only the first Provost to be elected by the Fellows. He was also the first who deserves to be remembered for achievements beyond the confines of College and Church. The son of a perpetual curate from the West Country, he spent most of his adult life at Worcester, where he had taken a first in *literae humaniores*. He had many connections with the Arts and Crafts movement. His cousin Emily Crabb Olive, whom he married, was an artist. She in turn was very close to her cousin, the painter and garden designer Alfred Parsons, who became a frequent visitor to Worcester and, as we have been reminded in an earlier chapter, redesigned the Provost's Garden in the Cotswold style. As Mavis Batey puts it in *Oxford Gardens*, 'There was a sundial in the centre of the garden and round it beds of roses, pinks and snapdragons. All the beloved "old-fashioned" flowers, the delphiniums, tiger lilies, peonies, sweet peas, wallflowers, larkspur and irises grew happily in the shelter of the stone wall that separates the Provost's lodgings from the main quadrangle.'

Parsons also designed the logo for the Daniel Press, showing – inevitably – Daniel in the lions' den. The Press was Daniel's greatest achievement. He was fascinated from childhood by the art of printing and he began crafting books on his own press nearly two decades before William Morris established the Kelmscott Press. In time, the Daniel Press would be acknowledged as the first attempt to raise the standard of printing in Victorian England. Daniel, who was a friend of Walter Pater, had a keen aesthetic sense. He shared the pre-Raphaelite vision of a return to the handiwork of the middle ages as a reaction against the dehumanising mass

Revd Charles Henry Oliver Daniel, Provost 1903–19, by William Rothenstein.

production of industrial and commercial modernity. The Arts and the Crafts should go together. If a writer has laboured to create beautiful words, then printer, illustrator and bookbinder should create an equally beautiful physical object. In 1876 Daniel started using a typeface known as Fell that had languished in oblivion at the Clarendon Press for a century and a half. Then in 1881 he produced *The Garland of Rachel*, in celebration of the first birthday of his daughter. Many of the best-known poets of the day made contributions: Andrew Lang, Austin Dobson, Robert Bridges, Lewis Carroll, Edmund Gosse. Emily Daniel provided large ornaments and illuminations. This volume was described in the 1921 history of *The Daniel Press* (itself printed on Daniel's press) as the first genuine sign of 'the Revival of Printing in this country'. Daniel went on to produce exquisite reprints of works of classical and Renaissance literature, matchless editions of Robert Herrick's poetry (1891), William Blake's *Songs of Innocence* (1893), the *Odes, Sonnets, and Lyrics of John Keats* (1895), and several volumes of plays and poems by his friend the future Poet Laureate Robert Bridges (see p. 145).

The writer Compton Mackenzie was for a time engaged to Daniel's daughter Ruth. He told the story of the affair in his novel *Guy and Pauline* (1915), along the way providing a charming pen-portrait of Daniel – poring over a seed catalogue or pottering in the garden – transposed from the Lodgings to an Oxfordshire rural vicarage. The novel also has a lovely description of the Daniels' houseboat on the Thames.

Daniel's later years were marred by ill health and the bitterness of the Great War, but he had as good an ending as a Provost could desire. In his final year the war was over and the Trinity Term was one of glorious and brilliant sunshine, during which he spent many hours in his beloved garden. He passed the Long Vacation at the cottage near Moreton-in-Marsh in the Cotswolds that his wife and daughter had found for him. He died on a warm early September day and, as the memoir in *The Daniel Press* puts it, 'his body was brought home to the Chapel which he had served so steadfastly, and thence, followed by troops of friends, was borne through the busy familiar streets to that sequestered corner of Oxford for which he had always felt a special fondness, the little Holywell Cemetery, and to his final peaceful rest.' Another future Laureate, John Masefield, wrote a poem in his memory called 'The Dream' in which he imagined going through the door of death and passing into 'a room / Where Daniel stood, as I had seen him erst, / In wisest age in all its happiest bloom. / Deep in the red and black of books immerst.'

Francis John Lys, born in 1863 and Provost from 1919 to 1946, was less happily married. His first wife was a formidable character who had a tendency to throw around the crockery in the Dining Room, though after her death he found comfort in a younger woman who became a charming hostess in the Lodgings. A College man through and through, he left a memoir called *Worcester College 1882–1943 and Some Account of a Stewardship* (1944). And stewardship of the College's grounds, estates and finances was indeed his lifelong passion. He devoted years to questions of drainage pertaining to the lake and the cricket field. He restored boundary walls and installed baths. He planted holm oaks to obscure the view of naked sunbathers on the roof of the newly built Ruskin College to the north. He objected to a City Council proposal that there should be an electric tramway running along Walton Street, since it would 'spoil the use of both Hall and Chapel'.

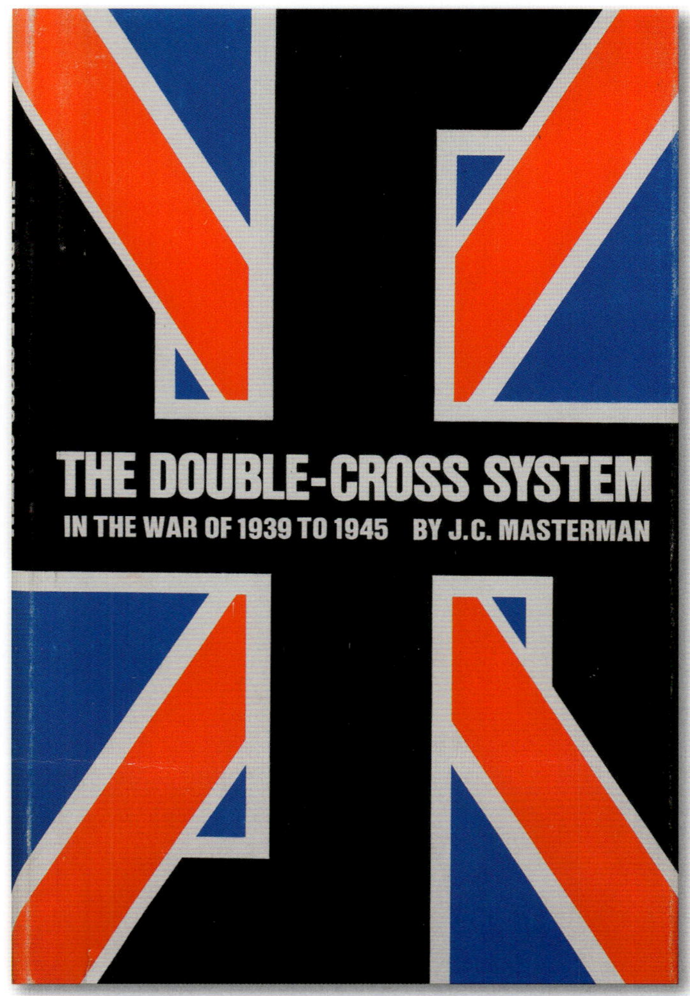

Left: *Sir John Cecil Masterman, Provost 1946–61, by Edward Halliday, 1952.*
Above: *Jacket image for* The Double-Cross System in the War of 1939 to 1945, *1972.*

The ninth and most intriguing Provost was Sir John Cecil Masterman, always known as J.C., who was born in 1891 and died in 1977. He held office from 1946 to 1961, having been a History Scholar of the College (with first class honours) immediately before the First World War. Interned in Germany during the war, in the 1920s he was a don at Christ Church. He might well have become headmaster of Eton in the 1930s, but chose to stay in Oxford. He taught, administered, became deeply involved in Oxford politics, but did not research or publish academic articles. He excelled at games – so central to the character-building of a gentleman in those days – to the extent that he played cricket at Lords', hockey for England and lawn tennis at Wimbledon.

Having missed out on the First War, he excelled in the Second. Called up in June 1940, he became secretary to a War Office committee. In his memoir *On the Chariot's Wheel* he recalls being asked by a general 'Can you write the King's English?' and replying that this was his only qualification. Before long he was in the intelligence corps and then MI5, where he chaired the new Twenty (XX) Committee that was established in January 1941 to trace and turn Nazi spies. Masterman claimed – and the evidence supports him – that for the entire length of the war every Nazi infiltrator who reached Britain was either eliminated or turned into a double agent.

Ian Fleming crossed his path: some say that 'M' is for Masterman (though several other candidates have been proposed). The XX Committee oversaw information about enemy agents and their traffic, making suggestions as to how they should respond (falsely)

Oliver Shewell Franks, Baron Franks, Provost 1962–76, by John Stanton Ward RA, 1975.

to their *Abwehr* controllers and devising increasingly elaborate schemes of deception. Masterman worked closely with the section chief, Major T.A. Robertson (known as Tar), made formidable use of his Oxford contacts around Whitehall, and chaired all the meetings with aplomb, ensuring that MI5 always got its way.

The XX Committee's greatest achievement was its role in Operation Fortitude, in which the Germans were led to believe that the invasion of France would take place in the Pas de Calais, led by the First US Army Group (FUSAG), an entirely fictional creation.

In 1945 Masterman wrote his top secret account of the committee's work, which was eventually published in 1972, amidst much controversy regarding the Official Secrets Act, as *The Double-Cross System*. For the first time, the public learnt about the motley crew of double agents such as the Serbian Popov, known as Agent Tricycle, and the enigmatic Catalan Pujol, who served under the codenames Bovril and then Garbo. At the heart of the committee's work was the decrypting of *Abwehr* wireless communications, but Masterman was Ultra-discreet in referring only passingly and obliquely to this Most Secret Source. The extraordinary significance of Bletchley Park only emerged after the revelation of the Enigma secret in 1974. As for the significance of Masterman's book, this is eminently apparent from a secret CIA report of the Cold War era, which was declassified in 1994:

> *Masterman's book is not exactly just a book 'on intelligence'. It's really a book about counterintelligence, that part of intelligence work which is concerned about what other peoples' spies and spy services are doing to you, using those spies to find other spies, to gain intelligence information, and to deceive the spy masters and those dependent on them. Masterman's book registers the coming-of-age in World War II of counterintelligence as a co-equal professional activity with espionage and political action, and in that fact rests its underlying significance. The book is a statement of a counterintelligence and security service's policy case, as well as the most informative recitation of the theory and practice of its counterintelligence accomplishments.*

Provost of Worcester might have seemed something of an anti-climax after the drama of wartime intelligence work, but Masterman's skills as a chairman served him well on Governing Body and then as Vice-Chancellor of the University. He stood up for the colleges and the humanities at a time when the central University and the sciences were beginning to dominate Oxford. He enjoyed robust debate, but didn't like troublemakers on his Governing Body or elsewhere: 'It is one, perhaps the chief, of the pleasures of university life that all subjects can be discussed and all views propounded, but it is clean contrary to university tradition that a militant minority should impose its will on the majority.'

He wrote a number of books, including a rather good Senior Common Room detective novel called *An Oxford Tragedy* (1933) and a somewhat whimsical guide to the structures and foibles of Oxford called *To Teach the Senators Wisdom* (1952). He was the archetypal bachelor don, inhabiting an almost entirely male society. On retiring from the Provostship, he moved to a College house on Beaumont Street, where he lived for the rest of his life. When he died, his ashes were scattered on the lake.

It was by way of Masterman's connections to MI5 that History don Harry Pitt became one of Oxford's leading recruiters for the security services. The next Provost, Oliver Franks, ennobled as Baron Franks of Headington in 1962, the very year of his election, also spent time

Asa Briggs, Baron Briggs, Provost 1976–91, by Derek Hill, 1989.

On His (and Her) Majesty's Service, but more openly. In the words of his biographer Alex Danchev, 'Profoundly reasonable and publicly austere, a figure of immense moral authority, Oliver Franks lived an exceptional life. He did not seek his various careers of don, mandarin, diplomat, banker, provost, pillar of state. They sought him. He did not collect committees, as some men do. Committees collected him. He did not pine for public recognition. Recognition came to him.'

Born into a scholarly household in Birmingham in 1905, he took a congratulatory first in Lit. Hum. at Queen's and became a tutor there, soon marrying one of his students, Barbara Tanner, from LMH. She had a Quaker upbringing and a fierce social conscience, devoting her life to public service as a magistrate, chairman of the boards of governors of Aylesbury and Oxford prisons (together with various other local young offender and probation institutions), chairman of the Oxford Citizens' Advice Bureau and of Age Concern, trustee of Oxfam, member of wages councils, and chairman of the management committee of the Nuffield Orthopaedic Hospital. In middle age, Danchev informs us,

> *She lost her shyness but retained her modesty. She practised yoga and tai chi. She liked to meditate. At seventy-five she learned to stand on her head. She was her own woman, an expression she would probably have deplored. At the same time she supported her husband in everything he did, just as he supported her. This was not a matter of form, but a grave moral obligation.*

When Oliver became Provost, Barbara brought along her old nanny and gave her a job of work to do, running a nursery on the top floor of the Lodgings.

Franks' extreme efficiency in the Ministry of Supply during the war led to various offers of leading public roles, from heading the National Coal Board to governing the Bank of England. But nothing could compare with the offer of the Provostship of his own College, Queen's, which he took up in 1946. Despite his remarkably young age (41) for the role, he cut a formidable figure. The story goes that he once interviewed a don over a disciplinary matter, leading the hapless Fellow to report 'I now know what the Last Judgement will be like, only I expect that God will be more human.'

Franks took leave of absence from Queen's for the small task of implementing the Marshall Plan for the comprehensive reconstruction of the war-shattered European economy. Then in 1948, departing from Oxford with a heavy heart, he felt duty-bound to accept the offer of the Ambassadorship in Washington DC, where without wasting any time he co-ordinated his fellow diplomats as they brought NATO into being. He said that this was child's play in comparison with chairing an Oxford Governing Body. Famously, in 1948 a Washington radio station telephoned foreign ambassadors and asked what each would like for Christmas. The French ambassador uttered some sugary platitude about world peace, the Soviet ambassador scored a cheap political point about 'freedom from imperialist enslavement', and Franks, perhaps deliberately, missed the point: 'It's very kind of you to ask,' he said, 'I'd quite like a small box of crystallised fruit.' He left DC in 1952, his farewell present from President Eisenhower being a rococo gilt mirror with American eagle on top, now hanging resplendent in the recently refurbished hallway of the Lodgings.

Having turned down the offer to be the first Secretary-General of NATO, he took on the Chairmanship of Lloyds Bank ('if you can run an Oxford college you can run anything', he quipped). This paid very handsomely, but still left ample time for the chairing of

Right and opposite: *Interior of the Provost's Lodgings. Major refurbishments, and restoration of an original Georgian style, have been presided over by the wives of Provosts Franks and Bate. Eisenhower's mirror can be seen on the left-hand side of the Hallway (right), where the portraits on the right are of the founder and his wife, together with Byrom Eaton and his daughter Sarah, a great female benefactor.*

commissions and inquiries. For nearly three decades, he was the go-to man when there was a sticky problem to solve, whether the governance of Oxford University, the limits of the Official Secrets Act or the conduct of the Falklands War. The first Provost not to be a Worcester man, he ran the College with effortless ease, though such were his distinction in public life and his austere demeanour that some undergraduates found him rather a remote figure. Others, though, were very fond of him and benefited from his tutoring in philosophy, which he took on even though he didn't have to. Lady Franks was adored: she entertained students for tea and showed great interest in all their affairs. Robert Kime, who went on to become one of the country's most distinguished interior designers, remembers buying antiques for her and admiring her great taste in the redecoration of the Lodgings.

He was a hard act to follow, but Asa Briggs, later Lord Briggs, was just the man to step into these giant shoes. A grammar school boy born in the West Riding of Yorkshire in 1921, not far from the Brontë parsonage, he read History at Sidney Sussex College, Cambridge, and simultaneously took a first in Economics via what we would now call a 'distance learning' degree from the External department of the University of London. During the war he worked at Bletchley Park, becoming a member of 'the Watch' in the now-famous Hut 6, where the Enigma code was broken (a nice link to J.C.). He came to Worcester at the end of the war, uniquely qualified to teach both History and Economics – with a little mugging up on Politics and Philosophy, he was capable of delivering PPE almost single-handedly. After a happy decade in the College, including the memorable summer in which he and Harry Pitt accompanied their student Rupert Murdoch as he drove his Ford Zephyr from Constantinople to Port Said, he went to a chair at Leeds and thence to the brand new University of Sussex just outside Brighton, where he quickly became Dean of Social Sciences, Pro-Vice-Chancellor and eventually Vice-Chancellor. He returned to Worcester on Franks' retirement in 1976 and remained Provost until 1991.

During his years as the College's History tutor, he published a pioneering book called *Victorian People* (1954), which brought alive the mid-19th century through a brilliantly eclectic series of case studies: the Crystal Palace, the public school regime of Dr Arnold, Samuel Smiles and his doctrine of self-help, Walter Bagehot on the English Constitution, and so on. He moved effortlessly between social, economic and cultural history, and was one of the first to make full historical use of literary sources such as the novels of Trollope. At Leeds he produced an immensely successful textbook, *The Age of Improvement, 1783–1867* (1959), which became familiar to generations of A-Level History students, including the present Provost. And at Sussex he followed up his earlier book with *Victorian Cities* (1963). The trilogy was completed with *Victorian Things*, published towards the end of his time as Provost (1988). Meanwhile, he had been commissioned by the BBC, with the full co-operation of Lord Reith, to write *A History of Broadcasting in the United Kingdom.* Published by Oxford University Press, this eventually ran to five volumes and was a foundational text for the serious study of the cultural influence of the media, a theme to which he returned in 2002 with *A Social History of the Media: from Gutenberg to the Internet*, co-written with fellow-historian Peter Burke.

Always passionate about education for ordinary people beyond the 'ivory tower' of academe, he managed to combine the roles of Provost of Worcester and Chancellor of the Open University

Briggs did, however, improve the quality of the food in Hall: 'an old member of the college, whom I had taught when I was a young Fellow, provided me with an anonymous but extremely generous benefaction provided that I, and not the Fellows, could use it in what I personally judged to be in the interest of undergraduates. I employed it to improve college food.' Inevitably, the rumour went round that this was Sainsbury money – perhaps even Sainsbury's food – but on this occasion they were not the donors. It was, however, during Briggs' time that John and Tim Sainsbury endowed the award-winning building by the lake that carries their name. Lord John, a devoted student from Asa's tutoring days, also made possible the Linbury Building (named for his Trust, which itself nods to the name of his wife, former ballerina Anya Linden) on the southern side of the College.

The Provostship of Richard Smethurst (1991–2011) was characterised by more building work, this time at the northern, Ruskin Lane, end of the site. The quality of student accommodation is now among the best in Oxford, and this may well be one reason – along with the incomparable gardens and the on-site sports field – why from 2007 to 2012 Worcester had more undergraduate applications than any other College. Dick Smethurst was born in 1941 and brought up in Liverpool. He read PPE and became tutor in Economics in 1967. He undertook a range of advisory roles in London – for the Treasury, the Prime Minister's Policy

– though this was sometimes at the expense of preparation for College meetings. He was often to be seen reading through a sheaf of papers on the way to Governing Body, though it was hard to tell whether he was acquainting himself with the agenda or correcting the proofs of his latest article.

In *Special Relationships: People and Places*, a memoir published in 2012 around the time of his 91st birthday, he explained the origins of the legendary Lodgings luncheons that came to be attended by the great and the good of the artistic, business, cultural and political worlds. Susan, his wife, was not given dining rights on his arrival, and indeed had to be accompanied into Formal Hall by a male Fellow. 'She had', as he puts it, 'no place in any college hierarchy':

> *I was determined, therefore, in 1976 not to rely solely on this traditional form of entertainment, although I made full use of it … My object was to open up the College to the outside world, an object that few of the College Fellows fully shared. Susan and I started to give Sunday lunch parties in the beautiful Provost's Lodge where the quality of the food (and drink) was guaranteed. None of it came from the College kitchens.*

The Induction of Provost Bate, October 2011.

Unit and the Monopolies and Mergers Commission, of which he eventually became Deputy Chairman. If these activites seem vaguely reminiscent of Franks, then his other major outside commitment was in the tradition of Briggs' work for the Open University: he directed the Oxford University Department of External Studies ('extra-mural' studies, as it used to be called) and became President of the local Workers' Educational Association and then the National Institute of Adult Continuing Education. He was renowned for his political skills within the University, becoming a Pro-Vice-Chancellor and steering the Conference of Colleges – the assembly of Oxford Heads of House – towards a system of binding votes. He saw clearly that with power and money shifting ever more towards the central administration, the colleges had, as he put it, 'to stand together or sink together'.

He once told an interviewer that 'Everything in my life happens entirely by accident', but there was a kind of inevitability about his becoming Provost, such was the combination of his administrative gifts with his long experience of, and deep loyalty to, the College. Among the more arduous tasks of his final years was a thoroughgoing revision of the College Statutes, consequent upon the decision in the 2006 Charities Act to remove 'exempt' status from the Oxford and Cambridge colleges, requiring them to report to the Charity Commission and to introduce certain checks and balances in governance that would have been viewed as anathema by an older generation of dons committed to the idea of a college as an entirely self-governing academic community (there was a time in the early 2000s when, amidst lively debate over the *University's* structures of governance, frustrated officials in Wellington Square began referring to 'The People's Republic of Worcester'). Undergraduates, especially those of a sporting disposition, meanwhile, will long remember Dick Smethurst for the Provost's Dinners that were regularly held in the Lodgings to celebrate victories in Cuppers and an array of other extra-curricular achievements.

The writer of this chapter is not the appropriate person to assess the early days of the 13th Provost. Suffice to say that Bate, who arrived in September 2011, is the first Provost in the College's history to have no prior connection with Oxford (beside the tenuous one of being a former student and Fellow of St Catharine's, Worcester's 'sister-college' in Cambridge, before going on to an academic career at Harvard, Liverpool, UCLA and Warwick). There is perhaps a resemblance to the arrival of Provost Inge, who came among the Fellows with a fresh pair of eyes and took some time to win their trust. But there is a difference: whereas Provost Inge was imposed upon the College, Provost Bate was merely identified and introduced by an external figure, who was tasked by the Governing Body to find a diverse shortlist of potential candidates from outside Oxford. It is surely, though, a sign of the times that the external agent in question was not the historic figure known as The Chancellor but the very modern one known as The Headhunter.

A Memory of Provost Daniel in the Lodgings

The life of an Oxford don has many advantages, but it has the disadvantage that the men of learning and general ability in the University are numerous and the prizes are few. And so to many, perhaps the majority, there comes a moment when they awake with a start to find themselves in the fifties and doing the same work, earning the same income, as in the thirties, and they feel discouraged. It was then a very real gratification to his friends as well as to himself when there fell to him the well-earned honour of the Headship of his College. The glory departed from the old house at the corner of Worcester Street, and it quickly disappeared. But Oxford became aware that the Provost's Lodgings at Worcester were unique – a dignified and delightful Adam house, the like of which no other Head of a College inhabited, and with all the appurtenances of a country house. The only definite alterations made were that the grate belonging to a magnificent Adam chimney-piece, which had been removed to the servants' hall, was replaced, and an interesting picture hung in a prominent position. But somehow a magic wand had touched the building, and its beauties so long obscured, unobserved, became obvious to the most casual visitor. If the architectural dignity of the Provost's Lodgings was great, there was no outbreak of dignity in its inhabitants. The warmth and ease of the old rambling house invaded the finely proportioned rooms at Worcester. And there, too, was a small intimate room – a floor lower than the front door, but opening into the garden under the unusual double flight of steps on the garden front. One supped there in the Long – a small party at a small round table, lighted by a tall red-shaded standard lamp, which stood on the paved space outside the open window. The big elms in the Provost's meadow dreamed dark and mysterious in the summer twilight; in the garden one divined the pink china roses overflowing their hedges of lavender. In the meadow the Provost's cow glimmered ghostly. We talked about the cow, and said that here at the back of Worcester one was not in Oxford but in the country. The cow thought otherwise. She demanded the real country, and had accepted an invitation to spend the rest of the summer with friends at Headington. And the cow was partly right. The back of Worcester, for all its rambling garden open to the meadows, and the sense of the river flowing behind the veiling trees, was not the country but Oxford. Oxford full of ghosts, of traditions. Close by, still warm with habitation, stood the cells in and out of whose narrow doorways had passed young Benedictine monks, which had rung to the noisy encounters of Greeks and Trojans when Erasmus dwelt in Oxford. The columned portico and the measured harmony of the stately buildings above us spoke of the 18th century with its strange mingling of coarse robust life with salt wit and courtly grace, and the famous College gardens breathed of the Return to Nature and the generation of the Romantics. Ghosts all, yet living spirits and part of the very body of Oxford. And now all we in our turn are mingling or have mingled with her ghosts, and it may be that in the summer dusk students yet unborn, leaning from the Benedictines' windows, may see a golden-bearded man in old-fashioned dress pacing the large College lawn and disappearing among the mysterious trees. And half awed, half thrilled, they will say to each other, ' We have seen Daniel the Printer'.

Margaret L. Woods, in *The Daniel Press* (1921)

13. Fellows and Tutors

Joanna Parker

When the College was founded in 1714, the role and the career of the academic were very different from what we recognise 300 years later. Indeed, the word 'career' is inappropriate for the earlier days of university teaching, when a college Fellowship was seen as a prize and, if connected to any career, belonged more to that of clergyman than of don.

At Worcester, there were four foundations supporting Scholars and Fellows, and when a vacancy in the Fellowship arose, it was filled from the pool of Scholars on the same foundation. In 1737, 'An election for Fellows was held. The Vacancys were three but, there being only two Graduate scholars, one of them being incapable of appearing as Candidate, from a disorder in his understanding, only Mr Wanley was elected.' Most Fellows had to take holy orders (there were exceptions in the Cookes foundation for two Fellows in law and medicine, and in the Clarke foundation for the Librarian), and all had to resign their Fellowships on marriage or on acquiring means above a certain level.

As a result, often a Fellowship was held only until some better position in the Church came up and enabled the holder to marry, so there was quick turnover of Fellows. Only a few spent the whole of their lives in Oxford. Not all Fellows held tutorial or other offices within the College and many obtained dispensations from residence: Edward Dandridge (elected 1760), for example, was repeatedly given leave of absence to pursue a legal career as a barrister in London. Teaching was one of the roles of the Fellows, but research, on which so much emphasis is laid today, was not a requirement, and although Fellows often had academic interests, they did not necessarily coincide with the curriculum. Vivian Green's words on the Fellows of Lincoln are pertinent: 'If the Fellows had scholarly interests, they were not in the precise sense of the word scholars … They read what the educated country clergy and squires of their time were likely to read.' Of the few publications by Fellows, most were sermons, for example those by John Tottie, elected in 1725, who later became a Canon of Christ Church and Archdeacon of Worcester.

Eighteenth-century Oxford has been defended lately from the charges famously levelled at it by Gibbon in his scathing account in the *Autobiography* of the 'dull and deep potations' of the Magdalen dons. One line of defence is that the University saw its role differently from today: not to find new knowledge, but to defend a body of known knowledge. Another is that the University did produce some fine intellectuals, such as Edmund Halley, William Blackstone, Robert Lowth, Thomas Gaisford and William Jones, and some conscientious tutors and well-read students.

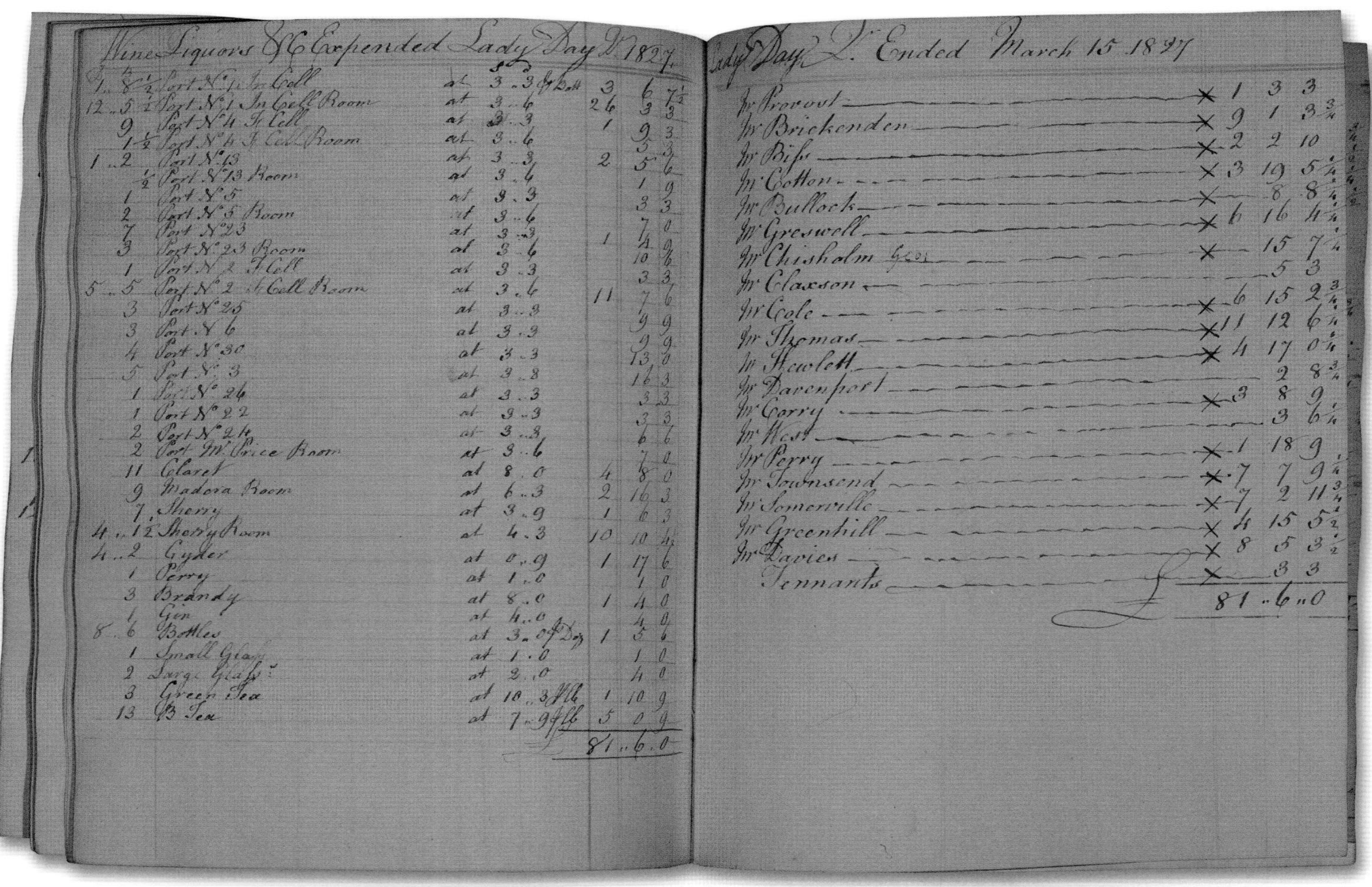

Wine Liquors &c Expended Lady Day Qr 1827			£	s	d
1..8½	Port No 1 In Cell	at 3..3 per Bott	3	6	7½
12..5½	Port No 1 In Cell Room	at 3..6	26	3	3
9	Port No 4 F Cell	at 3..3	1	9	3
1½	Port No 4 F Cell Room	at 3..6		5	3
1..2	Port No 13	at 3..3	2	5	6
½	Port No 13 Room	at 3..6		1	9
1	Port No 5	at 3..3		3	3
2	Port No 5 Room	at 3..6		7	0
7	Port No 23	at 3..3	1	4	9
3	Port No 23 Room	at 3..6		10	6
1	Port No 2 F Cell	at 3..3		3	3
5..5	Port No 2 F Cell Room	at 3..6	11	7	6
3	Port No 25	at 3..3		9	9
3	Port No 6	at 3..3		9	9
4	Port No 30	at 3..3		13	0
5	Port No 3	at 3..3		16	3
1	Port No 24	at 3..3		3	3
1	Port No 22	at 3..3		3	3
2	Port No 21	at 3..3		6	6
2	Port Mr Price Room	at 3..6		7	0
11	Claret	at 8..0	4	8	0
9	Madora Room	at 6..3	2	16	3
7	Sherry	at 3..9	1	6	3
4..1½	Sherry Room	at 4..3	10	10	4½
4..2	Cyder	at 0..9	1	17	6
1	Perry	at 1..0		1	0
3	Brandy	at 8..0	1	4	0
1	Gin	at 4..0		4	0
8..6	Bottles	at 3..0 per Doz	1	5	6
1	Small Glass	at 1..0		1	0
2	Large Glasses	at 2..0		4	0
3	Green Tea	at 10..3 per lb	1	10	9
13	B Tea	at 7..9 per lb	5	0	9
			81	6	0

Lady Day Qr Ended March 15 1827	£	s	d
Mr Provost	1	3	3
Mr Brickenden	9	1	3¾
Mr Biss	2	2	10
Mr Cotton	3	19	5¼
Mr Bullock		8	8¼
Mr Greswell	6	16	4¼
Mr Chisholm		15	7¼
Mr Claxson		5	3
Mr Cole	6	15	2¾
Mr Thomas	11	12	6¼
Mr Hewlett	4	17	0¼
Mr Davenport		2	8¾
Mr Corry	3	8	9
Mr West		3	6¼
Mr Perry	1	18	9
Mr Townsend	7	7	9¼
Mr Somerville	7	2	11¾
Mr Greenhill	4	15	5½
Mr Davies	8	5	3½
Tennants		3	3
£	81	6	0

SCR battels book, showing wine consumed between January and March 1827.

Worcester College started in 1714 with a small body of Fellows: only six in addition to the Provost could be supported from Sir Thomas Cookes' benefaction. The first six Fellows were Roger Bourchier, who had been a member of Gloucester Hall; Thomas Clymer from University College, where he had been a Bible clerk, and All Souls, where he was Chaplain; Robert Burd from St John's, who subsequently gained the degrees of B.Med. and D.Med.; William Bradley from University College and New Inn Hall; Joseph Penn of Wadham; and Samuel Creswicke of Pembroke, who afterwards became Dean of Bristol and of Wells. Under Cookes' bequest, precedence was to be given to candidates from various schools in Worcestershire, and in particular to those who could claim kinship with the founder, but of the first cohort only Bradley and Clymer were Worcestershire men. Bourchier, Clymer and Bradley had all been *pauperes pueri* or servitors; Penn was the son of an Oxford barber, a *privilegiatus*, sworn to the service of the University. Creswicke, on the other hand, was a member of the Creswicke family of Hanham Court, through whose Bristol connections he began his career in the Church. Blechinden nominated four of the first six Fellows; we don't know how the other two were chosen, but it is interesting that an attempt seems to have been made to select some less well-off and lower status candidates in accordance with the charitable aims of the founder. As was allowed by the statutes, two were not in orders; Bourchier and Burd. Penn appealed to the Visitor to be allowed to remain un-ordained, because he was debarred from taking orders by a speech impediment, but this was disallowed and he left in 1719. Bourchier, the senior Fellow, was the only one to stay long in the College, serving as Vice-Provost for lengthy periods until his death in 1751. The embittered Jacobite Thomas Hearne spoke well of him:

Dr Robert Bourne, Fellow 1784–96.

> *Mr Roger Bourchier, Fellow of Worcester College, is a Man of great Reading in various Sorts of Learning. He hath been always of that Place, having been entered there when it was a Hall, at his first coming to Oxford. He is not in Orders. Mr Colley of Christ Church says he is the greatest Man in England for Divinity.*

Hearne goes on, however, to say that Bourchier was 'fanciful', and later 'whimsical and crazed', because of his admiration for Charles Daubuz's commentary on the Book of Revelation. Bourchier's wide-ranging library of over 1,514 items was sold by auction in 1755. Clymer, who died in office as Bursar in 1725, comes out less well in Hearne's account. He was 'mightily addicted to Women, and was much in their company, tho' he was generally sly on those occasions, and some Stories goe about of him, which are believed to be too true'. At the time of his election he was involved in a bastardy case, of which he was acquitted, though 'all impartial People think and believe that he is not innocent'. He died of a fever in the house in St Aldates of a Mrs Dimmock, whose widowed niece he was courting. Provost Blechinden thought well of Clymer, however, and made him his curate at Nuneham Courtenay.

The College remained small for the first half of the century. Additional endowment for Fellowships came from the benefactions of Dr Finney in 1726 (two Fellows, confined to inhabitants of the moorlands of Staffordshire or, failing that, of other parts of Staffordshire or of Durham), George Clarke in 1736 (six more Fellows, aged under 30, preference to be given to 'persons as were born of English parents in the provinces of Canterbury and York' and to orphans of clergyman of the Church of England) and Sarah Eaton in 1739 (seven more Fellows, confined to sons of clergymen). The money was not forthcoming immediately; it was not until 1743 that the first Finney Fellows were elected; the first Clarke Fellows not until 1759 and the first Eaton Fellows not until 1773. By the end of the century, there were therefore 21 Fellows. (The figure remained approximately the same until 1858.) There were various disputes about the prerogatives of the Fellows on the different foundations, as to whether those on one foundation could elect scholars on another, and whether those on the Eaton foundation were eligible for the Provostship.

At the beginning of the 18th century, there were six scholars and ten commoners; at its end, there were 16 scholars, two exhibitioners, nine gentlemen commoners and 20 commoners. Very little material in the College archives sheds light on teaching and learning in College in the 18th century. The statutes of 1714 specify that there should be regular disputations held in the Hall and that weekly written themes should be set by the Dean; there should also be occasional recitations of Latin or Greek orations from classical authors as training in delivery, and Latin should be spoken in the Hall at all times. 'Shepilinda', in her account of Worcester in 1738, writes that John Tottie was 'the best Tutor in town'.

One 18th-century Fellow who had a career within the University was Robert Bourne (1761–1829). Bourne, educated at Bromsgrove School, was elected a scholar in 1777 and a Fellow in 1784. Having been trained in medicine at St Bartholomew's Hospital and possibly having studied in Holland, he developed a large practice in Oxford, and was active in modernising the Radcliffe Infirmary. In 1794 he became Reader in Chemistry and gave lectures showing how a knowledge of chemistry could be useful to doctors, landowners, MPs and manufacturers. He subsequently became the first Aldrichian Professor of the Practise of Medicine and later the Lord Lichfield Professor of Clinical Medicine. Unfortunately, his carefully kept

Revd Rowland Muckleston, Fellow 1837–56.

Edward Charles Adams, Fellow 1853–83.

records of patients were destroyed by his son. His publications included *An Introductory Lecture to a Course of Chemistry* (1797) and *Cases of Pulmonary Consumption etc. treated with uva ursi* (1805). Apparently he taught Classics at Worcester before becoming established as a medic.

The 19th century saw successive waves of reform to the University. With the new examination statute of 1800, the nominal oral exercises which were all that was needed to obtain a degree in the 18th century were replaced by more exacting exams for the BA, initially oral but later with the written element predominating. As the system got under way, the exam format settled into Honours degrees with three classes (with the fourth class added in 1830) and pass degrees, and a more focused approach to undergraduate learning was gradually brought about.

The classics (including ancient history and philosophy) were the staple of the curriculum in the first part of the century. Mathematics was initially included in the exam, but soon split away and could be taken as an extra. Teaching took place in college-based classes called 'lectures'; the tutorial was not yet a part of college teaching, though students could engage a private coach outside the college system for individual study and cramming for exams. Quite ambitious schemes of reading might be undertaken by individual students. The recently discovered memoirs of E.C. Adams, undergraduate and later Fellow of Worcester, give us pen portraits of the tutors in 1847, the year he came up, and rather unflattering accounts of the teaching. The tutors were Richard Greswell, 'greatly loved but little reverenced', Rowland Muckleston, 'very clever, very satirical and very lazy', Hibbert Binney, 'hard and dour and not much of a scholar' and William Andrew, 'of wonderful memory but little original talent'. Muckleston's method of taking classes is described in some detail:

Worcester proctors: back row, H.T. Gerrans 1895, W.H. Hadow 1898, R.W.M. Pope 1884; front row, H.J. Cunningham 1906, W. Chambers 1863, C.H.O. Daniel 1873.

Muckleston had the higher lectures, Aristophanes etc. but he let the men construe pretty easily without many observations and hustled them through 200 lines in the 45 minutes of lecture. If he had looked up the lecture beforehand, which I doubt, it must have been in the most cursory manner … He had also the important Latin Prose Lecture. Imagine 20 men in a large lecture room (now the upper Common Room) each with a large Spectator. Muckleston says, 'Turn to such a page, Mr. –', and then he would allot to each of us about 10 or 12 lines to be turned on the spot into Latin Prose for the next 20 or 25 minutes. Then each in turn read out his performance which was commented on, found fault with or improved. I doubt whether any of us derived much benefit – at least I certainly did not, but it could have been made most useful by a skilful and hardworking tutor.

Mark Pattison, too, speaks slightingly of Muckleston in his *Memoirs* in connection with examining with him in 1847, but Dean Burgon praises him in his poem about Worcester. Muckleston (first class 1833) was an early admirer of Scandinavia. He purchased a small estate in Norway, where he enjoyed salmon fishing and whence he brought back a sea eagle to Worcester, which he kept in the Fellows Garden and which was later stuffed.

Whether or not Richard Greswell (double first, Mathematics, 1822) was a good teacher, he was a learned man, who read German at a period when German authors were not much studied in Oxford (some of his German books are to be found in the Library) and had progressive ideas about education, supporting the study of science in Oxford. He published a pamphlet in 1854 which urged the setting up of a science museum with lecture rooms for science professors, laboratories and dissection rooms and a science lending library. In an earlier published paper (1844), he had urged the appointment of a professor of the philosophy of art, to encourage a branch of learning in which England lagged behind Germany, and to educate the sons of the English aristocracy to patronise the arts. Greswell was a supporter of Gladstone and was the chairman of his committee for the Oxford election of 1847, in which Gladstone was successful.

In the second half of the 19th century, the pace of reform hotted up, starting with the Royal Commission set up in 1850 by Lord John Russell. By the end of the century, Fellowship elections had become open and the clerical monopoly was broken; the 'don' was now becoming professionalised. New subjects were introduced: in 1850 Natural Science, Law and Modern History were added as extensions to *literae humaniores*. New schools were established: Theology in 1869, Law and Modern History in 1872, English in 1893, Modern Languages in 1903. However, the colleges managed to retain control over teaching, and to resist handing over much power to the professoriate. The commission of 1850 resulted in an ordinance for Worcester College, which opened its Fellowship elections (although Sarah Eaton's provisions were retained) and allowed one third of its Fellows to be laymen, though this was not converted into new statutes. It was not until 1882, and after a further commission (1872), that Worcester produced new statutes. These again stipulated that Fellowship elections must be made 'without any reference as to the place of birth or education' and dispensed with the necessity for the Fellows to be in holy orders, except for the purpose of giving religious instruction; marriage was now permitted to some of the Fellows, and the Governing Body could elect the Provost.

Like many College heads, Provost Cotton, who was Vice-Chancellor at the time of the 1850 Commission, was against reform. In the Hebdomadal Board's counterblast volume to the Commissioners' Blue Book proposing root and branch reform of the two ancient universities, he wrote a response challenging a number of its recommendations. He defended the system of closed Fellowships, arguing that it would be dangerous to go against the founders' wishes and lead to 'dissociation': 'The College becomes a collection of unamalgamated individuals, destitute of that sympathy and spirit of union and mutual regard which long connection in the same society tends to induce and foster.' In 1854 he wrote to Lord Palmerston arguing that the College didn't need new statutes: 'From the comparative lateness of its Foundation (1714) its Statutes are entirely free from those restrictive injunctions which press so heavily upon Colleges of a more ancient date. They contain nothing unreasonable, nothing calculated to impair the educational efficiency of the College.' There is a similar letter from the Vice Provost, Rowland Muckleston, signed by seven Fellows, including Greswell. In the same year, Cotton sent in a petition to Parliament signed by 14 Fellows, which urged that the Eaton Fellowship should be kept limited to the sons of clergymen.

A decade or so on, more of the Fellows favoured reform. C.H.O. Daniel, appointed a tutor in 1864, was a supporter, according to one of his memorialists: 'After his return to Oxford he soon became conspicuous among the academic Liberals of those days', largely supporting the report of the 1850 Commission. Daniel was one of the three Fellows appointed to negotiate the new statutes with the Commissioners. H.A. Pottinger, Lecturer in Law and Modern History from 1865 and not made a Fellow until after the revised statutes had been passed, was another supporter of reform. In 1863, he had defended Jowett from a charge of heresy brought against him by Edward Pusey over his contribution to *Essays and Reviews* (1860), by challenging the jurisdiction of the court. In his pamphlet *University Tests: a Short Account of the Contrivances by which the Acts of Parliament abolishing Tests and Declarations have been evaded at Oxford* (1873), he has some fun at Pusey's expense, and at the expense of the Hebdomadal Board report of 1853. Moreover, he calls for various reforms to end clerical dominance and make Oxford a fully national university. The evidence he gave to the 1872 commission is well worth reading: it is both outspoken and funny.

The Fellows of this period were politically Liberal. In the Oxford election of 1865, which Gladstone lost, they were 'strong for Gladstone', with 13 for, four against and three neutral. James

Above: *Thomas Watson Jackson, Fellow 1864–1914, by James Jebusa Shannon, 1904.*
Right: *W.H. Hadow, Fellow 1888–1909, by William Rothenstein, 1930, inscribed 'For my old friend and chief Henry Hadow ... (This is not a halo, but the ghost of a Doctor's cap!)'.*

Hannay, the Bursar, George Charles Bell, the Dean, and Pottinger sent a circular to the MAs of the College urging them to vote for Gladstone. One old member, R.B. Wright, wrote in disgust: 'I hope you will elect a good Conservative, who may hereafter take his place among the Fellows and stem the tide of Radicalism in the Common Room. Your unanimity must make it very dull just now'. Provost Cotton had tried to redress the balance by appointing C.H. Tomlinson (elected 1864, second class Mods, first class Natural Sciences, second class Mathematics) as Chaplain and Divinity Lecturer and also Tutor for the express purpose, as Tomlinson himself explained, 'of having one who would take charge of a certain number of the men and try to be a pattern of a "Conservative Churchman"'.

In the pre-Reform days, publications by the Fellows had been predominantly religious in character: largely sermons or tracts. In the second half of the 19th century, the range became broader, although the publications often date from after their Oxford days. Richard Crawley (a non-resident Fellow) published an admired translation of Thucydides; William Stebbing, a prolific author, published biographies, historical essays, a survey of English poets and anthologies of classical texts translated into English; his brother Thomas Roscoe Rede Stebbing published a translation of Longinus and wrote books on Darwinism and the crustacea, including *Report on Amphipoda* (1888) and *History of Crustacea* (1893); Edwin Wallace wrote on Aristotle. J.E. Thorold Rogers' book *The Economic*

Dessert in the Senior Common Room, *by William Rothenstein, 1936–7 (see p. 167).*

Interpretation of History (1888) was first given as lectures in Worcester Hall: though not a Fellow, Rogers, a friend and ally of Pottinger's, was Lecturer in Political Economy from 1873.

Across the second half of the century the Fellowship steadily reduced in number. The 1850 ordinance reduced the number to 15, and new statutes of 1882 further reduced the number to nine or ten. By the end of the 19th century, the number of Fellows was almost back to where it had begun in 1714, but the holders had a much older average age. W.H. Hadow (elected in 1888) wrote to his mother dispiritedly in 1899: 'At present we are in a very unsatisfactory transition state: the Provost growing more and more incapable, and six out of eight Fellows over 60.' These were: George Stott, Henry Moore, C.H.O. Daniel, T.W. Jackson, William Odling (the Waynflete Professor of Chemistry), H.T. Gerrans, H.A. Pottinger, and Hadow himself. Stott (1815–1911) was a remnant of pre-Reform Oxford. Educated at Bromsgrove, he was elected scholar on the Cookes Foundation in 1833, gained a third class in Classics and in 1839 succeeded to a Fellowship, which he held for 72 years. 'Beyond a regular presence at the stated college meetings he took little part in college affairs, and although he was ordained in 1839, feeble health precluded him almost entirely from active Church work.'

The Fellowship was too small a body to cover many of the new subjects, and Classics remained a staple. Tutors often taught a broad range of subjects. Inter-collegiate lectures were now replacing the college 'lecture' or class; and the 'private hour' or tutorial was becoming a key teaching method. Some subjects were taught by lecturers: for example (Sir) John Marriott (1859–1945)

Cartoons of the Fellows, *by Ralph Usherwood (Matriculated 1930). Clockwise from top left: C.H. Wilkinson, Fellow 1919–58, F.J. Lys, Fellow 1899–1919, Provost 1919–46, H.V. Somerset, Fellow 1921–57, W.A. Pickard-Cambridge, Fellow 1919–49, P.E. Roberts, Fellow 1919–49 and A. Bryan-Brown, Fellow 1922–67.*

taught Modern History and Political Economy from 1885; he was not made a Fellow until 1915. He was also a University Extension lecturer (by 1939 he reckoned he had given 10,000 lectures) and a prolific writer on history, his favourite of his own books being *The Life and Times of Lucius Cary Viscount Falkland* (1907).

The small group of Fellows and tutors contained some interesting men. Among the older Fellows were Thomas Watson Jackson (1839–1914) and Henry Allison Pottinger mentioned above. Jackson, from Balliol (first class Mods, second class Greats), appointed classical lecturer in 1864 and tutor in 1865, was the first Fellow who had not been a Worcester undergraduate. He never completed his work on Terence, but had strong interests in archaeology and art. He contributed to *A Provisional Catalogue of the Paintings exhibited in the University Galleries, Oxford* (1891), and made a slip catalogue of the Hope Collection of prints, of which he became keeper; he also re-catalogued part of the Douce collection of prints for the Bodleian. He donated to the Ashmolean his collection of potsherds and tiles gleaned from building sites (including material from under the site of Carfax Church) and also his library of books on art. Pottinger had graduated from Worcester with a first in 1846 and 'was a candidate for more than one Fellowship; but the Oxford of those days had no room for an enthusiastic adherent of the school of Cobden, and he presently withdrew from a competition the inutility of which was not obscurely hinted to him'. He became a private Honours tutor before getting the Lectureship at Worcester. According to Drake the Butler, 'he was never known to enter the College Chapel; it was said the nearest he ever got to it was when he stood on the steps outside at Dr Cotton's funeral'. The two young tutors were William Henry Hadow and Henry Tresawna Gerrans. Hadow, who was a Worcester undergraduate, with a first in Mods and Greats, taught classics. His interests were wide-ranging: he examined in Greats, Modern Languages and English, though his chief interest was in music, on which he wrote extensively, as well as composing. He was a virtuoso lecturer, never using a book or a note, although he gave chapter and verse for all his quotations. We also have an account of his tutorials:

> *When you took your weekly essay to him, you were always greeted cheerfully and a place was cleared for you at the end of a long table littered, in the most admired disorder, with every kind of book, paper, pipe or miscellaneous article. While you read your essay, he walked round and round the table (and you) drawing at, or relighting, his pipe. He seldom interrupted, till you had finished. His head was held high yet slightly bent forward, and his lips generally wore a kindly, tolerant and sometimes – at least so one hoped – an appreciative, smile. The reading over, he usually made some quick terse comment, such as, 'very good work in that,' or 'excellent, but you might have emphasised such and such a point.' He would then add, 'please take a note,' and resuming his eternal perambulations, pour out with effortless ease, a lucidly-arranged, illuminating and perfectly-phrased discourse on the subject of the essay … Hadow was generous in his praise, though his comment on bad or slack work could be scathing enough. It was always a privilege and a delight to work with him, and to come into contact with his amazingly ready, exact, generous and capacious mind.*

Alan Brown, Fellow 1937–77, by John Thomas Young Gilroy, 1974 (see p. 151).

Hadow left in 1909, and went on to have a distinguished career in university administration and as an educationalist, becoming Vice-Chancellor of Sheffield University and publishing the Hadow report on the education of the adolescent.

Gerrans, who was an undergraduate at Christ Church, with a first class in Mathematics, was elected in 1882. He had an encyclopaedic knowledge of his subject, as his mathematical library of some 3,000 volumes, now housed in the Maths Institute, attests. However, he never published on it, instead being a keen supporter of the study of German at Oxford, and producing an edition of two short stories by W.H. Riehl for the Clarendon Press. He promoted moderate

Schwabe
Worcester College
1945

Vere Somerset's room, with his scout George Hollis, by Randolph Schwabe, 1945.

reform in Oxford and was a supporter of higher education for women, serving on the Council of Somerville College.

The 20th century saw the largest change in the Fellowship: from a tiny body of nine teaching just a few subjects in 1900, to a large body of 40 Fellows in 1999, teaching the full range of disciplines. The Fellowship in 1910 is described by Masterman in *On the Chariot Wheel.* There were four elderly non-teaching Fellows: George Stott, T.W. Jackson, William Odling and Pottinger, and four Fellows engaged in teaching: Gerrans teaching Maths, F.J. 'Jackie' Lys teaching Classics, R.W. 'Bobby' Lee teaching Law and H.J. 'Jock' Cunningham teaching Ancient History. Masterman gives vivid sketches of these four and of Marriott, who taught him History but was not yet a Fellow. Masterman praises Marriott's teaching, but admits he could be egocentric: 'Once, when he had to leave a tutors' meeting before the business was ended he strode from the room and turned out all the lights as he left. "That", said Lys drily, "signifies the state of mental darkness in which we are cast by the absence of our colleague."'

During the inter-war period, the Fellowship remained small, though there had been some appointments in new subjects and a fixed group of subjects had now emerged with their specialist tutors. Classics was taught by A.N. Bryan-Brown, 'B.B.' (elected 1922) and the Greats philosopher W.A. Pickard-Cambridge (elected 1919); in History there were two tutors, P.E. Roberts (elected 1919) and H.V.F. Somerset (elected 1921 to teach Medieval History); English was taught by C.H. Wilkinson (elected 1918) – an unusually early appointment among Oxford colleges in this subject; and Law was taught by a succession of tutors. After Gerrans retired, there was no mathematician. There were no scientists, and the College bore some resemblance to the American liberal arts college. Students wanting to read other degrees were accommodated with tutors in other colleges. History had become a very successful subject for the College. Roberts was good at choosing candidates and getting good results, as R.B. McCallum writes in an unpublished memoir: 'Roberts' greatest gift was his choice of scholars. Again and again he picked out able boys, often from under the eye of New College and over the years he built up a reputation for Oxford historians.' A number of these went on to become academics or history writers, including R.B. McCallum, Roger Fulford, Philip Styles, Charles Wayland Lightbody, J.A.R. Pimlott, Michael Roberts, George Ramsay, Greville Freeman-Grenville, Douglas Johnson, Frank

South view of Worcester College, by William Delamotte, drawn in 1836 for Ingram's Memorials of Oxford, *1837.*

(U.F.J.) Eyck, Peter H. Ramsey, P.G.M. Dickson, Norman Longmate, and G.H. Le May. This foundation was built on by the later even more successful partnership of Harry Pitt and James Campbell. McCallum, who became Master of Pembroke, gives this assessment of Roberts:

> *Roberts was a very good quiet tutor, not outstanding but very conscientious and perhaps rather too kind. He not only tutored well and saw that you were examined fully in your subjects as you went along but he also took trouble to see that his better men were sent out to good tutors. Thus for two terms I was sent to L.B. Namier at Balliol and for two terms to Kenneth Bell.*

There have been many memoirs of this group of tutors in the *College Record*, and it is not possible to describe them all in detail here. Wilkinson in particular is remembered by all who came to the College because of his role as Dean and his larger-than-life personality. Some of the Fellows published books: Roberts wrote several books on British India and Wilkinson produced an edition of the poems of Richard Lovelace for the Clarendon Press. However, there was not the pressure to publish that there is today, with developments such as the Research Assessment Exercise far in the future. None of the tutors had doctorates, now seen as an essential step in an academic career.

It was after the Second World War that the College slowly began to expand. Asa Briggs was appointed in 1945 to teach both Politics and Economics. Unbeknownst to his Cambridge tutors, while at Cambridge reading History, he had taken an external London degree in Economics, and had been awarded first classes in both. As James Campbell wrote, this may well have appealed to the economical Provost Lys as 'two for the price of one'. Briggs was an enthusiast for PPE, which became a popular subject for the College. Geoffrey Dawes was appointed Fellow in Physiology in 1946; Richard Sayce was appointed the first French Fellow in 1950; J.R. Sargent was appointed the first full Economics Fellow in 1951 and Francis Price was appointed the first Physicist in 1954.

There had been Fellows with scientific interests in the 19th century, including Andrew Bloxam (1801–1878), who sailed on the *Blonde* as naturalist on its voyage to Hawaii in 1824 (several items he collected are now in the Pitt Rivers Museum) and T.R.R. Stebbing, mentioned above. But in the 1960s, the sciences became represented in full and became an integral part of College teaching. Fellows were appointed in Chemistry (John Danby 1960); Engineering (Raymond Franklin 1961); and Biochemistry (Charles Pasternak 1964). In the same decade the first mathematician since Gerrans was appointed in Tony Corner (1962); the first Music tutor was appointed with Edmund Rubbra (1963) and the first German tutor in Francis Lamport (1966). Later firsts in their subjects have been: Geology, Don Fraser (1979); Computing, Bernard Sufrin (1984); Biology, Peter Darrah (1992); Geography, Heather Viles (1996); Management, Nir Vulkan (2002); Psychology, Paul Azzopardi (2007). This expansion was encouraged by the Robbins Report of 1963 and maintenance grants for students, which provided an ever-increasing pool of applicants for places, so that student numbers have increased from around 100 in 1900 to over 400 today (not to mention the 200 or more graduate students). Another development has been the increase in the number of professorial chairs at the College, which now include the Nuffield chair of Orthopaedics (first holder H.J Seddon, 1941); the chairs of Comparative Philology (first holder G.E. Braunholz, 1927) and Modern History (first holder E.L. Woodward, 1948); and more recently chairs in Geophysics, Language and Communication, Pure Maths, Taxation Law, and Marketing.

As C.P. Snow remarked in *The Masters*, because the buildings and environment of a college stay the same and the past therefore has a strong presence, we wrongly assume life has gone on in the same way over the centuries; in fact the life of the academic has been transformed over the three centuries of the College's existence. Nevertheless, sometimes – say when reading complaints by early 19th-century tutors about the decline in standards or external interference with universities, or the late 19th-century minute books, which document academic and disciplinary problems encountered with students – one feels that some things at least are recurrent.

The Dog that wasn't a Cat

One of the most frequently cited myths in recent Worcester history concerns a fondly remembered History don and his beloved dog. Harry Pitt, so the story goes, was so attached to his dog, Flint, that in order to circumvent College regulations forbidding members from keeping dogs on site, he had Flint officially declared to be a cat by Governing Body. In 1975 the story of the Dean's dog who had become a cat made it to the letter page of *The Times*, the front page of *The Sun* (including a portrait), the San Francisco *Chronicle* and even, reportedly, the *Icelandic Press*, which confused the story even further by describing Pitt as 'the Headmaster of Worcester Grammar School in Oxford'.

Sadly, this wonderful example of Oxonian eccentricity was pure fabrication. There was indeed a ruling banning members from keeping dogs, and it had been in place since 1785. However, as the 1977 *Record* put it, 'it is a matter of unromantic fact that the Governing Body of the College has made no pronouncement on Flint or any other dog'. The whole saga had been set off by a letter from a student journalist to *The Times*, and the story was obviously too good to be dampened down by Pitt's response, which stated that 'Flint has asked me to assure your readers that he has suffered no legal change of species or ownership', while James Campbell added that 'I am the Dean of Worcester College, and my cat is not a dog'.

Notwithstanding his continued canine status, Flint was a well-loved member of College for 41 years, and the *Record* published an obituary when he died in 1982.

Jessica Goodman

Drawing of Flint.

Harry Pitt, Fellow 1949–90, by Patricia Knapp.

14. College Servants and Staff

Mark Bainbridge

In 1923, a Worcester College cricket team won the cup for the 12th time. W. Drake was the captain, W.C. Wyatt scored 107 runs, and F.J. Johnson took seven wickets for 27 runs. The names of these men are not to be found in the matriculation records of the College, but they were as much part of Worcester life in the last century as the undergraduates they served. For the cricket team was the Worcester College Servants' Cricket Team, the cup the Inter-College cup, and Drake the butler, Wyatt the scout, and Johnson the cook.

In his memoir *On the Chariot Wheel*, Provost Masterman likens the College to an opera, the undergraduates giving the performance and the dons providing the script and music. Yet, like any opera, the stage of the College needs plenty of behind-the-scenes work. This point was not lost on Masterman, who, continuing his analogy, wrote: 'the College servants are the dressers and the scene-shifters'. And indeed, in the history of the College, servants and staff have played an integral role. Staff achievements have often been commemorated in the *College Record* and the memoirs of many Worcester men and women include fond reminiscences on scouts and porters, whose personalities, in many cases, left as great a mark on the students they served as those of their tutors. As George Timpson recalled in his *Kings and Commoners*, 'Some of the liveliest memories which one carries away from school and college are of the domestic staff'.

The necessity of servants for the smooth running of the College was recognised in the 1714 statutes, which explicitly made provision for a *promus* [steward], *coquus* [cook] and *ianitor* [porter], the latter to be paid £8 a year, the others £6. A *tonsor* [barber], paid 20 *solidi*, was also required, his duties particularly necessary in the 18th century when the wearing of wigs or the curling of hair into a wig-like style for dinner was fashionable. The Bursar's Book for 1714 shows that these four staff were originally only assisted by a kitchen-woman and some servers in Hall, although by the late 19th century the staff had expanded to include gardeners, labourers, a hallman, shoeblack, a messenger, clerk, Senior Common Room boy, butler's assistant, coalman and bath-man.

Intriguingly, scouts (or bedmakers as they used to be called), who for most undergraduates must have been a major feature of life, rarely feature in the accounts books until the early 20th century. This apparent omission is explained in the memoirs of the College Butler, William Drake: it was only after the First World War that scouts were put on a weekly wage and the College provided them with cleaning materials. Before this, at the beginning of the 20th century, undergraduates were charged £8 per year for service:

Worcester College Servants' Cricket Team, 1920.

£5 to the College (which was then issued to the bedmaker three times a year), £3 as a gift directly to the bedmaker. The bedmaker could supplement his income by selling crockery, glass and bed linen to new undergraduates, in addition to providing milk for his staircase.

One scout who worked in this pre-First World War manner was Joseph 'Joe' Preston (1784–1873), whose father James had served the College for more than 50 years, and who was himself to give more than 60 years' devoted duty to Worcester. Preston was De Quincey's servant, and in his *Autobiography* De Quincey mentions how much he appreciated Joe, to the extent that at a time when 'half a guinea a quarter was the customary allowance' for scouts, De Quincey gave Preston 'a guinea a quarter, thinking that little enough for the many services he performed'. An early scout's duties can be pieced together from the memoirs of undergraduates and servants such as Drake: each scout had ten to 11 sets of rooms to look after, and would begin his day by lighting fires in each room at around 7am, and waking their occupants in time for Chapel. Since only dinner was served in Hall, breakfast, lunch and tea were brought to undergraduates' rooms by the scouts, who often did

Joseph Preston, artist unknown, 1857.

not leave College until 9pm. And it was not only the diet of his undergraduate charges that concerned a scout: when exams were approaching, William 'Willie' Elhirst's scout, the famous Wyatt, laid out dictionaries and books open at the relevant pages on the breakfast table in a none-too-subtle hint. Similarly, N.S. Power (1935), writing of College life in the 1930s (see the *Record* for 1991), recalls his scout Eaton asking him how he dealt with the questions in his Pass Moderations: 'I think you probably passed', was Eaton's judgement on his gentleman's performance. Masterman saw a touch of Jeeves in all this, and Elhirst's comment on Wyatt could also serve for Wodehouse's gentleman's gentleman: 'There is that about Wyatt that he doesn't only do what he's told, but he thinks for you as well.'

While undergraduates would come up to College for three- or four-year periods, many servants would stay for years, starting work with the College as a child or adolescent and spending the rest of their working life at Worcester, often even returning after 'retirement' either to perform some temporary work or to support the College at sporting events. One such figure was William Drake, who started at the College as a boy of 13 in 1881, retiring in 1946 after 65 years' continuous service. In 1916, Drake became College Butler, in charge of the Buttery, where he oversaw a type of unofficial club for College members, took responsibility for the serving of meals in Hall, and drew up undergraduates' food accounts in the large Buttery books, one of which he is shown holding in the foreground of Halliday's 1937 conversation piece.

For many servants such as Drake, the College was not just a place of work but also a social community, with Christmas parties and sports competitions (often against the Provost and Fellows) as annual events. It also provided several with homes, many in Worcester Place and surrounding streets in Jericho. In the mid-19th century, a small lending library also existed for the use of servants and their families. It is in sporting achievement, however, that Worcester's servants spent their leisure time most successfully: the Worcester College Servants' Cricket Team became one of the most successful in the University. When the (intercollegiate) College Servants' Cricket Challenge Cup was instituted in 1906, Drake started up a Worcester side, which went on to win the cup 13 times between 1906 and 1926.

The long service of men such as Preston, Wyatt and Drake, and their mention in the memoirs of Worcester men has given them a prominence in the College history, but to their names can be added the following: F.J. Johnson, College chef for 52 years from 1894 until 1946, who (in the words of one admirer upon his retirement) 'changed the statement of the pessimist that "there was nothing to eat but food" into a coveted aspiration of the optimist when the food was of his ordering'; W.G. Ward, gardener from 1906 until 1968, who took great pride in the fact that he had joined the College three years before Masterman came up as an undergraduate; N. Lord, scout and later SCR Butler, who served the College for over 30 years from 1919; W.H. Griffin, head groundsman, who died in service after 50 years in 1976; J. Bryant, Head Porter from 1934 to 1953, during which time he was also a Yeoman of the Guard, his legendary advice to undergraduates being, 'When you talk to me, son, stand to attention'; L.R. Carter, who joined the staff in 1924 and retired as SCR Butler in 1977, returning to work part-time until his death in 1981; and Mrs Daisy Smith, who as a scout from 1926–76 must have been one of the first women in what was until recently a predominantly male profession.

W. Drake, W.C. Wyatt and F.J. Johnson, fondly remembered by generations of Fellows and students alike.

15. Literary Worcester

Jonathan Bate

It is obvious, from his novels, bad as they are, that Hewlett suffered, all his adult life, from an incurable nostalgia for Oxford. Doubtless Worcester, with its austere eighteenth-century quad, and its swan-haunted lake, became for him a symbol of past happiness: the greatest – perhaps the only – happiness he had ever known.

Jocelyn Brooke (Worcester, 1927–8), *A Mine of Serpents* (1949)

On an autumn day in 1804 a Worcester undergraduate was in London, on his first trip up to town since matriculating at the College. He was suffering from violent toothache and excruciating rheumatic pains. By accident, he met a College acquaintance who recommended a dose of opium to ease the pain. 'Opium! Dread agent of unimaginable pleasure and pain! … I feel a mystic importance attached to the minutest circumstances connected with the place and time, and the man (if man he was) that first laid open to me the Paradise of Opium-eaters.' So began the addiction that led to the publication of Thomas De Quincey's celebrated memoir *Confessions of an English Opium-Eater*, which first appeared in the *London Magazine* in 1821 and was then reprinted as a book the following year. Melancholy as it is to report, Worcester's greatest contribution to English literature is the work of pyrotechnic imagination that inaugurated the drug culture.

Born in Manchester in 1785, De Quincey was a highly strung young scholar, obsessed with the latest Romantic poetry. He turned up in Oxford in December 1803, tried and failed to blag his way into Christ Church, then fetched up at Worcester because he had heard it was less expensive than other colleges. This was an age when undergraduate life was dominated by gambling, boating, riding, private parties, coffee-houses and taverns. De Quincey lived in rooms 'on Staircase No.10 in the front quad, up one pair of stairs to the right' (Rupert Murdoch occupied the same set a century and a half later). The rooms cost six guineas a year. He was constantly broke, spending far too much on books – the latest literature, not his set texts. His College servant Joe Preston recalled that De Quincey 'was always buying fresh books and was sometimes at a loss how to find money for them. In those days men dressed for Hall and De Quincey, having one day parted with his one waistcoat in order to purchase some book or other, went into Hall hiding his loss of clothing as best he could'. The high point of his undergraduate career was the arrival at the Worcester Porter's Lodge of two letters from William Wordsworth, whom he would soon visit in the Lake District and would idolise and write about. The chance to stay with Wordsworth and Samuel Taylor Coleridge meant that he spent far more time out of Oxford than in it. When

Thomas De Quincey, by James Archer.

it came to his Finals, his Latin examination led the examiner, Edmund Goodenough of Christ Church, to go down to Worcester and announce that De Quincey was 'the cleverest man I ever met with'. But the combination of ill-health, opium and nerves led De Quincey to flee Oxford before his *viva*, with the result that he never got his degree – though this did not stop him becoming one of the most prolific all-round writers of the age.

For a time Worcester had a De Quincey Essay Society, but the more enduring College literary society, formed in the Victorian period and active for much of the 20th century, was named instead after the most illustrious poet to have been educated at Gloucester Hall. Richard Lovelace (1617–57) was the son of a Kentish gentleman. He matriculated as a gentleman commoner on 27 June 1634, 'being then accounted', according to the *Athenae Oxoniensis* of the not always reliable Anthony à Wood, 'the most amiable and beautiful person that ever eye beheld, a person also of innate modesty, virtue and courtly deportment'. Wood alleges that he was awarded an MA after only two years as a result of having won the favour of a 'great lady belonging to the queen'. He apparently took the degree on the occasion of a visit to Oxford by King Charles I and Queen Henrietta Maria, for whose acting company he wrote a (now largely lost) comedy called *The Scholars*, which revealed him as a precocious poet. If Colonel Wilkinson, who devoted much of his academic life to the study and editing of Lovelace, was correct in identifying Lovelace as the bejewelled and begloved subject of the portrait that now hangs in the Provost's dining room, he was indeed a gorgeous boy.

He served as ensign and later captain in the 'Bishops' War', then retreated to the family estate in Kent. But in April 1642 he and some other hotheaded royalists disrupted a quarter session at which parliamentary supporters were debating the pro-monarchy 'Kentish petition'. Captain Lovelace tore up the parliamentary counter-petition and then led his supporters to London, where he and a friend delivered their petition to parliament. For his pains he was confined to the Gatehouse at Westminster, from where he may have written his famous poem 'To Althea, from Prison', the most celebrated verses ever penned by a member of the College.

His movements after his release are uncertain, but his loyalty to the royal cause was never in doubt and his lyric poems circulated widely in Cavalier circles. In 1648 he was once again imprisoned by the parliamentarians. His volume of poems called *Lucasta*, including the renowned lyric 'To Lucasta, Going to the Wars' and some richly complex royalist verses entitled 'The Grasshopper', was published the following year, around the time of his release. He died in 1657, short of money but firm in his opposition to Cromwell.

Worcester has not yet produced a poet to rival the celebrated Cavalier of Gloucester Hall, though literary history may come to judge the multi-award-winning Glyn Maxwell (born 1962) as one of the most accomplished verse technicians of the late 20th and early 21st centuries. His work's rootedness in the best traditions of English poetry – seen for example in a beautiful sequence in memory of the First World War poet Edward Thomas – is testimony to the training he received doing an English degree at Worcester, while his bold experimentation and gift for grand narrative – poems in response to 9/11, for example – owes a debt to the great Caribbean poet Derek Walcott, who taught him as a graduate student in the United States. Maxwell is a remarkably versatile writer, a playwright, critic and anthology editor as well as a poet. He has even written an

Lovelace's 'To Althea, from Prison'

When Love with unconfinèd wings
  Hovers within my Gates,
And my divine *Althea* brings
  To whisper at the Grates;
When I lie tangled in her hair,
  And fettered to her eye,
The Gods that wanton in the Air,
  Know no such Liberty.

When flowing Cups run swiftly round
  With no allaying *Thames*,
Our careless heads with Roses bound,
  Our hearts with Loyal Flames;
When thirsty grief in Wine we steep,
  When Healths and draughts go free,
Fishes that tipple in the Deep
  Know no such Liberty.

When (like committed linnets) I
  With shriller throat shall sing
The sweetness, Mercy, Majesty,
  And glories of my King;
When I shall voice aloud how good
  He is, how Great should be,
Enlargèd Winds, that curl the Flood,
  Know no such Liberty.

Stone Walls do not a Prison make,
  Nor Iron bars a Cage;
Minds innocent and quiet take
  That for an Hermitage.
If I have freedom in my Love,
  And in my soul am free,
Angels alone that soar above,
  Enjoy such Liberty.

Richard Lovelace as a student at Gloucester Hall, attributed to John de Critz the Elder.

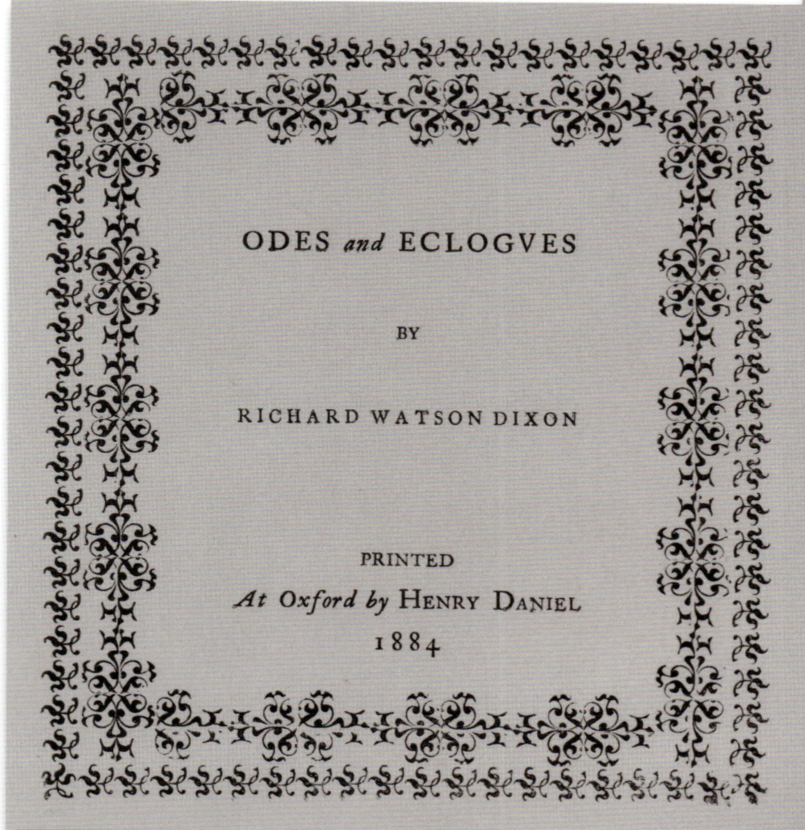

ODES *and* ECLOGVES

BY

RICHARD WATSON DIXON

PRINTED

At Oxford by Henry Daniel

1884

xxij

O fleſh and blood/ comrade to tragic pain
And clowniſh merriment: whoſe ſenſe could wake
Sermons in ſtones/ and count death but an ache/
All things as vanity/ yet nothing vain:
The world ſet in thy heart thy paſſionate ſtrain
Revealed anew: but thou for man didſt make
Nature twice natural/ only to ſhake
Her kingdom with the creatures of thy brain.

Lo Shakeſpeare/ ſince thy time nature is loth
To yield to art her fair ſupremacy:
In conquering one thou haſt ſo enriched both.
What ſhall I ſay? for God—whoſe wiſe decree
Confirmeth all He did by all He doth—
Doubled His whole creation making thee.

Daniel Press books: Richard Watson Dixon, Odes and Eclogues, *1884; Robert Bridges,* The Growth of Love, *1890.*

exceptionally witty sequel to Shakespeare's *Twelfth Night,* told from the point of view of Malvolio (*Masters are you mad?*, 2012).

Worcester writers have, indeed, thrived in many different literary genres. John Lahr (born 1941) is both a theatre critic and a superb biographer – of his father Bert Lahr (the Cowardly Lion in *The Wizard of Oz*), of Noel Coward and Frank Sinatra, and most notably of the astonishingly talented playwright Joe Orton, who was battered to death by his lover Kenneth Halliwell. That book, *Prick up your Ears* (1978), was made into a fine movie. Again, Toby Litt (born 1968) was nominated in 2003 as one of *Granta* magazine's 'Best of Young British Novelists', but he is more than just a novelist: he has published a range of innovative short stories, non-fiction writing and even an interactive short story created via Twitter. His 'Thought-heavy, flash-light' website reveals that the title of his first book began with the letter A, the second B, and so on. At the time of writing, he has reached K.

Dons, too, can show a certain versatility. Christopher Ricks was born in 1933, went to Balliol, was English Fellow at Worcester in the mid-1960s and subsequently held the King Edward VII Chair of English Literature at Cambridge (where he taught the present Provost). Knighted in 2009 for his services to scholarship, he is widely regarded as the most dazzling literary critic of our time, the authentic successor to Cambridge's William Empson. His versatility lies in his range: he is equally adept preparing a rigorously scholarly edition of Tennyson's or T.S. Eliot's poetry, writing with fleetness of foot about *Milton's Grand Style* (1963) or *Keats and Embarrassment* (1974), and making the case for Bob Dylan's lyrics as great poetry (*Dylan's Visions of Sin,* 2003). W.H. Auden described him as 'exactly the kind of critic every poet dreams of finding'. Richard Cobb (1917–96), meanwhile, came to Worcester in the 1970s as Professor of Modern History, having spent years as an independent

Above left: *Jocelyn Brooke,* A Mine of Serpents, *dustjacket of first edition, 1949.*
Above right: *Elanor Dymott,* Every Contact Leaves a Trace, *cover of 2013 edition.*

scholar working in French archives. Made a member of the Légion d'Honneur in recognition of his contribution to the history of the French Revolution, he also had a gift for travel writing – the posthumously published collection of short pieces *Paris and Elsewhere* (1998) offers wonderful evocations of France between the wars – and for quirky memoir, whether of childhood in Tunbridge Wells (*Still Life,* 1983) or a schoolfriend who (gruesomely) murdered his mother (*A Classical Education,* 1985). To judge from his letters to fellow-historian Trevor-Roper (*My Dear Hugh,* 2011), he had a somewhat mixed view of Worcester, as well a Merton man might.

Provosts can also be versatile. Masterman wrote a play about Marshall Ney in addition to his memoir, his account of the XX and his detective novels. Bate is a critic, biographer and editor of Shakespeare, but has also written a novel (*The Cure for Love,* 1998) and a one-man play for the actor Simon Callow (*Being Shakespeare*), which has been performed at the Oxford Playhouse up the road from the College, as well as at the Edinburgh Festival, in the West End and in New York and Chicago.

Worcester undergraduates who have gone on to become novelists are no less lacking in range. There has been everything from Victorian light fiction – *Peter Priggins, the College Scout* by Joseph Hewlett (1800–47) – to 21st century 'chick lit' – *Bergdorf Blondes* by Plum Sykes (born 1969) – by way of *Watership Down,* the massive international bestseller by Richard Adams (born 1920).

The two finest stylists among Worcester novelists were up in the 1920s. The Anglo-Russian William Gerhardie (1895–1977) published *Futility*, his first (and arguably his best) novel, in 1922, while he was an undergraduate at the College. He shared rooms with John Rothenstein, son of the painter William Rothenstein, and regarded Worcester as unquestionably the best of all the colleges, largely on account of its gardens. He had a slight tendency to exaggeration, saying that the College had remained unchanged for 1,600 years, retaining the spartan conditions of the original monks 'who lived in these rooms to expiate their sins; and nothing was ever altered since for historical reasons'. He added that an American undergraduate at Worcester, on being shown round the ancient buildings and told how very old they were, 'remarked very wisely, "Then why the dickens don't you pull them down and build new ones?"' One of the other things he liked about Oxford was that the College servants were as servile as the serfs before the Russian Revolution. Evelyn Waugh once said to Gerhardie, 'I have talent, but you have genius'. He was the primary inspiration for the figure of the writer Logan Mountstuart in William Boyd's superb 2002 novel *Any Human Heart*. Gerhardie was sometimes described as the English Chekhov.

Jocelyn Brooke (1908–66) was a delicate child from Kent, homosexual, obsessed with orchids and fireworks. He only lasted a year at Worcester (1927–8), where he got a place (he believed) because he was the great-grandson of Joseph Hewlett (he of *Peter Priggins, the College Scout*). As an 'aesthete', he inevitably had his room trashed by the College 'hearties', but he was fortunate to be present on the famous occasion when T.S. Eliot came to the College and read 'The Waste Land'. Brooke had rooms in 19 Beaumont Street and wrote articles for the *Isis* student magazine on such subjects as 'Decadence: its Symptoms and Cure', where he characterised modern 'degenerates' – i.e. himself and his friends – as the sort of people who have sexual abnormalities and a penchant for free verse. He and another Worcester man, Jonathan Curling (whose printed letterhead read Jon Querlin in advertisement of his own queerness), started their own avant-garde magazine called *Flux*, which was banned by the Proctors. Brooke's single year at Worcester (Provost Lys sent him down after a dire performance in Prelims) is lightly fictionalised in a very funny, if *Brideshead*-influenced, sequence in *The Mine of Serpents* (1949), the middle part of his 'Orchid Trilogy', the autobiographical masterwork that led some to regard Brooke as a kind of English Proust.

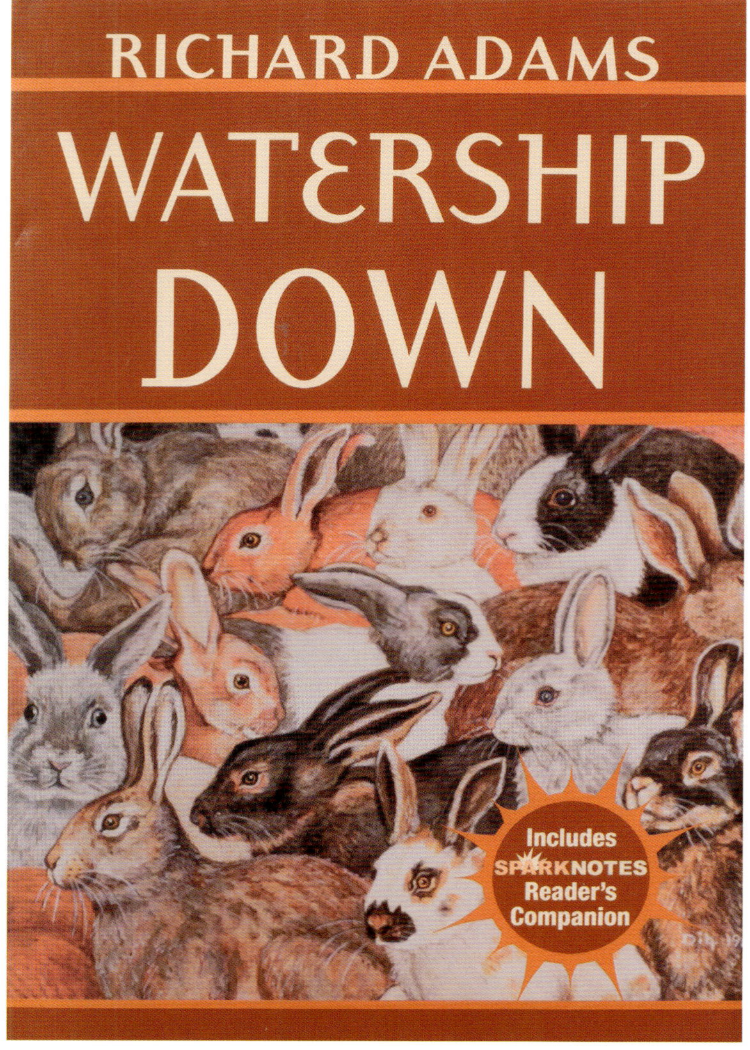

Richard Adams, Watership Down, *dustjacket of a 2004 book-club edition.*

Novelists from grander colleges have sometimes attached their fictional characters to Worcester, in order to place them on the margins and make them into outsiders. Thus Alan Hollinghurst of Magdalen makes the tellingly named Nick Guest, narrator of *The Line of Beauty* (2004), a Worcester undergraduate, while John Fowles of New College signals the failure of the son of the protagonist of *Daniel Martin* (1977) by making him a philosophy don at Worcester. It took a Worcester woman, Elanor Dymott (born 1973) to make the College itself into the protagonist of a novel: *Every Contact Leaves a Trace* (2012) is a beautifully written high-class murder mystery that in its descriptions of lake and quad, secret garden and Senior Common Room, Commem Ball and tutorial encounter, will strike a chord with every former Worcester student.

It remains to be seen whether Dymott or someone else will become the first great female novelist from Worcester. But no account of the College's literary associations would be complete without noting our link with the two finest female comic novelists in the English language. Nancy Mitford's great love Gaston Palewski, who appears in lightly fictionalised form as Fabrice in *The Pursuit of Love* (1945) and *Love in a Cold Climate* (1949), was a Worcester man. And so was Harris Bigg Wither. He was still an undergraduate at the College when he had the temerity to propose to Jane Austen. She accepted, slept on it, and came down in the morning to announce that she had changed her mind. So she did not become a Worcester wife. She went on to write some rather good books instead.

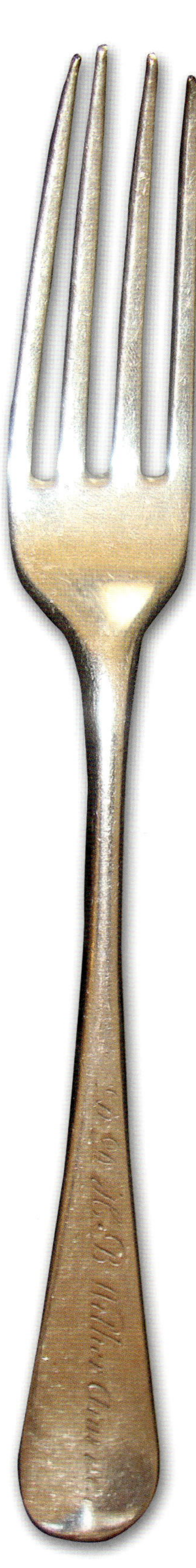

LEFT: *Glyn Maxwell,* Masters are you mad?, *2012.*
ABOVE AND RIGHT: *His proposal to marry Jane Austen having been first accepted and then refused, Harris Bigg Wither returned to College, completed his degree and donated a set of 12 silver forks to his* alma mater.

Lydgate of Gloucester?

John Lydgate was born in Bury St Edmunds in the early 1370s, and became a monk of the abbey in 1389. He continued to describe himself as a 'monk of Bury' throughout his life, despite being rather better-travelled than most. He spent the first decade of the 15th century studying at Oxford; since Gloucester College was the chief Oxford house of the Benedictines, with known connections to Bury St Edmunds Abbey, the College was most likely his home. Gloucester College may have had a slightly easier regime than some – there are records of trouble-making students moving there after being thrown out of another college – and perhaps it suited the poet-monk, who wrote of his boyhood that he spent all his time on practical jokes and fighting, while inventing lies to explain his absence from Matins. Nevertheless (or as a result?), at Oxford he gained the attention of the young Prince Henry, Shakespeare's famously feckless Prince Hal, who later became Henry V: the prince wrote to Bury Abbey in about 1407, to demand that they allow Lydgate to stay longer in Oxford. He produced any amount of poetry during these years – love lyric, devotional works, fables – but when he set to work on his greatest compositions, he entered the political sphere of court patronage and propaganda. He claimed Prince Henry as patron for his *Troy Book* and *Siege of Thebes*; during the 1420s and into the 1430s he accepted a variety of commissions, supporting the legitimacy and grandeur of the Lancastrian line, and the infant Henry VI. His greatest work, the 36,000-line *Fall of Princes*, was written under the patronage of Humphrey, Duke of Gloucester, uncle to the king. Lydgate ended his life back in the abbey in Bury, where monastic poverty must have been somewhat ameliorated by a generous royal pension.

Lydgate's connections with Oxford are frustratingly thin on textual evidence, and indeed his only poetic references to university are his 'Verses on Cambridge'. Here we may suspect him of showing a subtle sense of humour in response to a commission. He argues straight-facedly for Cambridge's foundation in the sixth century BC, but observes that, at least, no one ever accused the place of heresy. Oxford, in painful contrast, had been the home of John Wyclif (*d.* 1384), regarded as the founder of the Lollard heresy, whose works and all discussion of them had been banned by Archbishop Arundel in 1409.

> Cambridge was founded long or° Christ was borne – (*before*)
> Five hundred years, thirty and eke° nine. (*also*)
> In this matter ye get no more of me,
> Rehearse I will no more at this time.
> These remembrances have great authority,
> To be preferred of long antiquity;
> For which by record, all clerks say the same,
> Of heresy Cambridge bore never blame.

Laura Ashe

Lydgate presenting his manuscript, Siege of Troy, *to Henry V, Digby Manuscript,* c.*1420–35.*

16. Worcester and the Law

Francis Reynolds

Although the study of law is long-established in Oxford and Cambridge, the Doctorate of Civil Law being the second most senior in the University, after Doctor of Divinity, the undergraduate schools that we know now date from the mid-19th century. The School of Law and Modern History (described by one contemporary source as 'an easy school for rich men') dates from 1853, and Law later became separate as the School of Jurisprudence, for which the first examination was set in 1872. The syllabus then was slanted towards other traditional Oxford subjects, and so contained a considerable amount of Roman law and legal history.

Worcester, despite its small size at the time, had a Law lecturer in post from 1865, H.A. Pottinger, who had obtained a first class in Classics in 1847. He was first a History lecturer, but became a Law lecturer in 1865. He was elected a fellow in 1883 and Librarian in 1884. It is stated that the first class of the Jurisprudence school was 'for many years almost the monopoly of his pupils'. He was 'a mine of exact information in the details of history, the genealogies of Europe, for example'. He defended Benjamin Jowett, the Master of Balliol, when Jowett was attacked by Dr Pusey and others for heresy, and his various writings included an attack on the Statutes of Keble College, and a pamphlet criticising the Board of Studies of the School of Jurisprudence in 1876. He retired from teaching law in 1900 and died in 1910.

Pottinger was succeeded by Robert Warden Lee, the writer of a book on Roman Law still in use in the 1950s. Lee took a first in Classical Moderations in 1888 and in Lit. Hum. in 1891. He first joined the Ceylon Civil Service for three years, but left it on medical advice. After teaching for Civil Service examinations, he was called to the Bar and took the BCL (Bachelor of Civil Law) soon afterwards. His career was partly based on knowledge, doubtless acquired in Ceylon, of Roman-Dutch law, in which he practised before the Privy Council and held a chair at UCL (simultaneously with his post at Worcester) from 1906. In 1914, he became Professor and Dean at McGill University, Montreal, where he remained for seven years, becoming a KC in Canada. He returned to the Chair in Roman-Dutch law at All Souls in 1921. His departure from Worcester had not been entirely trouble-free. He would have liked a year's leave of absence to try out the Canadian venture, but the College, while initially sympathetic, did not in the end permit this. Despite what must obviously have been a tricky episode, he remained well-disposed towards Worcester and did some teaching there between the 1920s and the 1950s, when he retired at the age of 87.

The was something of a hiatus in Law teaching at Worcester from Lee's departure at the beginning of the First World War, though it seems that P.A. Landon of Trinity, a figure of the old school who

Above: *Stained-glass window in the Library depicting Henry Pottinger, designed by Reginald Otto Bell of Clayton and Bell, 1950.* Right: *Francis Reynolds, Fellow 1960–2000.*

was still lecturing in the 1950s, did some teaching for the College. But in 1927 the College appointed J.L. Parker to a Fellowship. He had taken a first in Modern History in 1926 and care was taken in his appointment: he was allowed three terms to work in chambers with a barrister before taking up his post. However, his time as a Law tutor did not prove successful, as various published reminiscences of the College at the time testify, and he was persuaded to resign his Tutorial Fellowship in 1937, though he remained as a Supernumerary Fellow till the end of the Second World War, when some documents refer to his doing 'Government work' in London.

Alan Brown (see p. 133) was appointed to succeed Parker in 1937, the first Law Fellow who actually had graduated in Law. He was a Rhodes Scholar from Queensland who had in 1935 obtained a first in the BCL, together with the Vinerian Scholarship, a distinguished qualification. He had practised in Australia between his graduation and the Worcester appointment. He started out with an energy that must have provided a most satisfactory contrast with his predecessor: he founded the College Law Society, the minute book of which is still extant, and the College Law Library, which for some time was in a small separately accessible annexe at the back of his room, though it was later moved to its present larger rooms in what had been the Bursary. He introduced mooting: his first moot was on the facts of the *Victoria Park Racecourse* case on which he had worked in Australia immediately before. (It involved the construction of a tower to look in at proceedings on the racecourse.)

The Terrace, scene of many a Law tutorial and now (at lower ground level) of the Law Library. Watercolour by Bernard Gotch.

Like the First World War, the Second made a break to the College's activities for most, but after service in the Scots Guards, Brown returned with renewed energy. The College Law Society was revived, a leading member of the time being Iain Glidewell, later a Lord Justice of Appeal (in modern times, the Society only exists to organise an, albeit very successful, annual Law Dinner for present and past members of the College). Brown undertook innumerable public activities, by which his law teaching was bound to be affected, over about the 15 years from the end of the war. He was Senior Proctor in 1951, Alderman and subsequently Mayor of Oxford (the title 'Lord' had not then arrived) in 1953, and was at varying times Domestic Bursar, Estates Bursar and Senior Tutor. A London Toastmaster was reported as saying that 'the best two after-dinner speakers I have heard are Lord Birkett and a fellow called Brown from Worcester College Oxford'. He knew everyone in Oxford and more Old Members of the College than anyone. He supplied vigour to what may have been at the time a somewhat closed institution. But such energy takes its toll and it was much regretted when he had to reduce his activities very considerably from about 1964, though he remained a Fellow and lived in Worcester Cottage, to which he was much attached, until 1978.

Meanwhile, he had procured in 1958 the appointment to a Lecturership of Francis Reynolds, who had obtained firsts in Jurisprudence and the BCL in 1956 and 1957 respectively. The original appointment was effected by cables between Oxford and Chicago, where Francis was a Teaching Fellow, reminiscent of Evelyn Waugh's *Scoop*. Reynolds became a Fellow (without further advertisement) in 1960 and retired in 2000. At that time the Law faculty was maturing, and the degree of instruction required for success in examinations was far beyond what had been thought appropriate in 1937. It has become even more so since 2000. Reynolds' job was to create a new framework, and, whatever the merits of the framework, from the late 1960s the success of Worcester lawyers, and of Law in Worcester in general, can certainly be claimed as considerable.

Reynolds' appointment had created a second Law Fellowship, and this was later held from 1968 by Bryan Gould, later an MP and subsequently Vice-Chancellor of Waikato University, New Zealand; he was succeeded in 1975 by Paul Craig, who was a Fellow for 23 years and moved to the Chair of English Law at St John's in 1998. In 1978 the election of Andrew Ashworth meant that the College had for a time three Law Fellows. In 1988 Ashworth moved to a Chair at King's College London and subsequently to the Vinerian Chair at All Souls. He was succeeded by Jeremy Horder, who became a Law Commissioner in 2005 (though remaining a Fellow till 2010) and subsequently was appointed to a Chair at the London School of Economics.

For a short period at the end of 2011 there were two members of the Supreme Court of the United Kingdom who had read Law at Worcester after 1958. It was for some years possible to sit a three-man Court of Appeal from Worcester (though not all of those involved had read Law), and there have been several other distinguished High Court Judges and Lords Justices of Appeal. Lawyers tend to think of judges as indications of prestige, since they hold notable public offices, but there are also many senior and prestigious solicitors (some of this stemming from days when Freshfields, now Freshfields Bruckhaus Deringer, Simmons & Simmons, who funded a scholarship, and sometimes other firms used to interview in Reynolds' room); also two Members of Parliament, two First Parliamentary counsel, senior civil servants, prominent figures in the City and academics.

A Female Scout in a Male World

The surroundings were in complete contrast to my factory days, beautiful, peaceful, quietly elegant, toffs would saunter between staircases and underground bathrooms wearing paisley bathrobes and cravats, the bathrooms were like dungeons with rusty old pipes and baths, concrete floors none too clean. Sid, the bath attendant, took no pride in his work and was rarely to be seen, I think that he was the bookies runner for all the scouts' bets …

When I was placed in charge of my own small staircase, it was a dream come true. The old scouts were not best pleased, their male bastion had been breached by a woman, mere girl really, they saw only the direst consequences, they eyed me suspiciously and frowned upon my light-hearted bantering with the toffs; no good would come out of such familiarity … but I felt flattered, wanted, feminine … I could be taken into a gent's arms to be given an impromptu dancing lesson, quickstep or rumba, played on an HMV record on an old gramophone with a horn; I'd only looked in to do his cups …

Most of them had been to public school or in the Forces, they were used to being away from home. They were expected to come to Oxford; although obviously relieved that they had gained a place, there was not the dread of the unknown and the awful responsibility of having to do well. They were mainly in their second year and had chosen the set of rooms and the other people to be on the staircase alongside them. With first year exams behind them, sport (the outdoor variety) cricket, rugby, tennis, soccer, played an important role, they wished to do well for their college, maybe even Varsity. They were healthy, balanced, and for me to be welcomed and drawn into their circle was to me a second education, ever on-going. I shared their sometimes foolish pranks, was let into some little plot to deflate an ego, nothing too drastic, just gentle teasing, teach the pompous ones a lesson. I was again moved by the consideration of these men, just as my fellow workers took me under their wing at the factory, so did the students. I remember going to work one day with a sad tale. A pair of new shoes that I had managed to buy at the cost of 15/-, not an untidy sum to me, had almost fallen apart after a drenching as I was caught in a thunderstorm while cycling home. I was very upset at being told by the shopkeeper, from whom I had bought these shoes that, 'they were not made for cycling in wet weather, but for summer wear'. My protests about being caught out fell on deaf ears and I was dismissed accordingly. It was to me then, a major blow. I honestly did not know where the next pair would come from. There was a lovely toff, a real one, in the room next to my pantry, he was a wet bob (a rowing man) and would be up early every morning to train. We would sometimes share a cup of tea and a chat, light stuff nothing too serious, but on this particular morning I, still resentful of my cavalier treatment by the shopkeeper, told him a few facts and concluded by saying, 'I bet they wouldn't treat you like it'. He listened, head on one side, shook a finger and walked away saying, 'we will see'. I thought nothing of it, why on earth should a chap bother his head with such mundane stuff? However on leaving his room the next morning he said quite casually, 'Oh by the way, take that pair of shoes back to the store, there will be a new pair waiting for you, or if you prefer, a full refund.'

***From the unpublished memoir of Ruby Sandberg* (d. *October 2009*)**

17. Worcester Women

Jessica Goodman

Matriculation in 1979 was an historic occasion, different from every matriculation ceremony that had preceded it over the previous few hundred years. For the very first time, the cohort of undergraduates that left the Worcester lodge to process down to the Sheldonian on a bright October morning did not consist solely of nervous young men in suits. That year, 30 of the incoming students were female. The matriculation photograph marks the end of a very long era, and the beginning of a new one: 1979 was the year in which Oxford became truly a mixed University.

In October 1974, five male colleges had for the first time admitted women, at a stroke doubling the number of colleges open to female applicants. Three years later, separate entrance exams for women were abolished, and 15 colleges, including Worcester, agreed to admit women from 1979. At the same time, two of the all-female colleges began admitting male undergraduates.

Among the women in that first group of female Worcester undergraduates was Rosanne Murison (née Wetenhall). Convent and grammar school educated in the North of England, she had won a scholarship to study PPE at the *alma mater* of both her father and her grandfather. The welcome for the first women to arrive as freshers was overwhelming: 'There was a sense of it being an honour, and we definitely received extra attention. Even when we arrived for our interviews, within seconds of putting our bags down the undergrads appeared to show us round college. We got wined and dined an awful lot in our first year; all the third years were keen to meet us.'

That year was a whole series of firsts: the first female scholars to be inducted in the Chapel, the first female undergraduates to take Prelims, and the first women's boat to compete at Christ Church Regatta. If the male faction of the Boat Club had harboured any doubts about the potentially harmful influence of female boaties, these were soon put to rest by a storming first place performance. Rosanne, a key member of that crew, credits their unprecedented victory in the competition to the efforts of her friend and teammate, Princeton alumna Kate Bucknell (now a bestselling author and scholar of the Auden-Isherwood generation), who 'whipped a frankly fairly un-athletic group of English schoolgirls into shape'. And indeed, then Boat Club captain Fergus Murison – formerly one of the most vocal opponents of the female rowing contingent – was so impressed that he eventually ended up marrying Rosanne.

Not everyone had been so easily persuaded of the benefits of co-education. The Governing Body had seen some stolid opposition to the change, not least in the form of well-loved History Fellow Harry

Worcester College Freshers 1979.

Pitt. But Rosanne might just have been responsible for changing that brilliant but stubborn mind:

> *I was brought to see Worcester when I was considering applying. It was a beautiful June day, and my father introduced me to a lot of his old tutors. At one point we bumped into Harry Pitt. Apparently [according to former Provost Dick Smethurst], that was the moment that he realised that Old Members had daughters as well as sons, and that letting girls in might not be so bad after all.*

Part of the worry over the arrival of female students had concerned the practicalities of their life in College, but Rosanne recalls the women's sanguine reaction to sharing bathrooms with herds of rugby-playing men. 'The showers would often be full of mud, and I suppose when they were really filthy we would moan a bit. But really after an awful lot of fuss as to how the College was going to change, everyone seemed to adapt instantly.' The food, on the other hand, was a different story, and within two terms most of the women had smuggled gas rings into their College rooms, where they would hold dinner parties to avoid what Rosanne describes as 'ghastly' College fare. Happily, in 1982 another Old Member, Dick Bowes, whose daughter Sarah was to attend Worcester, made the gift to Provost Briggs that allowed him to improve the quality of the food and make it more affordable, and since then the food in the Hall at Worcester has achieved University-wide renown for good rather than bad reasons.

Rosanne speaks of her tutors with particular fondness. Copper Le May, Michael Hinton and David Begg, she says, never treated their female students any differently from their male colleagues. Indeed, one of her most cherished memories is the nervous anticipation of waiting to discuss a carefully crafted tutorial essay, worked on long and hard over the preceding week. She does, though, acknowledge that the tutorial system could pose some difficulties for female undergraduates:

> *Debating and argument are very important, and I think women are less argumentative by nature and nurture. Now girls do better at school than boys, so when you come up to university girls are probably more academic and better qualified. In our time the girls had been educated differently – for the first few years I think the College was quite disappointed at the academic results of the girls in*

Sabina Lovibond. In 1982 Dr Sabina Lovibond joined Worcester as a College Lecturer; two years later she became the first woman to hold a Tutorial Fellowship, retiring in 2011.

general. And I think that's because the girls had just been brought up differently. Perhaps people just didn't expect so much of us.

Nonetheless, Rosanne loved her time at Worcester, and credits the tutorial system with furnishing her with immensely valuable skills of quick thinking and self-confidence.

And the female class of 1979 certainly proved their worth: Rosanne herself won a Kennedy Scholarship to study in the States and now has a highly successful international career with diamond merchant De Beers, while her contemporaries include not only author and academic Kate Bucknell, but also BAFTA and Emmy-nominated production designer Maria Djurkovic, and film composer Rachel Portman OBE, the first woman to receive an Academy Award for a film score.

Rosanne's memories of Worcester are largely rosy: time spent with friends, her ill-fated organisation of food for the 1981 Commemoration Ball, witnessing an infamous chocolate mousse fight during Boat Club Dinner. They are, as she points out, the memories of any undergraduate, male or female, then or now. Her experience as a 'first' was, after all, rather ordinary, though no less special on a personal level. There is only one incident that jars that perfect view: when she ran for treasurer of the JCR Committee, her opponent implied that she was under-qualified because of her sex. But Rosanne charitably puts that down to the Parliamentary debating style of JCR politics, in which any excuse is found to attack opponents. Whether or not the debate format can be blamed, the JCR does seem to be one of the last bastions of male domination in the College. Rosanne does not recall a single female JCR Committee member during her time in Worcester, and though the committee is now invariably more balanced, the Presidential role has only been held by a female a handful of times since 1979.

Today, the gender balance of the student body is close on 50/50. And elsewhere in College life, while women have yet to achieve complete parity, enormous strides have been made. The Governing Body (made up of Fellows) now has 11 female members out of 49. But the SCR was entirely male until 1977. This was the year in which Lesley Le Claire, until then Assistant Librarian, was given the role of Librarian and became a member of the SCR, despite not being a Fellow of the College. Her memories of that experience form a later chapter of this book.

The first female Fellow was philosopher Sabina Lovibond, who retired in 2011 from a Tutorial Fellowship which, with the two-year Lectureship that preceded it in 1982–4, spanned nearly all of Worcester's first three decades as a mixed college. She was also the first holder of the office of Tutor for Women (1992–5), and describes herself as witness to a slow but significant evolution:

> *I think I can claim to have witnessed the College's metamorphosis from a male institution with a sprinkling of female faces into something more genuinely co-educational – though of course there is still a long way to go at Governing Body level. Undergraduates of both sexes seemed to gain confidence over these years in the live discussion of philosophy, but it was a particular pleasure in recent times to see women students throwing themselves into tutorials and seminars with an unselfconscious forthrightness that my own generation would have found it hard to match.*

Rosanne agrees that some things have definitely changed since that first fresh-faced matriculation photo: 'The fact that women are

Female undergraduates now make up around 50 per cent of the student body.

now a true 50 per cent of College in every sense will have changed the culture, which was still very masculine when I was here. I know from my experience in business that female-dominated companies go about things in a more collaborative way.' However, when she returned to Worcester to meet current undergraduates a few years ago, she was surprised to discover more continuity than she had anticipated, in both a positive and a negative sense:

> *I thought the girls would be generally much more ambitious, and much more frightening. I've been reasonably ambitious, having a career and family, but a lot of the girls were surprised that I'd managed to do that. Sadly, there still seems to be a perception that high-flying jobs in business are for men, because of the demanding lifestyle. So I came away thinking that people were a lot more similar to my contemporaries than I'd expected. In the business world I see a sector of today's graduates who are ruthlessly ambitious and focused, but what I realised in talking to undergraduates was that there is actually a nice range of people, with lots of different skills and different plans for their lives. They are much more like people I remember when I was here.*

Nonetheless, Worcester's modern females certainly more than hold their own academically against their male counterparts. In 2012, when 45 per cent of finalists University-wide were female, just 38 per cent of first class degrees went to women. At Worcester, 51 per cent of finalists were female, and so were 51 per cent of firsts. Equality, it seems, has arrived.

18. Worcester and the Wider World: International Students

Jessica Goodman, Josh Grehan and John Hood

It was in 1998 that the first cohort of JYAs arrived at Worcester: six Junior Year Abroad students from Amherst, Bates, Bowdoin, the University of California at San Diego, and Cornell, who would make the College their home for a semester. That November saw the first Worcester Thanksgiving dinner, featuring a pumpkin pie recipe that had been meticulously researched by the catering team. Now an unmoveable feature of the annual College calendar, the dinner is just one sign of the multinational community within Worcester's walls, as international students arrive at the College from all over the world.

A high proportion of the undergraduate international students come via the JYA programme. From the initial cohort of six, the scheme has expanded to accommodate 25 to 30 visiting students every year, with about 20 in Oxford at any one time. The programme now covers a range of institutions across the States, though there is a particular connection with Princeton, whose students make up around one-fifth of the intake. JYA students are taught within the tutorial system, following the same lectures and receiving tutorials from the same tutors as permanent undergraduates, although they do not sit University exams. English, PPE and Maths are some of the most popular subjects, and Brian King, Philosophy Fellow and the 2011–13 Visiting Student Programme Director, notes that academic adaptation can pose some problems: 'In general, I think it takes them a while to adjust to the generally cooler form of praise that Oxford (or perhaps British) tutors give. One student spoke of her heart swelling with pride when an essay was described as "very competent".'

A central tenet of the JYA experience is the opportunity to play a real part in Worcester life. Kevin Newbury was in that very first cohort of American students. He left his home and university state of Maine to study at Worcester, and after an initial bout of homesickness (and having got over the strangeness of having a room all to himself) he dived headfirst into the College and University drama scene, directing several plays during his year here. His favourite memory is rehearsing by the lake, also his preferred spot for study-break strolls. Now a globetrotting opera director, he credits his time in the UK with providing him with the independence required for success in such a demanding field:

> *I loved the more autonomous approach to education. When I returned to the US, I felt that I was being baby-sat, and I missed the deep, meaningful learning that happened working with a professor alone in a room. Granted, it was intimidating at first, but it helped me build up confidence in my ideas and my writing. But my time in*

Worcester also taught me to be self-sufficient in a wider sense: to make a home anywhere, to occupy my alone time to the fullest.

The postgraduate student body is inevitably more internationally diverse than its undergraduate counterpart. The nature of graduate study requires students to seek out the best supervisors with whom to work, and 63 per cent of full-time postgraduates across the University come from outside the UK. Worcester is no exception, and the Middle Common Room community is currently home to graduates from 22 different countries besides the UK.

Certain of these students arrive in Oxford via specific links Worcester has with institutions in United States, including the Martin-Wilson scholarship through Williams University, and the Sachs Scholarship through Princeton, while others are part of the University-wide Rhodes scholar scheme. Here, two international students recall their Worcester experiences.

The quad from Staircase 6. Josh Grehan's favourite view of Worcester.

Josh Grehan, Sachs Scholar 2010–12, MPhil in Economic and Social History

Attending Oxford had always been a dream of mine; it's just such a historic educational institution. It was a little intimidating at first, but once I was accepted for the scholarship it was incredible how quickly I found myself to be part of a small family. Various winners from previous years reached out and contacted me. I took classes in lots of different departments, and I really appreciated that flexibility within a graduate programme. My supervisor did a brilliant job both guiding me through the programme and helping me with my thesis.

I remember the morning I arrived. It was the most beautiful sunny day when I dragged my cases into the College after a long flight. I can still recall the pattern cut into the grass of the front quad: it was diagonals, a bunch of diamonds etched in different shades of emerald green, and that was my first memory. I obviously had a lot of ideas about the old buildings, and the rowing, but Oxford was much more urban than I'd expected; this is actually the biggest city I've ever lived in. I grew up 24 miles outside a town of 30,000 people in Western Canada, and Princeton was only 7,000 students in a little town that grew up around it.

But I quickly made a lot of friends – I'm definitely a joiner, and my main activity was rowing. The MCR is a very special community, but it's also just a very small part of Worcester. The vast majority of the people who attend Worcester, and row, are undergrads. As a result through rowing I came to know more of the student body as a whole, so I felt more comfortable when I walked through the College; I suddenly knew more of the student body than I would have otherwise. And from there, whether it was serving as Welfare rep on the MCR or doing other voluntary activities in the community, I was always involved. There's a lot to do at Oxford and I think it's a shame if you don't take advantage of it.

Above: *Josh Grehan (far right, in sunglasses).* Right: *John Hood.*

All in all Worcester has helped me grow. I believe that your world is in large part made up of the people that you know. Everyone has their own little spheres that they operate in. By coming here I have had the chance to meet amazing individuals and develop close friendships with incredible people from the UK and around the world. Because we're friends, my life is part of their life and their life is part of mine; it has just provided me with a much more global experience.

I can't help but stop every time I reach the top of Staircase 6, from the Provost's Yard into the main quad, and look around, where there are rose trellises on the walls, beautiful buildings around the quad, and just think 'how is this my home?'. For two years I've had the chance to call something so beautiful, 'my place', and I'll never forget that.

John Hood, Rhodes Scholar 1976–8, MPhil in Management Studies, Vice-Chancellor of the University 2004–9

I knew a lot about Oxford historically from general reading, and I knew it was a place I very much wanted to go. When I was younger I'd grown up next door to a returned Rhodes scholar, and my parents always had all these books on the bookshelves with the Oxford imprint or the Clarendon Press imprint on the spine. In those days when you applied for a Rhodes scholarship you had to nominate three colleges, in order of preference, and of course coming from 12,000 miles away in the mid 1970s one had no idea of what colleges one should apply to or why. But I was aware that several New Zealand Rhodes scholars in preceding years had come here, and I was also much taken by the fact that the College had its sports ground within the College enclosure, so all that suggested this was where I should come.

It was a grey foggy cold day when I arrived, but actually I found the beauty of the place captivating from the outset. A college experience is a unique experience. You are part of an intimate community of undergraduates, and in those days relatively few graduates; people right across the disciplinary spectrum, local and international. Some of my closest friends are people that I knew at Worcester. And there was a closeness to the SCR too, so I got to know several dons whose subject areas were not related to the courses that I had an interest in. So that opportunity to have a broad

Visiting students 2010–11: Back row (l-r) Jasmine Jimenez, Jane Abbottsmith, Laura McKeon, Sarah Schriber, Amy Savard; Middle row (l-r) Ani Kodzhabasheva, Chenyu Zheng, Katie Joachim, Michael Ward, Amy Murdoch, Chang Liu; Front row (l-r) Katie Punsly, Zachary Mollengarden, Maggie Cooper, Dr Elisabeth Dutton, Ashley Trebisacci, Trevor Ezell, Jessica Yao.

range of disciplinary exposures and to build, if not long-standing friendships, at least university-time friendships, with people from a wide range of age groups, through academic interests, cultural interests and sporting interests, was just absolutely unique.

And I don't think things have changed all that much. You have the sense that that special culture that Worcester prides itself on, around engagement, participation, friendliness, has persisted well, and I think that's a credit to all of those who have been part of the College over the 35 years or so. I think you cannot forget that this is first and foremost an academic institution, so there was always the sense of academic depth and quality and achievement: the intellectual discipline that Oxford seminars and tutorials encourage has served me better in my life that anything I learned in my upbringing to the age of 25. But beyond that there was always a very humane character about the place: those in Fellowship positions were interested in the students at the College, were interested in them for who they were and who they are, and for their scholarly interests and also for their other interests.

THINGS

19. The Pictures

Joanna Parker

Portraits

It seems appropriate to start an account of the College pictures with representations of the founder, Sir Thomas Cookes. A recent bequest – well-timed for the Tercentenary – from Mrs Quita Pollen, whose husband was a descendant of Sir Thomas, has produced two fine oval portraits of Sir Thomas and his first wife, Lady Mary Cookes, and a double miniature of them both (see pp. 32 and 47).

It is not known when the College acquired the large whole-length in the Hall, which seems to be a version of a portrait by Kneller or Dahl (now in the Bodleian Library), but in 1812 the College paid the Oxford picture framer James Wyatt £60 to have this reframed 'in a very large Rich bold Carved French Frame and gilding the same, with College Crest carved at the top and Arms on Shield'.

An account-book kept by Provost Gower in the College Archives reveals that in October 1740 Gower made two journeys to Islip 'to enquire after the Founders Pictures', and on 29 October he 'paid Mr Wall for 1 whole Piece & 1 half Piece of the Founder 31.17.6'. This was presumably Dr John Wall, the founder of the Worcester Porcelain Factory, an amateur painter and an Old Member; Gower owned a picture by him of 'The Judgement of Erasistratus', which he left to the College in his will. Frustratingly, none of these pictures have survived.

The final and perhaps most interesting portrait of Cookes is the large picture that hangs in the Lower Library lobby, given by a former Fellow, Samuel Wanley. Painted by Robert Edge Pine (1730–88) in 1773, this shows Sir Thomas standing arrested by a bust of King Alfred, the legendary founder of University College, who is presumably inspiring him to found a college; a structure intended for the buildings of Worcester is in the background, with the inscription 'ΑΡΕΤΗΙ ΚΑΙ ΠΑΙΔΕΙΑΙ', 'for virtue and knowledge'. An account made by an unnamed visitor to Oxford in 1785, preserved in the Bodleian, has confused later commentators:

> *Library*
> *Sir Thomas Cookes, WL [whole length] standing, … leaning long wig – 1714 – This picture was sent to Bath to be copied by Mr Pine who returned them a picture totally unlike the original picture being tall and thin, this rather short, round and fat.*

(The reference here is to the figure of Sir Thomas.) Two documents in the Archives now make us think that what happened was that the College sent to Pine in Bath either the portrait in the Hall or possibly the image painted by John Wall, to form the basis of a new

Above left: *The portrait of Sir Thomas Cookes that hangs in the Hall.* Above: Sir Thomas Cookes contemplating the bust of King Alfred, *by Robert Edge Pine, 1773.*

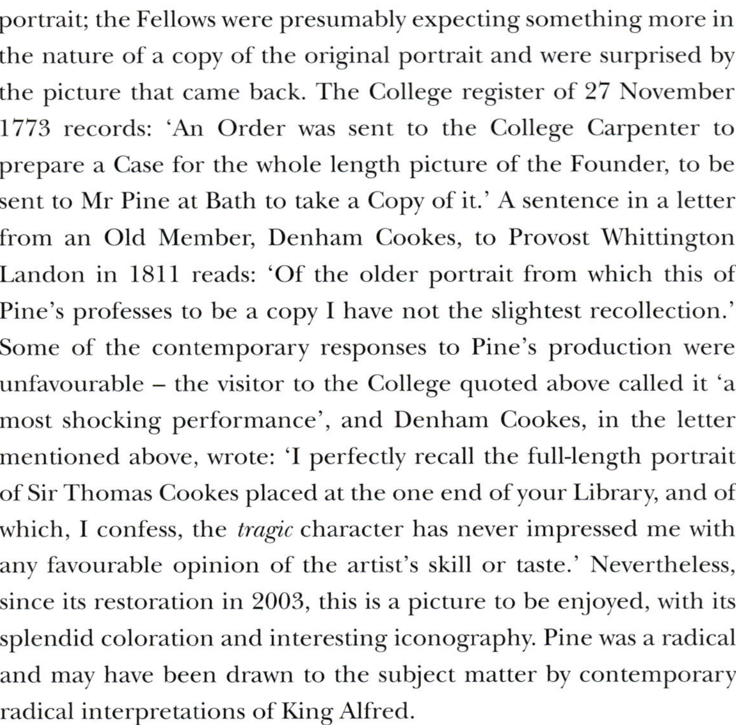

portrait; the Fellows were presumably expecting something more in the nature of a copy of the original portrait and were surprised by the picture that came back. The College register of 27 November 1773 records: 'An Order was sent to the College Carpenter to prepare a Case for the whole length picture of the Founder, to be sent to Mr Pine at Bath to take a Copy of it.' A sentence in a letter from an Old Member, Denham Cookes, to Provost Whittington Landon in 1811 reads: 'Of the older portrait from which this of Pine's professes to be a copy I have not the slightest recollection.' Some of the contemporary responses to Pine's production were unfavourable – the visitor to the College quoted above called it 'a most shocking performance', and Denham Cookes, in the letter mentioned above, wrote: 'I perfectly recall the full-length portrait of Sir Thomas Cookes placed at the one end of your Library, and of which, I confess, the *tragic* character has never impressed me with any favourable opinion of the artist's skill or taste.' Nevertheless, since its restoration in 2003, this is a picture to be enjoyed, with its splendid coloration and interesting iconography. Pine was a radical and may have been drawn to the subject matter by contemporary radical interpretations of King Alfred.

The College also owns several portraits of George Clarke – 'almost our founder', as the inscription on the silver cup he bequeathed reads – by Kneller's studio, but none in Kneller's own hand, according to the experts. There is a fine miniature (see p. 91), 'my own Picture in Water-Colours, and set in Gold', which Clarke left in his will to John Michel; it is engraved with his monogram and the following inscription: *'hanc sui ipsius picturam testamento reliquit Geo; Clarke ar: Joh: Michel amico coaevali MDCCXXXVI'* and was given to the College by Clarke's executor Dr Robert Shippen, Principal of Brasenose in 1739. In Clarke's print collection there is a preparatory drawing for an engraving of a double portrait of Clarke acting as secretary to Queen Anne's consort, Prince George of Denmark; the original painting – a genuine Kneller – is at All Souls.

Left: George Clarke with the Prince of Denmark *by Godfrey Kneller.*
Above: *Richard Smethurst, Provost 1991–2011, by Jennifer McRae, 2004.*

The portraits of all 12 past Provosts of the College have recently been hung in the Hall. The latest is the portrait of Richard Smethurst by Jennifer McRae. This shows him in a less formal style than his predecessors, seated jacketless in a white shirt, but clues are given to his academic status and interests: his Pro-Vice-Chancellor's white tie and bands lie on the table beside him together with the teapot, and his gown is hanging up behind him. The books on the shelves are on economics and international relations, and the one at his left elbow is Susan Gillingham's *One Bible, Many Voices.* Jennifer McRae admires the symbolism of Tudor portraits. The portrait was painted in the Provost's study in the Lodgings, with the sitter looking towards the window into the Provost's garden, but since the painter liked the cottages, she has added in a window with a view of them from one of the staircases on the Terrace!

As well as portraits of Provosts and Fellows, the collection contains two early portraits of servants: the first, painted in 1816, depicts Anthony Cooper, Common Room servant of the early 19th century, and the second is a small oval portrait of Joseph Preston (1783–1865) aged 73, who was servant first to De Quincey and then to the SCR (see p. 140); it was presented to the Common Room in July 1857 by W.H. Griffiths. Preston is mentioned in Dean Burgon's poem about Worcester ('Who knows not old Joe Preston?' … 'fraught with viands, bread and beer') and his recollections of De Quincey's time as a student were recorded by W.E. Daniel in *Our Memories,* the book of Oxford reminiscences printed by C.H.O. Daniel on his private press. The tradition of representing long-serving College staff has continued: a pencil sketch by Randolph Schwabe, presented by Major G.F.G. Cumberlege in 1945, commemorates William Drake, who worked for the College for 65 years from 1881–1946, becoming College Butler in 1916. There are also an oil portrait of Leslie Carter, SCR Butler, by Oliver Thomas (1946) and a pencil sketch of his successor in the post, Roger Whiteman, by Malcolm Sparkes.

Perhaps the most interesting portraits of all are the three conversation pieces. Two of these were commissioned in 1936–7 by C.H. Wilkinson to represent the SCR and JCR; they were celebrated in an article entitled 'Academic Chat' in *The Times* for 17 August 1937: 'The pictures together give a glimpse, and a most attractive

Above: *Anthony Cooper, College servant, 1816.* Right: *William Drake, College Butler, by Randolph Schwabe, 1945.*

one, of the leisure moments of the members of one of Oxford's most beautiful colleges'. William Rothenstein's picture of the SCR (reproduced on p. 131), presented to the College by R.E.M. Coke Harvey, shows the Fellows seated at dessert in the Lower SCR: some of the College's pictures can be seen behind them on the wall. From left to right they are the historian and Vice-Provost Paul Roberts, the philosopher W.A. Pickard-Cambridge (not to be confused with his brother the classicist A.W. Pickard-Cambridge), the English tutor and Dean C.H. Wilkinson, the classicist A.N. Bryan-Brown and the Provost F. J. Lys. This represents over half the Fellowship of the time: the historian H.V. Somerset, the Professor of Comparative Philology G.E. Braunholtz, the lawyer J.L. Parker and the chaplain R.L.P. Milburn are not portrayed. Edward Halliday's picture (reproduced on p. 190) shows a group of 16 undergraduates grouped outside the Hall with the Porter James Bryant and the Butler William Drake, and the shadow of the Dean on the grass. Various props – tennis rackets, golf clubs, a copy of *The Sporting Times*, bagpipes, a tankard, a pipe – suggest sporting and other activities; the figure holding a gown represents learning. As with Van Dyck's huge group portrait at Wilton, the figures are carefully posed and give a slightly stylised effect. In a letter to Harry Pitt, G.V.R. (Jim) Grant, who can be seen in the left of the picture in a dressing gown holding a towel and sponge, described how the picture was executed:

> *The painting was carried out individually in the Library; my pose was rather painful since I had to stand on my left leg with my right heel well up in the air, my left hand held upright, twisted to the left to shew the sponge and my head and shoulders turned to the right as I was supposed to be greeting Ford. My right thigh was against a table to give me a small amount of support.*

The two scenes (together with the later picture by Halliday of undergraduates, drawn largely from Eton and Winchester, in a room, commissioned by Wilkinson (see p. 189) in 1952) provoke reflection on the huge changes that have taken place in the College in the post-war period.

LEFT: Edge of a Forest with a Grainfield, *by Jacob van Ruisdael,* c.*1655.*
BELOW: The Last Supper, *attributed to Sebastiano Ricci,* c.*1715.*

BEQUESTS

The picture collection is perhaps unusual among those of Oxford colleges in that it contains many pictures besides portraits; these have been the result of the generosity of its Old Members and friends. An early bequest was that of the Reverend Treadway Russell Nash (1725–1811). Nash was an undergraduate in the 1740s; in 1749, he made the grand tour together with his eldest brother Richard, who had been at Christ Church. We learn from Chambers' *Biographical Illustrations of Worcestershire* (1820) that

> *In March, 1749, he accompanied his brother Richard on a tour, for the recovery of his health, to the Continent, where, after remaining in Paris for about six weeks, they spent the remainder of the summer on the banks of the Loire; in the month of October and the following year, they visited Bordeaux, Thoulouse, Montpelier, Marseilles, Leghorn, Florence, Rome, Naples, Bologna, Venice, Padua, Verona, Milan, Lyons, and again Paris, from whence Mr Nash returned to Oxford the latter end of the summer of 1751.*

On returning to Oxford, Nash resumed his Fellowship, which he combined with being Vicar at Eynsham; he served as Bursar and Dean, and was 'the first who projected a carriage road from Oxford to Witney'. Extensive diaries by Nash of his travels abroad and in England survive at Eastnor Castle; they also include excerpts he copied out from Inigo Jones' annotations to Palladio in the College Library.

As a third son, Nash might have expected to continue the life of an Oxford don and country clergyman, but in 1757 he resigned his Fellowship on unexpectedly inheriting the family estates in Worcestershire. (He added the Russell to his name on inheriting the estate at Strensham from his brother's widow.) In his new role as a country gentleman, he wrote a two-volume *Collections for a History of Worcestershire* and edited a de luxe edition of *Hudibras* by Samuel Butler, another Worcestershire man. A fire caused by a bottle of aqua-fortis in a carriage unfortunately destroyed 'a very curious and valuable selection of drawings and prints, which he and his brother had purchased in France and Italy'. What might the College have missed out on here? Nash's wealth at his death in 1811, excluding his landed property, was around £60,000. He left to the College a group of pictures that it has generally been assumed he bought during his tour of the Continent (though it may be noted that most of them are Dutch or Flemish School and some by painters who worked in England). There seem to have been ten paintings. The most famous is the beautiful *Edge of a Forest with a Grainfield* by Jacob van Ruisdael, which has been loaned to many exhibitions of Dutch art and which features in E.H. Gombrich's bestselling *Story of Art.* Others are a *Last Supper* by Sebastiano Ricci; a *Nativity* by the studio of Bassano; two still-lifes, one by a member of the van Huysum family and the second by one of the Verelsts; an Italianate landscape by Frederik de Moucheron, and a landscape with ruins and figures most recently attributed by Martin Eidelberg to Henry Ferguson (or Vergazoon);

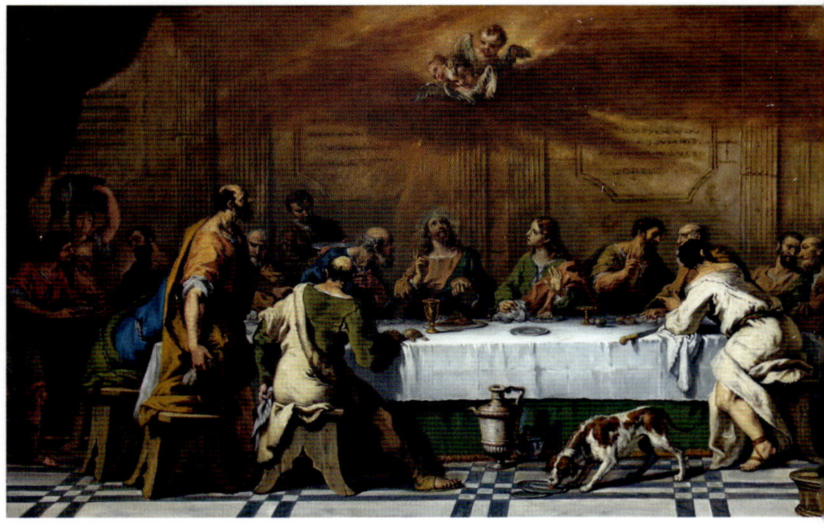

Left: Arthur's Castle, Tintagel, Cornwall, *by William Turner of Oxford, 1868.*
Above: *The cottages, by Bernard Gotch,* c.*1930.*

two genre scenes of an old man and old woman spinning and of a man and a woman selling fish; and a *Magdalen* by the studio of Guido Reni, which prior to the refurbishment of the Chapel by Burges served as an altarpiece. An invoice from James Wyatt dated 1812 shows that the College took immediate care of the ten pictures, purchasing five new frames and having the other frames mended, all the pictures cleaned, and ten labels made as required by the testator. James Wyatt (1774–1853) was an Oxford carver and gilder, who operated from 115 High Street, and became Mayor of Oxford in 1842.

From the New Testament scholar Robert Henry Lightfoot, Dean Ireland's Professor of the Exegesis of Holy Scripture at Oxford (matriculated 1902), came a collection of oils and watercolours by William Turner of Oxford and a Michael 'Angelo' Rooker. William Turner (1789–1862) was born in Black Bourton, near Bampton, and later moved to his uncle's estate in Shipton-on-Cherwell, the setting for many of his pictures. After a period in London as a pupil of John Varley, he returned to Oxford and made his living by giving lessons in the University and the county; in 1831 he moved into 16 St John Street, where he lived until his death. Throughout his life he made regular summer sketching tours to all the picturesque parts of the British Isles (he never travelled abroad); the resulting pictures were exhibited at the Society of Watercolours' annual exhibitions. Turner's pictures are varied in style; he was often drawn to empty landscapes portrayed with a low horizon and changing weather; other pictures are in brighter colours and offer lusher or more fertile visions of nature. In 1851 in the fifth volume of *Modern Painters* Ruskin wrote: 'I am sorry not to have before noticed the quiet and simple earnestness, and the tender feeling, of the mountain drawings of William Turner of Oxford.' Our Turners include several Oxford scenes, a picture of Cherwell lilies, and scenes from Cornwall, Wales and Scotland.

More recent bequests have been those of Arnold Osterman Dyer (whose father was at Worcester) in 1972, H. John Paris (1932) and Harry Pitt. From Arnold Dyer came a group of mainly sporting pictures, including some by John Frederick Herring Senior and Francis Sartorius the Elder. From John Paris, who was Director of the National Gallery of South Africa, came a group of 19th-century British paintings, and from Harry Pitt about 60 mainly 18th- and 19th-century British watercolours. It is not possible to mention individually all the paintings that the College has received as gifts, but they have added immensely to the richness and variety of the collection. An important subset of the collection consists of views of the College, among which are nine pleasant watercolours by Bernard Gotch (1876–1963).

JCR Pictures

The JCR acquired some fine items at the beginning of the 20th century, among them the set of ten Oxford scenes in watercolour, pen and pencil by Thomas Rowlandson, with caricatured figures in the foreground and attractive topographical backgrounds of University and College buildings, many of which Rowlandson copied from the Oxford Almanacks. They were made into aquatints by Ackermann in 1810. This set was purchased by subscription in 1930 in memory of Maurice Lockitt. In 1942, Paul Nash was commissioned by Derek Adams (1926) and Peter Adams (1930) to paint a picture of wartime Oxford. It shows tanks from the Senior Training Corps' mobile column advancing westward, with a view of the city in the background, aeroplanes overhead, and the clouds mirrored by puffs of smoke: a pastoral landscape overtaken by war. In a letter to Captain Adams, Paul Nash wrote of the commission:

> *At first it rather alarmed me I will confess but, largely owing to the imagination of Colonel Wilkinson, I was guided in a direction which almost immediately opened up a true pictorial prospect. From the heights above Ferry Hinksey we reviewed the scene. It struck me that now was the moment to portray – so far as the landscape was concerned – before the winter elms lost their architectural value and became merged into domes of leaves. The next day I made my 'blitz Krieg' in spite of every threat of rain and useless weather. Whereupon God gave me not only a first-class natural design but a colour scheme thrown in. It was really handsome!*

In 1947, the JCR started a picture fund, 'with the object of purchasing works of art and particularly contemporary British paintings':

> *As an immediate aim, it is felt that emphasis should be laid on purchasing the paintings of contemporary British artists, and this for two reasons: first, because the prices would be more within our present range; and secondly, because it is desirable to afford a permanent home and encouragement for contemporary British art. If, as is hoped, the scheme spread to other Colleges, the University would be able to provide patronage, and perhaps a strong impetus, to British painting. There are even prospects in the future of a permanent exhibition in Oxford of pictures selected from JCR collections. This, then, is an important aim of the fund, but in no way over-rules the collection of older works of art.*

An arrangement was made for JCR members to contribute £1 a year if they wished, and Lord Methuen agreed to act as advisor.

Above: A south view of the Observatory at Oxford, *engraving after Thomas Rowlandson,* c.*1890.* Opposite: Oxford During the War, *by Paul Nash, 1942.*

Worcester was one of the two first (the other was Pembroke) among many other colleges that started similar funds around this time. A patriotic interest in British painting in the immediate aftermath of the war was clearly one motive.

Among Worcester JCR's first purchases was a watercolour of Melrose Abbey by H.W. 'Grecian' Williams (1773–1829) in 1949 from Ryman's Exhibition of English Water Colours, to complete the décor of the JCR, which was then hung with a number of Oxford scenes. In 1951, they began to build up a library of modern pictures to be lent to contributors to the fund; purchases included a John Piper of the Provost's Lodgings, commissioned by Adrian Sherwood, in 1950, and a maquette for *Mother and Child* by Henry Moore in 1952, which the sculptor kindly sold very cheaply. Unfortunately, as was the case with many of the other colleges, enthusiasm waned (most JCR picture collections fell into disuse during the very different era of the 1970s); the collection was not properly looked after, and responsibility for it was eventually taken over by the Curator of Pictures.

Under the curatorship of David Landau, a great patron of the arts who was for many years a Supernumerary Fellow of the College, all the College pictures were entered on a database, which will ensure that they can be properly maintained for the future. The holdings of oil paintings have recently been included in the National Inventory of Oil Paintings organised by the Public Catalogue Foundation; images are to be found on the BBC's 'Your paintings' website.

20. The Treasures

Joanna Parker and Kate Colleran

George Clarke's Collections

Some of the College's greatest treasures are to be found in George Clarke's collections of prints and drawings. The drawings collection falls into two parts. The first group consists of 17th-century drawings by Inigo Jones and others that Clarke bought some time at the beginning of the 18th century. The group also contains six drawings by Andrea Palladio. Jones' drawings had passed to his pupil John Webb, who in his turn had left them to his son William in his will, with the injunction that they were to be kept 'intire together, without selling or imbezzling any of them'. Nevertheless, they began to appear upon the market at the end of the 17th century. One group was eventually purchased by Lord Burlington from the Talmans in the 1720s; the masque designs are now at Chatsworth and the architectural drawings at the RIBA drawings collection, now housed in the V&A. The other group was acquired by Clarke probably in about 1703 from William Webb's widow. Which of the drawings are in the hand of Jones and which in that of Webb is a matter for much debate. In the 18th century, they were mostly ascribed to Jones in such publications as Isaac Ware's *Designs of Inigo Jones* (1730) but today the number of autograph drawings by Jones is believed to be much smaller.

Opposite: *Inigo Jones: Design for a ceiling for the Duke of Buckingham.* Above from the left: *Design for the New Exchange in the Strand; Design for completing the central tower of Old St Paul's; Design for a catafalque for James I.*

Inigo Jones' architectural drawings are highly important. They record designs, such as the new Palace of Whitehall, which were never built because his chief patron Charles I was notoriously short of money, and designs which were built but are now destroyed, including the Prince's Lodging at Newmarket, the Corinthian portico which he added to old St Paul's Cathedral, and the chapel and the interiors at Somerset House. Only four major buildings survive: the Banqueting House in Whitehall, the Queen's House in Greenwich, the Queen's Chapel at St James's Palace and St Paul's Church Covent Garden, and even these have been altered. Jones was a key figure for the development of art and architecture in 17th-century England, but he put much of his effort into that most ephemeral of all art forms: the masque. The drawings are thus even more than for most architects a major source for understanding his style and development. Worcester has two precious early drawings, before Jones went to Italy in 1613–14, which show his earliest response to Italian ideas, before he had assimilated Palladio's conventions for architectural drawing. One is a design for the New Exchange in the Strand, and the other a design for a new top on the tower of old St Paul's Cathedral, which had lost its steeple in a storm. Neither was executed.

Jones' drawings are also beautiful works in themselves; particularly so the design for a catafalque for James I, which shows his mastery of Italian sources, and the ceiling design for the Duke of Buckingham, one of his few coloured drawings. Some of the finest drawings are the many studies of heads, often copied from prints of Parmigianino, Titian and others. Jones taught himself to draw when he began designing masques, and he continued to draw into the last years of his life for his own pleasure and for practice. Figurative art was very important to him, as it was part of his attempt to exalt the role of the architect from craftsman to artist, a maker of designs: as the theatre and art historians Stephen Orgel and Roy Strong put it, 'Jones takes his place as the first person in the history of British art who realised the value of being able to express himself through draughtsmanship. By cultivating this accomplishment he was able both to assimilate visual information and realise his own ideas.' According to Webb, Van Dyck praised Jones' drawing style: 'In designing with his Pen [he was] not to be equalled by whatever great Masters in his Time, for *Boldness, Softness, Sweetness* and *Sureness* of his *Touches*.'

The second group of drawings consists of those which Clarke acquired through his participation in the many building schemes which took place in Oxford during the late 17th and early 18th centuries. These include drawings by Henry Aldrich, Nicholas Hawksmoor, John James, John Talman, Sir James Thornhill, Sir John Vanbrugh and others; there are also many by Clarke himself. Later drawings for buildings at Worcester have been added to these, including many designs by William Burges for Chapel and Hall.

George Clarke also assembled a large collection of prints. He did not buy old master prints but contemporary reproductive prints – the equivalent of the modern art book. Though not so valued by collectors today, these are both historically interesting and also often beautiful. Clarke's impressions are often early ones and in excellent condition, and he chose the finest contemporary prints available, by the most prized engravers, of the subjects that interested him. He bought prints of buildings – Roman, Italian, French and English – interior decoration and garden design; of paintings – Italian, French and English, especially Raphael and Poussin but also Hogarth and Watteau – and of portraits of 17th- and 18th-century figures. He bought many foreign prints, and he patronised all English efforts at printmaking. Some striking examples of English prints are two medley prints by George Bickham (see p. 96), and the set of South Sea Bubble playing cards (see p. 93), which satirise the mad schemes for making money that ended in financial collapse in 1720. Clarke's bookplate (see p. 91) was designed by Simon Gribelin, a Huguenot print-maker who had settled in England.

The ownership of a priceless collection of this nature presents a major problem of conservation to a college with limited funds. By the 1980s, interest in architectural drawings was increasing and conservation approaches to collections were also changing, moving towards less interventionist techniques. In 1986, Dr David Landau, Supernumerary Fellow at the time and founder and editor of *Print Quarterly*, invited conservator Kate Colleran to the Library to be shown the drawings by the Librarians James Campbell and Lesley Le Claire, in order to draw up a conservation condition report and plans. But it was not until three years later that the success of the Inigo Jones exhibition in New York, later transferred to the Royal Academy in London, provided the impetus for serious fundraising. Here Kate Colleran recalls her experience.

Joanna Parker

A Conservator's View

I could hear the whispering across the centuries: 'I hear my good Lord Buckingham has a drawing prepared by Mr Jones himself for his ceiling for his new abode in Essex.' I was gazing in wonder at a garden flipped to the ceiling, executed in silver and gold and red and blue. It was feeling a little sorry for itself in a miserable British Council frame (lent for an exhibition in Florence in 1948), 'foxed' in places, dusty but still magnificent. Is the blue a true ultramarine, I wondered, made from lapis lazuli, the costliest of minerals, brought to England from Afghanistan to be ground into pigment in Mr Jones' workshop? Did he *have* a workshop? Did he really draw those precise, miniaturist lines himself, or was it his assistant?

As these thoughts scudded across my mind, two enormous leather-bound albums were heaved onto the tables. These albums contained the rest of the drawings by Jones and Webb, bound into this backbreaking format in the 1930s by Colonel Wilkinson, Fellow Librarian of fearsome repute.

Although the albums were diabolically heavy and difficult to view, he probably saved the drawings from physical damage. What he did not know – could not have known – was that the quality of the support pages was such that in a relatively short time they would turn extremely acidic. By the time I saw them, the acid was migrating into the drawings. Another album of more modest dimensions, but with most of its 18th-century binding intact, contained Hawksmoor drawings; there were also drawings in boxes by Dr Clarke, several drawings by Palladio, and some 100 presentation and working drawings by William Burges. There were magnificent albums containing prints.

Approaching the task of conserving some 1,000 drawings – if we include Burges' designs for the Chapel and the Hall – was a daunting task. I remembered John Harris' Preface in the catalogue for the New York exhibition: 'In the past, an architectural drawing has been studied in three ways: for its aesthetic merit (the Old Master syndrome of colour and prettiness), for the building for which it was drawn, or as a representation of the drafting style of the architect.' What approach should we take to ensure their physical stability without compromising the complex primary evidence of their making and their history?

Jones' and Webb's drawings are on mellow Italian papers, while Hawksmoor and Dr Clarke drew mainly on Dutch papers. Burges used beautiful English handmade watercolour papers for presentation drawings, and machine made paper for transfer drawings. They are all very different, with different fibre furnish, different methods of making and different characteristics. The designs are drawn in inks using quill pens; the inks are mostly iron gall or black carbon or brown ink of varying intensity and colour. Often, there are graphite underdrawings and the measurements are drawn with a stylus and the lines punctuated with dots. Many have washes of inks or watercolours. There are corrections – little tabs – attached for variations in the design. Some drawings still have blobs of red sealing wax on their verso by which they were attached to the drawing boards.

A drawing can be viewed purely as an information carrier, while the object itself is almost superfluous. On the other hand, the object may be viewed as a corpus of data and a source of complex primary evidence. It is the profound alteration of this primary evidence that is of concern to the historian and therefore to the conservator.

Jones' and Hawksmoor's architectural drawings are valuable both as objects and sources. An architectural historian may wish to use the drawings as an information carrier to look at the design; but he would

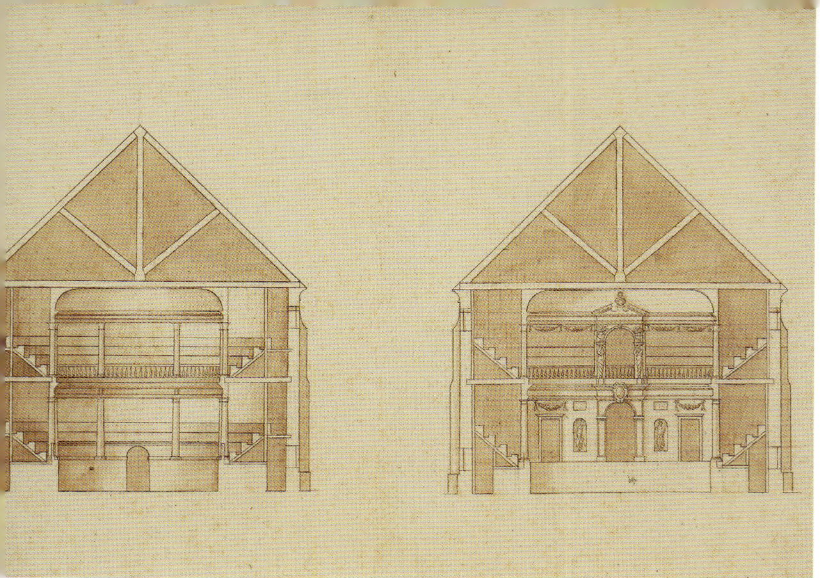

Above: *John Webb, theatre drawings: transverse sections.* Right: *Brooch designed by Vicki Ambery-Smith after the theatre drawings in the collection.*

also wish to consider the alterations and lift those delightful little flaps that indicate alternatives. He will want to know what part of the design is in the original hand and what has been added by a later one. Searching for these clues, he is looking at a corpus of data. A student researching 17th-century pigments, inks and drawing techniques, or the paper historian, would also wish to see the unaltered complex primary evidence, which holds a myriad of clues.

An original album binding provides primary evidence of book structures, binding materials and techniques; its unmodified content allows us a glimpse into the mind of an 18th-century collector. What did he collect? Why this image and not another of the same period? Why did he arrange his prints in this particular way? What were the ideas informing his collecting?

In time, it became clear that the purpose of the conservation project should be the twin tasks of conservation: firstly, to manage change, therefore to retard ageing – and to do so without loss of either information or of the corpus of data – and secondly, to provide a controlled and managed environment. Over 12 summers, a conservation studio was set up in the Library. Working as a team of four, consisting of three interns and myself, we removed dirt and dust from the surfaces of the drawings, repaired hundreds of them to prevent further physical damage, smoothed out their wrinkles, discovered drawings on their hidden backs and finally, mounted and boxed them in the best available conservation materials.

There are secret joys for a conservator. Handling the beautiful papers of the 16th and 17th century, creamy or slightly pink, the result of the papermaker's rotting of his precious linen before turning it into pulp; the curly imprints of the pressing felts when the paper was still damp. And what do I see here? but a hair, light brown, trapped in the paper. And here is an impression of a papermaker's thumb as his hand slipped into the freshly cast damp leaf. I match my thumb to his and say 'hello' across the centuries. Would he approve of me trying to save the paper he so laboriously made?

And what of the plethora of watermarks, some known, some mysterious. Who was 4M, whose monogram appears below a shield? Were these secret religious signs, as some historians claim, or papermakers leaving their mark for trade and posterity? Theirs was a secretive trade.

Inevitably one is drawn to certain images: the New Exchange in the Strand, which glares at the viewer with menacing 'eyes' of deep brown colouring its 17 arcades.

Or the equally strange new top to the tower of old St Paul's Cathedral, which looks more like a design for a skilful jeweller to turn into a grand silver table centre-piece than a real building.

And here is the Catafalque of James I, bedecked with flags, and the large dome supported by masculine Doric Orders for a not-so-masculine King; the whole design inspired, but not slavishly copied, from its Italian precursors. Imagine this huge painted hearse with 12 statues of the Virtues in mourning flanking the dome, only two of them now, standing forlorn in brown ink on the page.

Then there is the beautifully detailed drawing of the interior of a theatre, executed in pen and ink with brown wash of varying density to give the illusion of depth. It is being used as the basis for the Globe Theatre's reconstruction of an indoor 17th-century playhouse. It also inspired Vicki Ambery-Smith's striking gold and silver brooch, given to me by my friends at Worcester College upon the completion of the conservation project, and which in time will come home to the College.

Above and left: *Inigo Jones, studies of Old Master drawings.*

Or look at Jones' *Heads*, his copies of old master drawings, of Raphael, of Parmigianino, in which he imitates their dense crosshatching until his pen scratches through the paper. In a beautiful double-sided drawing, he draws the same heads in different positions. There is a sketch of a hand with splayed fingers just above a wonderfully realised head of a man, copied from a print; it looks as if he had grown wings at the top of his head. A demure woman – or is it a boy? – looks on …

But my favourite is a little sketch revealed during conservation. Drawn with crumbly graphite without scale, in freehand on the back of a formal drawing, so different from the measured pen and ink drawings. One can almost hear him thinking, 'Quick! Where is my stick? I must draw this before it escapes me … '

But where is Mr Jones? He is here, stuck in one of the print albums, IGNATII IONES MAG: BRIT: ARCHITECTI GENERALIS, VERA EFFIGIES, engraved by Hollar, based on a beautiful drawing

Above: *Wenceslaus Hollar, portrait engraving of Inigo Jones, after Anthony Van Dyck.* Top left: *Inigo Jones, Sketch elevation probably for Sir Peter Killigrew's house, Blackfriars, London.* Left: *Ivory carving of Inigo Jones.*

in black chalk by Van Dyck at Chatsworth. The print is in reverse but true to the drawing. It shows a man of 67, a man old for his time, with a slightly melancholic, puzzled expression, as if interrupted in mid-thought.

He is also present in his own annotated copy of Palladio's *Quattro Libri dell' Architettura* of 1601. As an architect, he is struggling to find the English word for 'loggia', an architectural concept unknown in England. He covers the margins in his neat hand, the script running to the edge of the page. He comes alive as a man in his obsessive concern with his health, his digestion, his kidney stones

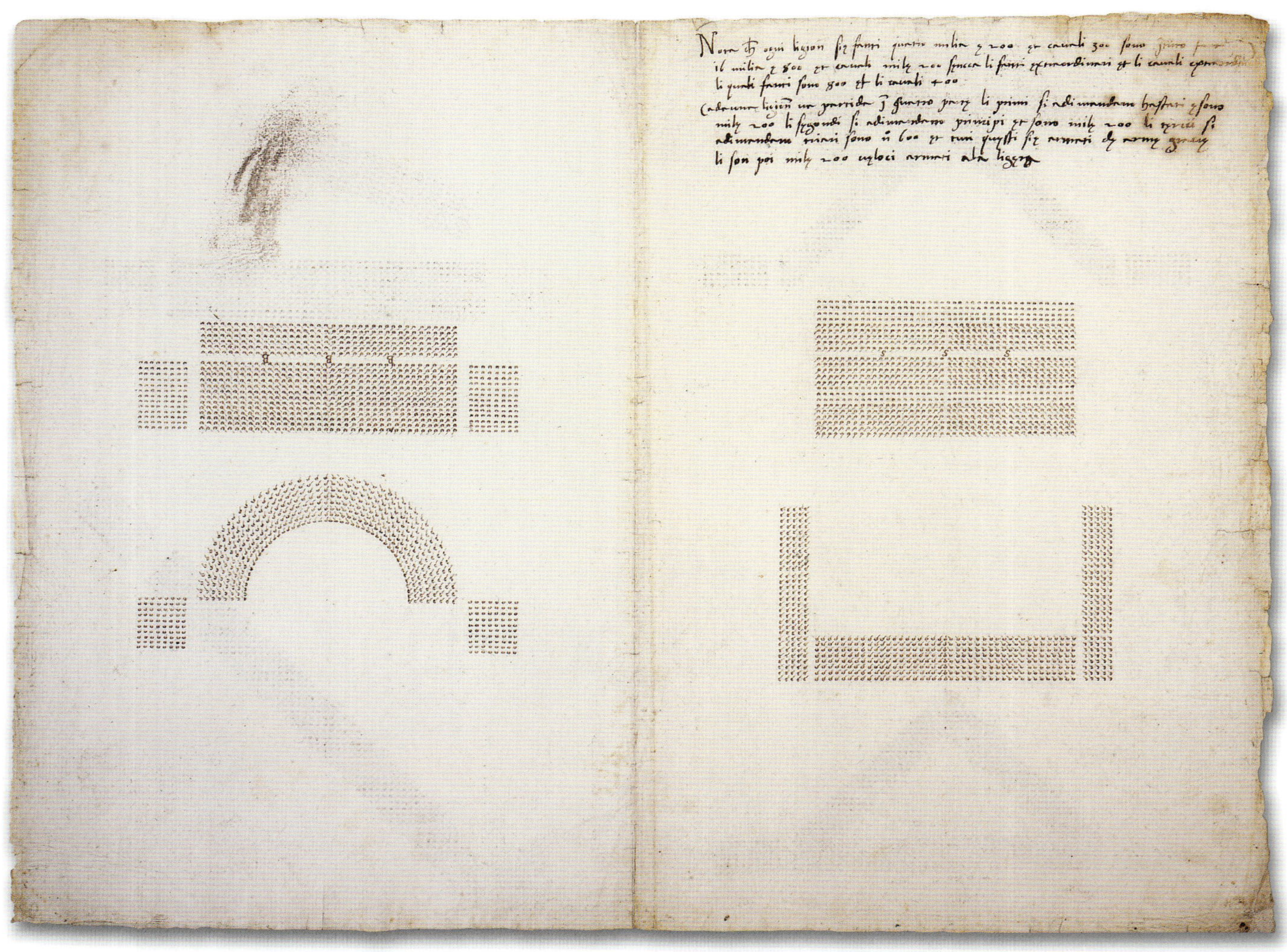

Andrea Palladio, plan of military formations. The annotations are in Palladio's own hand.

and, movingly, with 'dimness of sight'. The flyleaves of the book are full of remedies:

> *Mr Deuall a paper to wear for dizines in the head*
> *Take too Oualles of bronepaper and between them putt this take a smale gripe of sage dried but not much, and on dragma of Cloues beaten together and quilt them between thes too papers, and weare it on the top of your head a littell warmed this will hould good a seaune-night and then make a new*

We meet him again in 2011, in a small auction house, as a fine ivory carving copied from the engraving. The lines of his hair and collar are stiff and more formal as ivory is a hard material to carve. It is probably by a Netherlandish artist working in England in the late 18th or early 19th century, but the provenance is lost. It is now at the Lodgings, a gift of Lesley Le Claire to the College.

And what of his mentor, Palladio? We have six of his drawings, three recently identified as by him. One of these, drawn on thick white paper, is not of a building, but of military formations, based on ancient sources, with notes on the formation of a Roman legion in Palladio's own handwriting.

More and more treasures. In a large album bound in the 18th century in a typical Oxford binding, we have a glimpse of George Clarke's association with Hawksmoor. Many of the drawings in this album are by Hawksmoor, and there are other unbound drawings by him, including a proof of his contribution to the design of

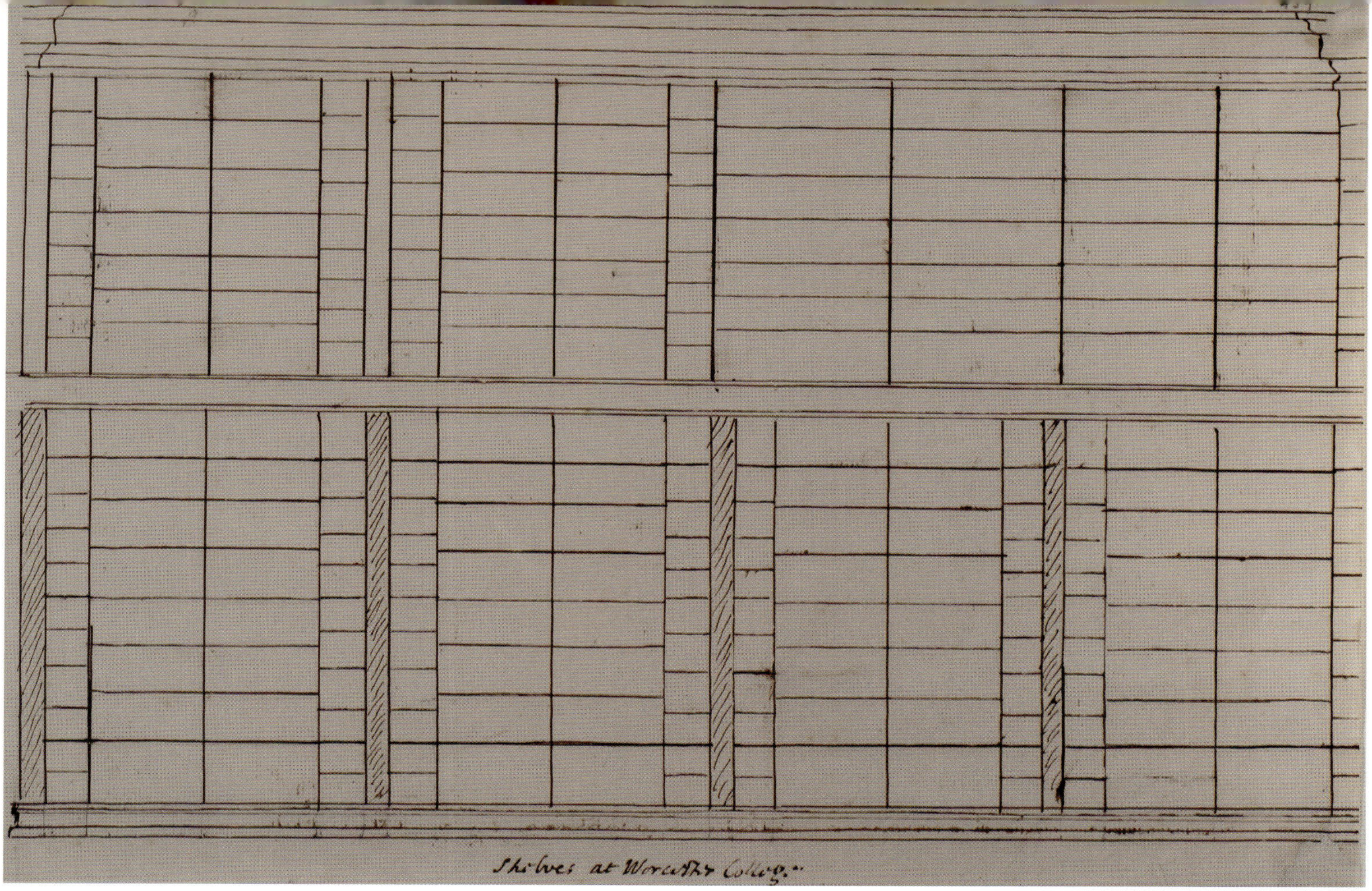

Above: *Design for shelving in the Library by George Clarke.* Right: *The shelving* in situ *today.*

Worcester's Library. 'Equall Bay's', he instructs under the pen-and-ink shaded arches, before adding his credentials for the source of his design 'Arc sur le Pont du Xaintes'.

Behind all these treasures and pleasures stand the Clarkes: Sir William, the father, and Dr George, the son, whose joint collections are the glory of the Library. George's design for the shelving in the Library remains unaltered to this day.

Clarke is a busy man. In 1710 he takes over from Dean Aldrich in the design and production of the Oxford Almanacks. Under his influence, they change from depicting allegorical figures copied from old master painting and prints to a record of the changing face of Oxford colleges. 'Dr Clark has a compleat set of the Oxford Almanacks for Worcester College Library – a great rarity', it was said.

And finally we find an image of the benefactor, a man of importance and taste, framed in an elaborately designed cartouche in the 1741 Almanack (reproduced on p. 48), in a great tableau of operatic design. He stands in the company of other benefactors with two putti energetically pointing towards him, holding the plan of the Library – Worcester's greatest treasure.

Kate Colleran

LIFE

21. Out of Hours: Student Activities to 1960

Emma Goodrum

At the time of the College's foundation, student leisure activities were predominantly those of the country gentleman – riding, hunting, shooting and dining. However, the development of team sports in early 19th-century public schools was inevitably carried through to University level, and sports clubs and inter-collegiate competitions, as well as literary societies and clubs dedicated to the performing arts, soon began to flourish.

It is sport that features first in the Worcester chronology. The earliest recorded involvement at University level was in 1825, when a crew first entered the Eights and finished third of four boats, behind Exeter College and Christ Church and ahead of Balliol; this was only the ninth year of racing in Oxford and the first to be conducted in the modern manner. Worcester did not feature again until 1830, when its crew finished fourth of six boats, but in 1834 they rose as high as second on the river, their highest-ever position, and a feat repeated in 1848. The first ever Torpids in 1838 saw the Worcester second VIII finish head of the river and the College has entered crews into both competitions each year since 1843.

Initially, there were no uniforms for rowing crews, but as the number of boats increased and it became difficult to distinguish between them simple colours were adopted. The first Worcester jerseys were white with pink stripes, but at a Boat Club meeting in 1856 the uniform was changed to 'puce velvet caps and puce-trimmed jerseys – much to some men's chagrin'. Minutes of the following meeting record, perhaps unsurprisingly, that 'the boating spirit of the Club … [is] at a very low ebb' and by 1861 the colours had been settled as the more familiar black trimmed with pink, with a badge showing a pink Maltese cross.

Although the origins of other 19th-century sports clubs are obscure, the Cricket Club appears to have been in existence by 1844 when Walter Marcon (1842) became the first Worcester man to represent the University (against Cambridge at Lord's he batted number five, scoring 24 and 8* in a match drawn because of rain). By 1862, both the Cricket and Boat clubs had run up serious debts and had to be bailed out through donations from the Provost and Fellows. As a result, a member of Governing Body was appointed to each committee to oversee their finances. Edward Adams (Fellow 1854–83) did rather more than that while a member of the Cricket Club committee and played several times for the College XI, the only don in Oxford to do so at the time. Adams may have been required to play due to lack of undergraduate members – records reveal that the club was unable to fulfil a single fixture in 1863. Potential cricketers may have been discouraged by the long distance

Above: The Old Buildings of Worcester College, Oxford, *by J.V. Richardson, showing an archery target,* c.*1850.* Right: *Silver blades awarded annually to the winner of races held by the Worcester College Boat Club.*

to the College cricket pitch at Cowley Marsh: a late-19th-century petition from undergraduates for a new cricket pitch states that Worcester was further from its ground than any other college in Oxford and that 'consequently … either the College Cricket suffers or the reading of those who play; and often both'.

It appears that the first sports to take place within the grounds of Worcester were archery and fives. A drawing dated 1850 shows an archery target established on what is now the Nuffield Lawn, but it is impossible to say whether these were a permanent or temporary fixture. In 1856, a more permanent addition to the College was built in this area at the request of undergraduates – a Winchester-style fives court, almost certainly the first of its kind in the country as it predated those at Winchester College by six years. The Prince of Wales, later Edward VII, had a standing invitation to play at the court during his time at Christ Church in the early 1860s and it is known that he did so on at least one occasion, borrowing equipment from Edward Adams, who had been using the court when the Prince arrived.

Worcester's influence on sporting innovations was not confined to fives however. Although sliding seats had been used in the University Boat Race of 1873, opinion on them was divided and there was a strong possibility that the University Boat Club would revert to fixed seats in the following year. As Eights week of 1873 began, the Worcester crew was one of several colleges still using fixed seats and, although Worcester rowed over on three consecutive nights,

Above: *Worcester College VIII, 1899.* Right: *'Arrival of the Worcester togger', 1888.*
Below: *Programmes for concerts by the Worcester College Music Society, 1884 and 1885.*

they did not get near the boat in front of them. On the third night, the President of the Oxford University Boat Club approached the Worcester captain, John Gibbons (1871), and asked him to switch his crew to sliding seats to prove their superiority. Gibbons, despite misgivings of mutiny, agreed. As the next day was Sunday and there were no races, the Worcester crew was able to practice on its new seats, a session described by Gibbons as 'not very encouraging'. Despite approaching Monday's races in 'a rather depressed frame of mind', once the Worcester crew started it became clear that it was easily keeping ahead of Keble College, and Gibbons soon found that 'we were beginning to dance in the wash of the boat ahead of us and realised we were near them … there was an increasing noise on the bank and our bell began to ring, the noise on the bank increased, we jumped about more and more in the wash of the boat ahead – and then came, opposite the Barges, the thrilling shock of the bump!' Until the previous day, only the Captain and Stroke of the Worcester crew had ever been on a sliding seat, but their sudden success in achieving what was claimed as the first legitimate overbump in the history of the Eights confirmed the use of sliding seats at Oxford. Early success, however, was short-lived and by the 1880s, Worcester had sunk to the bottom of the rankings for Torpids and Eights alike.

As with the Cricket Club, the earliest records of the social clubs and societies have not survived, but it can be said with certainty that by the 1860s both the Debating Society and the Worcester College Musical Society were in existence. The Debating Society

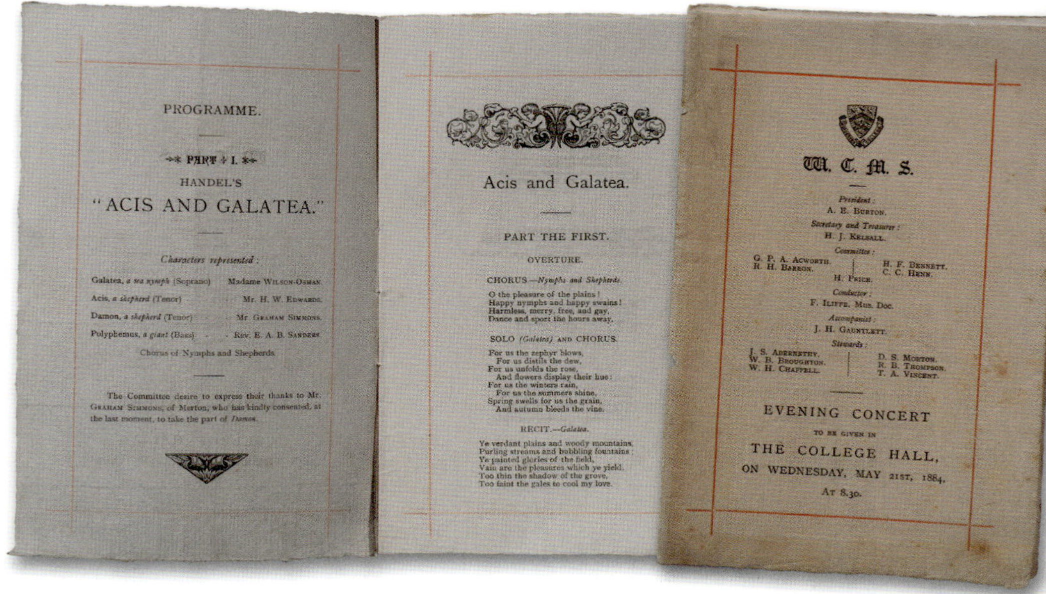
PROGRAMME.

PART I.
HANDEL'S
"ACIS AND GALATEA."

Characters represented:

Galatea, *a sea nymph* (Soprano) — Madame Wilson-Osman.
Acis, *a shepherd* (Tenor) — Mr. H. W. Edwards.
Damon, *a shepherd* (Tenor) — Mr. Graham Simmons.
Polyphemus, *a giant* (Bass) — Rev. E. A. B. Sanders.
Chorus of Nymphs and Shepherds.

The Committee desire to express their thanks to Mr. Graham Simmons, of Merton, who has kindly consented, at the last moment, to take the part of *Damon*.

Acis and Galatea.

PART THE FIRST.

OVERTURE.

CHORUS.—*Nymphs and Shepherds.*

O the pleasure of the plains!
Happy nymphs and happy swains!
Harmless, merry, free, and gay,
Dance and sport the hours away.

SOLO *(Galatea)* and CHORUS.

For us the zephyr blows,
For us distils the dew,
For us unfolds the rose,
And flowers display their hue:
For us the winters rain,
For us the summers shine,
Spring swells for us the grain,
And autumn bleeds the vine.

RECIT.—*Galatea.*

Ye verdant plains and woody mountains,
Purling streams and bubbling fountains;
Ye painted glories of the field,
Vain are the pleasures which ye yield.
Too thin the shadow of the grove,
Too faint the gales to cool my love.

W. C. M. S.

President:
A. E. Burton.
Secretary and Treasurer:
H. J. Kelsall.
Committee:
G. P. A. Acworth. R. H. Barron. H. Price. H. F. Bennett. C. C. Henn.
Conductor:
F. Iliffe, Mus. Doc.
Accompanist:
J. H. Gauntlett.
Stewards:
J. S. Abernethy. W. B. Broughton. W. H. Chappell. D. S. Morton. R. B. Thompson. T. A. Vincent.

EVENING CONCERT
to be given in
THE COLLEGE HALL,
ON WEDNESDAY, MAY 21st, 1884,
At 8.30.

was run on the same principles as the Oxford Union, and debates covered a wide range of topics. Motions proposed in 1883 include, for example, the disestablishment of the Church of England; the abolition of restrictions on the sale of land; Home Rule for Ireland (lost by 13 votes to four); the abolition of the monarchy (carried with the President's casting vote); and that 'the woman is, and must continue to be, inferior to man'. This last motion was thrown out and an amendment 'that in the nature of the case no such comparison is possible' was carried by 19 votes to six.

The first physical artefact of the Worcester College Musical Society, a concert programme, hails from 1863, but it was not until the presidency of William Henry Hadow (Fellow and Classics Tutor 1888–1909) that the Society truly began to flourish. Hadow could be critical of the Society and its audiences, remarking in a letter to his parents that on one occasion 'everybody played and sang abominably – myself included' but that the audience were unaware of the deficiencies: 'confound them, when will they learn the difference between good and bad?' Despite Hadow's occasional condemnation, in the late 19th century the Society became renowned in the University for its high standards and ambitious programmes. Concerts typically followed a two-part format with a long interval between. The first part generally consisted of a longer work such as Brahms' cantata *Rinaldo*, performed in 1899, or Mendelssohn's incidental music for *Oedipus at Colonus* in 1890. The second part contained shorter instrumental and vocal items and the gardens and cloister were lit by lanterns. Unusually for Oxford at the time, the summer concerts of the Worcester College Musical Society contained very few external performers except for female soloists and, occasionally, a hired conductor. Undergraduates also had the opportunity to have their own compositions performed for the first time and many took it, including the composers Sir Percy Buck (matriculated 1891) and Richard Owen Beachcroft (1894).

ABOVE: *J.C. Masterman with F.J.G. Whittall and A.H. Hardy in the gardens, 1911.*
BELOW LEFT: *The De Quincey Society in 1895.*

A number of other clubs existed during the 1880s but the only evidence for these rests in the 'College News' section of the *Oxford Magazine*. Among those at Worcester were the Sunday Evening Society, which heard papers from visiting speakers on matters of religion; the Anthological Society; the Scriveners Essay Society; and the Shakespeare Society, which met four times a term to conduct play readings. Other clubs established in this period include two named in honour of literary figures with connections to the College. Formed in 1878, the De Quincey Essay Society discussed any topic with the exception of religion. Early matters considered included cremation, reform of spelling, and war. The Lovelace

Above: *College cricket, 1914.* Right: *R.S. Thatcher and H.V. Wilkinson, 1911.*

Club was founded in 1884 in order to 'perpetuate the memory of Colonel Richard Lovelace, sometime of Gloucester Hall, and to further the study of Letters'. At its first meeting it considered 'whether or no one great poem such as "stone walls do not a prison make", can justly entitle its author to high poetic fame'. Although the outcome is not recorded, the club continued to commemorate the memory of Lovelace for the next 70 years. More could be said about each of these clubs, and a great many more besides, making the contemporary remark that 'at times [Worcester's] clubs have seemed to be as numerous as its members' seem less of an exaggeration.

In the period after 1900, the undergraduate community continued to add to the number of clubs and societies, the most important of which was the Buskins. Named after the high, thick-soled boot worn by actors in ancient Greece, the club was formed in 1902 by Roland Braddell (1901), initially for the purpose of 'reading plays once a week in various members' rooms'. By 1908, the Buskins, still meeting weekly, were also producing plays; Richard Sheridan's *The Rivals* was staged in that year.

The high level of sporting participation in the late 19th century is shown by the establishment of the Amalgamated Clubs in 1883. The umbrella organisation was formed to regulate club spending and prevent debt, and the founders included clubs dedicated to rowing, cricket, fives, athletics and lawn tennis. These were swiftly followed by rugby union in October 1883, association football in 1886 and hockey in 1902. An increase in sporting interest and the expense of maintaining the cricket ground at Cowley Marsh in a fit condition for play prompted a written request from undergraduates that the meadow in the west of the College grounds be developed into a sports field. Costs initially proved prohibitive, leading to a short-lived scheme to split the cost with Trinity College and share access, but by May 1896, fundraising among undergraduates and Old Members had attracted sufficient funds to allow work on the meadow to start in the Long Vacation. Parts of the field had been drained and raised by 1898 and in the following year it was used for cricket, tennis, rugby and football; the pitches, however, were not full size, as parts of the field were still required for the Provost's cows. In 1905, the Bursar wrote to Provost Daniel asking if the cows might be moved 'as both football teams are confined at present within more uncomfortable limits than the cows would be if they gave up the part which the football teams covet'. As it stood, not only were the pitches too small to host Cuppers matches, but the newly completed

Left: *Lovelace Club cup.*
Right: *Carroll Wilson, Rhodes Scholar,* c.*1911.*

pavilion was in danger from rugby balls. After the cows had been moved to the confines of the Provost's garden, Worcester became unique within Oxford as the only college to have full-sized sports pitches within the main college grounds.

The activities of all the undergraduate clubs and societies ceased during the First World War as the College and the University as a whole rapidly emptied. In 1919, although there were only three undergraduates in residence who had been at the College before the outbreak of the war, many of the clubs and societies were re-established and continued much as they had before. This period bore witness to some notable successes. The Buskins' first production after the war, *The Tragedy of Pompey the Great* by John Masefield, is recorded as having drawn 'a warm tribute of admiration from the author', who, at this time, lived at Boars Hill. The Buskins also became known for their collaborations with the Exeter College Fellow and theatre producer Nevill Coghill. He directed several Buskins productions in the Worcester gardens including, in 1934, a version of *The Tempest* in which the entire cast, with the exception of Ariel and Caliban, departed on a galleon that rowed out into the darkness of the lake. The more famous Coghill production of *The Tempest* in the gardens, in which Ariel appeared to run across the surface of the lake (thanks to some duckboards submerged just beneath the surface), was an Oxford University Drama Society production in 1949.

Other clubs and societies also flourished in the period after the First World War and new ones continued to be added to the ranks. Worcester literary societies welcomed a number of distinguished guest speakers including T.S. Eliot, who read 'The Waste Land' to the Philistines in 1928, and J.R.R. Tolkien, who read a story entitled 'The Legend of Worming Hall' to the Lovelace Club in 1938. The minutes of the Lovelace Club record that the well-received story was a 'witty and charming fantasy'; Tolkien would, in 1949, publish it under the title *Farmer Giles of Ham.* Among the new student organisations were the Walsingham Society, a historical group named after Thomas Walsingham, the 14th-century historian who may have studied at Gloucester College, and the Benedictines, a group of left-wing undergraduates established for the discussion of 'current political and literary topics'. The Benedictines was originally established in opposition to the College Essay Society, which at that time was patronised by the Dean, Cyril Wilkinson.

Sport, in comparison, struggled to re-establish itself after the war due to a lack of numbers and experience. In 1919, Worcester was forced temporarily to amalgamate with Hertford for hockey, and with Hertford and Keble for rugby. The Boat Club managed to enter a crew into Torpids that year despite 'extreme shortage of numbers and … the fact that no member of the College had a very

The Buskins production of The Tragedy of Pompey the Great *by John Masefield, 1920; Programmes for the Buskins production of* The Merchant of Venice, *1935;* Tamburlaine the Great, *part II, 1933;* The Merry Wives of Windsor, *1936;* The Tempest, *1934.*

efficient knowledge of rowing'. Despite this inauspicious start, the Torpid went on to enjoy particular success in the inter-war period, going head of the river in 1922 and 1930. Success was rewarded with a number of Bump Suppers, riotous occasions that often led to fines and other discipline. After one particularly exuberant supper in 1927, the JCR president felt it necessary to write to the Provost and apologise for the interruptions made during his speech. On the letter, Provost Lys has noted other acts committed, such as 'bread throwing from the beginning, and a good deal of noise ... many windows broken, tables in pavilion burnt (goal posts put away), some pillar roses badly broken, vases at entrance to garden destroyed'. This was not the only occasion where celebrations exceeded their proper dimensions. William Drake, College Butler, recorded in his memoir that:

> *Anything is likely to happen towards the end of a Bump Supper. I remember one when the Chef had unthinkingly put on as one of the sweets dishes of meringues. These were just the thing to throw at one's friends, also the people who were not! ... I saw many a dinner jacket spoilt when a meringue smashed on their shirt front and the cream ... splashed over them or hit the panel at the back if you were able to dodge one.*

Undergraduates in a College room, *by Edward Halliday, 1952.*

In addition to sports dinners there were also a number of clubs devoted solely to dining, including the United Dining Club (UDC), known to non-members as the United Drunken Club. The UDC had its own plate, cutlery, wine glasses and dessert service in green and gold, and would dine in College at 6pm before adjourning to the Randolph and Eyles billiard rooms. Its members would then return to the College by 9.15pm, where they were entertained by a pianist and a comedian. The captains of the sports clubs formed the OK Club and would take it in turns to host a large breakfast in their rooms, a meal that would often last all morning and include dishes such as pheasant, wild duck, ham, tongue, galantine of veal, eggs, and pigeon or game pie which would be complemented by tea, coffee or lager.

Official inter-collegiate competition was again suspended during the Second World War but, due to the introduction of short courses for servicemen, Oxford did not empty as it had in the previous war. Sport, music and drama all continued in some form, including radical alterations to previous convention. In 1944, the Buskins conducted a reading of *King Lear* with members of Somerville College and in *Romeo and Juliet*, their first production after the war, the female roles were taken by members of St Hugh's College and St Hilda's College rather than by external professional actresses. Three members of Somerville College were also involved in the 1960 Buskins revue *Next Time Yes*, which became the first Oxford college production staged in London when it was taken to the Lyric Theatre, Hammersmith.

In 1945, Worcester continued its association with Somerville though the establishment of the Worcester-Somerville Musical Society, which gave concerts throughout the year, including a carol concert and at least one large-scale opera. The society also organised and sponsored professional concerts, including a recital of Elizabethan music by Julian Bream and Peter Pears in 1964; Pears also returned in a memorial concert for Benjamin Britten on the first anniversary of the composer's death. The Worcester-Somerville Musical Society survived the admittance of women to Worcester in 1979 and men to Somerville in 1994 but came to end in 1997, when the Worcester College Music Society was re-established.

Other societies gradually declined in the years after the Second World War as gate hours were extended and undergraduates mixed more in the University. Participation in sport continues to grow, however, undoubtedly aided by the convenience of having sports facilities within College grounds.

The Halliday Re-creation

How do these things ever get started? With alcohol, typically. In the Buttery one evening with a few other sporty types, the conversation turned to the famous painting. Someone suggested that the Halliday boys were our spiritual ancestors – or words to that effect. The remark struck a chord. Just like us, this happy band of brothers were obviously bent on enriching themselves outside the confines of a library; they just had this fantastic insouciant style. Anyway, another someone (might have been me) came up with the notion of delving into the dressing up box and redoing the whole thing. The thought of filling all those different roles was a tad daunting, but fortunately there was no shortage of suitable candidates in situ. Worcester circa 1979 boasted a dozen blues and half blues across all major sports, as well an impressive number of clubbable types who were only too happy to 'strike a pose'.

Casting correlated to the members' favourite sport or hobby. Failing that, you got the role if you possessed a suitable prop. Chris Harrison, for example, was an avid golfer. John Knight was a gifted tennis and cricket blue. Bill Dixon was one of 12 people on the planet who actually still subscribed to the *Sporting Life*. And so on. There were a few stumbling blocks, inevitably: no one owned a set of bagpipes; the best we could do was to install a Scotsman, Gavin Melluish, in the spot. The Bursar's Office kindly loaned one of the old accounts ledgers, but not the College Butler, so it was left to Owain Rees to blow out his cheeks and stuff a pillow up his shirt.

Everyone agreed that the honour of playing the painting's central figure and focal point, 'Tankard Man' should go to Captain of Boats Fergus Murison. Sure, plenty of men in college were enthusiastic beer drinkers. But the hop never seemed to inspire them the way it inspired Fergus. He invited us to think about the old Boat Club traditions in all kinds of new and exciting ways. Who would have thought that JCR furniture could be set alight while people were still sitting in it – or that beer glasses weren't just for drinking out of, but eating too? The Halliday men would have thoroughly approved of Fergus, we all felt.

Nick Harding

Top: Conversation Piece, *by Edward Halliday, 1937.* Above right: *Re-creation of Edward Halliday's* Conversation Piece, *1979. Dramatis Personae (from l to r). Background figures: Andy Hockey (fresh out of the shower); Steve Hartnell OBE; Martin Scott. Middle Ground: Ray Porfilio (with pipe, pretending to be interested in the* Sporting Life*); Bill Dixon (black eye, don't ask, actually interested in the* Sporting Life*); Chris Harvey (jodhpurs); Neil Swann; Jerry Howe; Richard Stovin-Bradford; John Knight; Ross Mitchell; Nick Harding. Foreground: Fergus Murison (tankard man); Stuart Gulliver (seated, couldn't keep a straight face); Ron Zeghibe (standing, ditto); Chris Harrison; Gavin Melluish (sans bagpipes); Owain Rees (laughably faux College Butler).*

COLL. VIGORN.

MENU, JUIN 20, 1871.

POTAGES.
A la Brunoise. Puree au Petit Pois.

POISSONS.
Turbot. Saumon. Salad d'Homard.

ENTRÉES FROID.
Anguilles la Tartare. Gateaux de Veaux.
Soles aux Mayonaise.

ENTRÉES CHAUD.
Ris de Veaux à la Dauphine. Petit Timbales a la Reine.

RELÉVÈS.
HANCHE VENAISON.
Poulets la Vouilles. Langue de Bœuf.
Jambon la Essence. Quartier d'Agneau.

RÔTS.
Oeson. Caneton. Cailles.

ENTRÈMETS.
Gelée à la Macedoine. Crêmes de Marasquin.
Chartreuse de Fraise.
Corbeilles de Patisserie. Gateaux à la Louise.

RELÉVÈS.
Poudings glacés à la Marquise Lorne.
Talmonees au Lucre. Pouding à la St. Clare.
Ramequins à la Royale.

Worcester College Gaudy,
JUNE 27th, 1889.

Menu.

Soup.
Clear Turtle. Green Pea.

Fish.
Salmon. Whitebait.

Entrées.
Sweetbreads. Aspic of Petit de Foie gras.

Haunch Venison. Lamb.
French Beans. Asparagus.

Ducklings. Quails.
Peas.

Westphalia Ham and Peas.

Sweets.
Ice Pudding.
Fruit Jellies. Apricot Cream.
Cheese Cakes.

Ramaquins.

COLL. VIGORN.
CONVIVIVM GAVDIALE
a.d. vii. Kal. Iul. MDCCCCXIV

Promulsis
Lanx satura Trimalchionis

ORDO CENAE
Ius testudineum liquidum
Asparagi liquamen

Rhombus elixus cum squillarum condimento

Coturnicum patella Vatelica
Altilium iecora congelata

Armus Agninae pratensis arsus
cum pisis viridibus et tuberibus hornis

Perna Eboracensis cum fabis patulis

Cerasorum scriblita cum cremore
Persicae Cartusianae

Crusta Baroniana

Bellaria glaciata

Pinot Gris, Kientzheim-Kaysersberg, Alsace 2011

Ch. Labadie, Medoc 2008

Domaine du Fresche, Moelleux, Anjou, 2010

Quinta de la Rosa' Colheita 1997

Menu

Duck Consommé with Beetroot

-oOo-

Saffron Risotto with Scallops

-oOo-

Fillet of Beef with Wild Mushrooms
Parisienne Potatoes
Spring Vegetables

-oOo-

Plum Brioche Pudding
with Crème Anglaise

-oOo-

Dessert

-oOo-

Coffee & Truffles

Worcester menus across the years. Clockwise from the top left: *Menu for 1871 Gaudy; 1889 Gaudy; 1914 Gaudy; and 2013 Gaudy.*

22. The Kingsley Club

Jean-Pierre Schweitzer

When Henry Kingsley, brother of the author of Water Babies, *was up at the College (1850–3) he was 'noted more for his addiction to athletics and exuberant social pleasures than to academic pursuits'.*

Kingsley did not take a degree, but he was celebrated for his remarkable physical fitness and ability as an oarsman, and noted for his ability to run a mile, row a mile and trot a mile all within 15 minutes. A tankard which Kingsley won as cox at the 1852 Worcester Regatta Severn Cup remains in the College today, and he later went on to win the Diamond Challenge Sculls at Henley. Aside from sport, he and Edwin Arnold (1833–1904) were co-founders of an absurd and short-lived secret society called the Fez Club, whose pursuits included donning fezzes, smoking oriental tobacco and wildly rejoicing in misogamy, misogyny and 'celibate freedom'.

It is perhaps this legacy, and not his sporting pedigree, which initially led 11 Worcester undergraduates to meet on a Sunday in April 1894 to prescribe the rules for a new College dining society, to be called the Kingsley Club. They agreed to dine together each term, bringing with them a guest who was not a member of the College. Dining societies were a familiar part of College life, created as a means for socialising with other students who enjoyed eating and drinking.

By 1907 the Kingsley Club had shared its 89th dinner, but as the club's finances fell into disorder it suffered periods of bad favour with the College. During the 1914–18 war, as debts grew and members dwindled, the club was forced to break up. Once the war had run its course and the College began to fill up again, students attempted to reform the club. Realising that they would be subject to the old debts of the club until 1922, they met as 'The Jokers' until they were cleared of this burden. But the new members were just as profligate. Worcester's longest-serving butler, William Drake, describes in his *Memoirs* the annual stream of 'irresponsible undergraduates' who left Oxford to work in the civil and colonial

Kingsley Club cigarette box.

The Kingsley Club 1934: Back row (l-r): W.E. North Lewis, A.M. Conradie, J.D. Firth, J.O.E. Hood, A.H.M. Humble, J.C. North Lewis; Front row (l-r): W.H. Migotti, C.G.F. Bryan, J.R. McCready, C.J. Hitch, G.H.W. Goode.

services in all parts of the globe with outstanding wine accounts to the College. In an attempt to control this excess, the College wrote to Old Members requesting that they pay fees, and it was ruled that members would not be permitted to dine with the club until bills from the previous term's dinner had been settled. Despite Drake's irritation, he was a good friend to the club. A menu from a ten-course Kingsley dinner in February 1932 has several messages of thanks to Drake, and serves as a testament of his service to the College. One Kingsley member writes 'Drake old man, a wizard show'; J. Smith writes 'A grand show Drake – I am at peace with the world'; and another 'The best of the College, W. Drake and the Wine'.

The Kingsley Club's popularity has waned across the decades. The legendary Richard Cobb was particularly supportive of the club during his time as a Professorial Fellow of the College, when the Kingsley Club held a popular summer garden party for University students. The only evidence of the club's existence in the later years of the 20th century is a bound menu from 1985 and a record in the log book of the club which notes a 1986

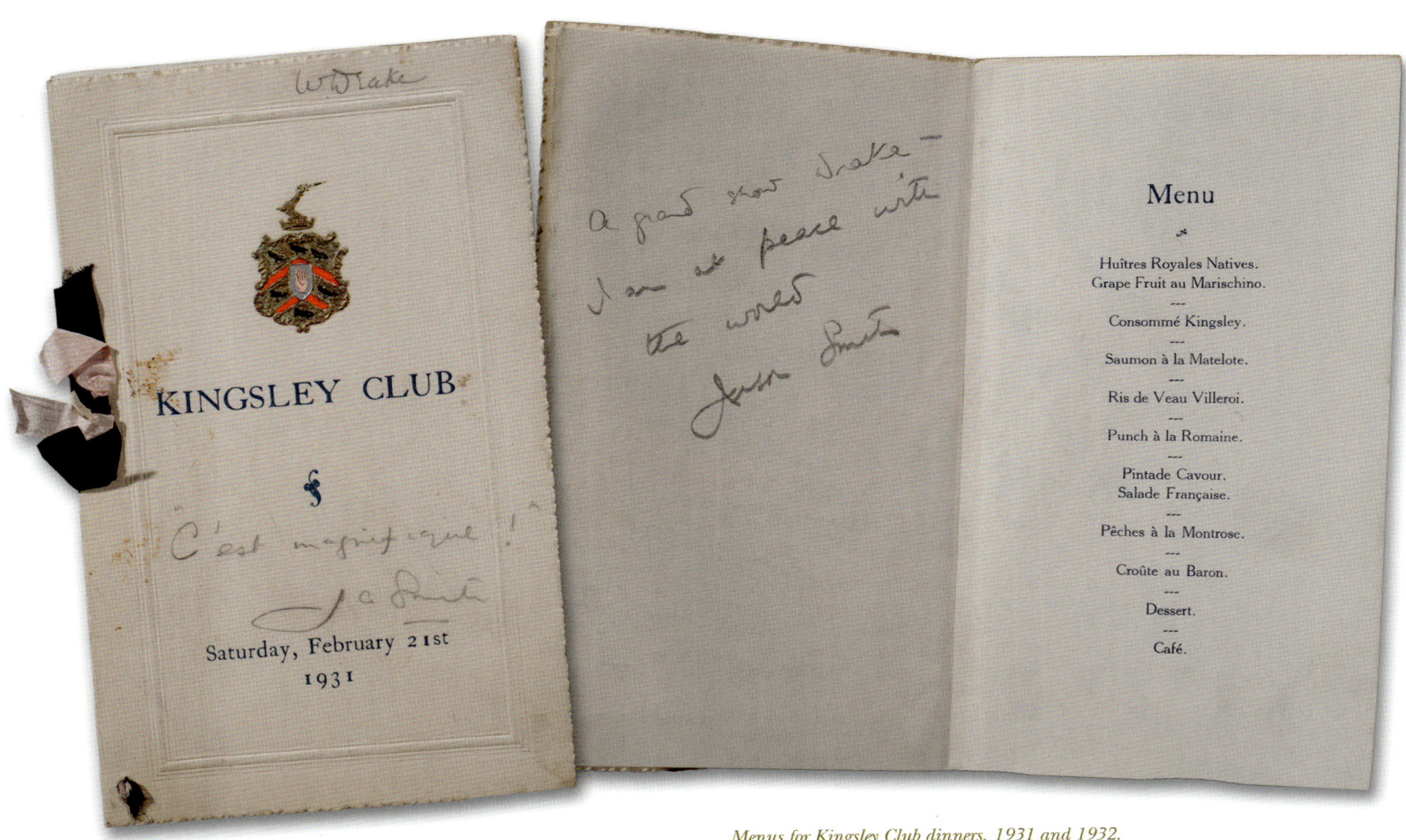

Menus for Kingsley Club dinners, 1931 and 1932.

reunion of 1955–6 members at Boodle's, St James's, where 'a toast was drunk to the continuing prosperity of the club'. Later still, a 1997 JCR report in the College Records describes the revival of an old tradition by which 'Wednesday Formal Hall of fourth week acts as a midpoint of term celebration for those who don Matriculation garb, a pink carnation and bring port to toast the Kingsley Club President'. Recent attempts to reform the club have met with limited success, though termly dinners were recently reinstated.

Ironically, it is not the dining element but rather Kingsley's sporting legacy that has done the most to keep the name of the club alive. Although membership was only open to members of Worcester College, it was agreed that anyone who could emulate Henry Kingsley's 15-minute triathlon should become an honorary member of the club. This became know as the Kingsley Challenge. We believe the first time this occurred was in 1953, following a wager made between the then Dean of Worcester College, Colonel C.H. Wilkinson and the then President of the club, Lord Nicholas Gordon Lennox. Wilkinson had criticised modern youth and claimed that it would take two or three men to do now what one Henry Kingsley had done a century ago. Lennox undertook to prove him wrong, and so on 3 December 1953, Peregine Pollen of Christ Church made an attempt to equal Kingsley's feat on the banks of the Isis at Port Meadow. He sculled a measured mile downstream 'dodging swans and sailing dinghies', then ran back to the start, finally mounting a mare called Garth Royal and riding the final mile back to the post. The time elapsed was a little under 14 minutes. The event was witnessed by Provost J.C. Masterman and N.G. Lennox, and also reported in the *Spectator* by Peter Fleming, under his nom de plume 'Strix'.

In the 1990s, Sebastian Roberts, who had lived with two Kingsley members while he was at Balliol, resurrected the Kingsley challenge by setting it to the 1st Battalion of the Irish Guards, of which he was then in command. David Hannah, a Radley and Durham oarsman, was successful. Then in 2006, when Sebastian, now a Major General, was commanding the whole London military district, he repeated the challenge with soldiers from all regiments in his command.

NB: We should be most interested to know whether anyone has any more information regarding the Kingsley Club, particularly if anyone has since emulated Henry Kingsley's triathlon.

Eights Week between the Wars

The one-minute gun sounded. The boatman pushed the boat out into the river.

'Touch her up stroke side,' called Renner.

The four oars pulled through the water, slowly and without an ounce of wasted energy.

'Hold her bow and three.'

The boat swung to its position.

'Thirty seconds.'

Not a man in the boat moved. They had learned the value of resting during the last few seconds.

Another gun. The timer began to count.

'Ten seconds … Nine … Eight … Seven …'

'Come forward to row,' Renner shouted.

'Five … Four …'

'Are you ready?'

'Two …'

The starting gun!

Eight oars flashed in and out of the water so rapidly they resembled the fins of a giant fish that had been angered by stabbing thrusts. Renner shrilled the numbers. There was no other sound from the Worcester men. No other sound except Vaughn's stinging voice as he called from the bank. It drove like a curling whip. Renner did not allow the stroke to drop. He fought his crew until their red faces became splotched. By the first bend in the river, Worcester was within a quarter of a boat length of Christ Church. Magdalen was far behind. The race of the final day was between Christ Church and Worcester.

The prize was the headship of the river.

Only a quarter of a boat's length separated the two crews, and there was three-quarters of a mile to race. Renner called the good news – It broke the spell.

No human bodies could stand the whipping these men had given theirs. Christ Church saw the momentary slack and her coxswain demanded a spurt. Three yards were gained. But the members of the Worcester crew did not know it. They thought they were still within a quarter of a length. And Renner did not tell them. He saw his mistake and immediately began to swear at his men and to fight them into a forgetful fury.

They did not respond. Their minds called on their bodies and their bodies refused. Christ Church was holding her lead when the half-mile post was passed. Vaughn motioned to Renner and the coxswain was silent. The captain leaned forward.

'Worcester. Worcester,' he called in a low voice.

'Worcester. Worcester,' screamed little Renner.

The boat seemed to tremble. Then almost to rise from the water and hurl itself at the boat ahead. The men no longer crept out slowly – slowly – and threw back their bodies. They crept forward, poised, and hurled their bodies and their hopes of immortality against the ends of their oars.

'You're going up. Going up. You'll do it. I swear it. I swear it. Fight, Worcester, fight. Now. Now. Spurt. Give her ten. One…Two…'

From far ahead of them came to their dulled ears the pleading from the barge.

'Worcester-er-er-er-er Worcester-er-er-er-er.'

As the air surged in and out of their tortured lungs the men in the boat snorted like animals. Two of them were sobbing.

'Harder back, you swine. Harder back. Fight. Fight. You're babies. There's not a man in the boat.'

Renner saw the sunlight suddenly shine full upon the white face of the man directly before him. He turned his head. When he looked back the tears showed in his eyes. Still he cursed them.

The boats were passing the Worcester barge. There was a quarter of a length between them. And three hundred yards to go. Worcester was creeping up. Inch by inch.

'You'll be head of the river if you fight,' shouted Vaughn.

'Worcester. Worcester.'

'A spurt'll do it,' screamed Renner, as he began to bawl the driving numbers.

Each man in the boat pledged his soul to his God for that bump.

The stroke became faster and harder.

'You're on them. You're on them. If you spill your guts they can't get away. Fight, you swine. Harder back. Fight. Fight. Fight.'

The eyes of one of the men in the boat were set. He stared unseeingly before him. Another chewed his tongue. Steele's chin showed red with blood from his bitten lip.

Vaughn leaned forward.

'Ten strokes'll do it. Worcester. Worcester.'

'Worcester-er-er-er-er Worcester-er-er-er-er.'

'It's the head of the river for Worcester. Worcester. Worcester. Now. Now. Now.'

Just before Steele fainted, he saw the pale face of little Renner as he leaned sideways to pull the rudder to make the bump that put Worcester head of the river.

From the novel* Laurel and Straw *(1927)
by Worcester Rhodes Scholar James Saxon Childers (1923)

23. Music at Worcester

Robert Saxton

For over a century, music has contributed to the reputation of Worcester College, as both an aspect of worship and as an academic discipline. The Chapel, as part of the statutory bedrock of the foundation, has produced a roster of distinguished organ scholars as impressive as that of any Oxford or Cambridge college. Sir Percy Buck, organ scholar 1891–4, Director of Music at Harrow and Professor at the University of Dublin for ten years, was appointed to the Royal College of Music, where he taught and wrote about music theory, as well as acting as Music Advisor to the Education Committee of the influential London County Council, while Henry Colles, later music critic of The Times, *held the organ scholarship from 1899 to 1902, to be followed a few years later by Sir Reginald Thatcher who, having been awarded the MC in the First World War, became an important administrator in the early years of the BBC Music Department, ending his career as Principal of London's Royal Academy of Music.*

Post-Second World War organ scholars have distinguished themselves impressively, from Christopher Dearnley (1948–52) and James Dalton (1952–5) (later Tutorial Fellow and Organist of The Queen's College, Oxford), to two of today's outstanding conductors: Steuart Bedford (1961–4), who directed the premieres of Britten's *Death in Venice* and *Phaedra* during the composer's final illness, and Nicholas Cleobury (1968–71), director of the Oxford Bach Choir and founder-director of the Britten Sinfonia. Sholto Kynoch (1998–2000) went on to found the prestigious Oxford Lieder Festival and, in the past six years, organ scholars have been appointed to post-graduate organ scholarships at Canterbury and Norwich cathedrals. Tom Allery (2008–10) is now Assistant Organist at Magdalen, Oxford, where he is also Tutor to the Choristers at Magdalen College School. In the early years of the 21st century, Worcester's Chapel community boasts three incumbent organ scholars (reading Music in all three undergraduate years) and two choirs, one with boy trebles from Christ Church Cathedral School and the other a mixed-voice choir with

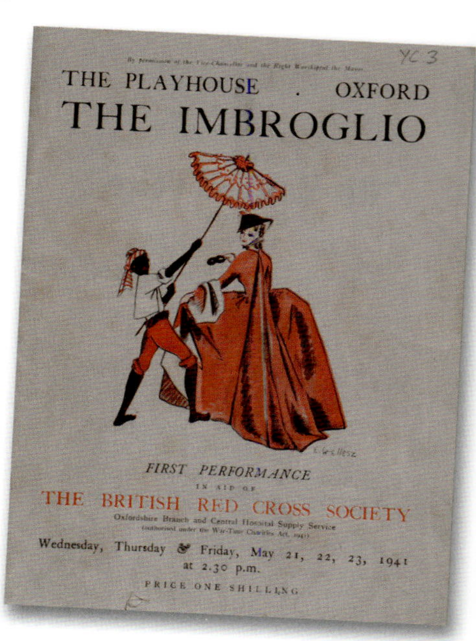

Opposite page: *Poster for* The Imbroglio, *the opera written by the History tutor H.V.F. Somerset.* Left: *Musical entertainment at the JCR Garden Party.* Above: *CDs produced by Worcester College Choirs.*

women sopranos. Several commercial CDs have been produced, one of which was awarded best Christmas CD by the 2012 BBC Music Magazine and, due to the good offices of the Chaplain, Revd Dr Jonathan Arnold, himself a distinguished singer (The 16 and the Tallis Scholars) the choirs have broadcast several services on BBC Radio 4.

As for the academic side, Worcester has been 'on the map' since Sir W.H. Hadow (Fellow, 1891–1909) lectured on behalf of Sir John Stainer, the then Heather Professor of Music, and subsequently became Vice-Chancellor of Sheffield University; to this day, some instrumental award holders are Hadow Scholars. After the inception of the Faculty of Music following the Second World War, Worcester appointed Dr Edmund Rubbra, Gustav Holst's 'star' pupil and one of England's greatest 20th-century symphonists. On his retirement in 1969, the principle of appointing a composer as Tutorial Fellow continued with Kenneth Leighton, an outstanding composer of liturgical and concert music who, after two years in post (1968–70) took up the Reid Professorship at Edinburgh University, to be followed by Dr Robert Sherlaw Johnson. The latter, having blazed a trail as a pianist by making, for Argo, the first complete recording of Messiaen's *Catalogue d'Oiseaux* and producing prize-winning compositions, moved to Worcester from the newly founded, path-breaking department at York University; for 29 years, as University Lecturer and Tutorial Fellow, he presided over the burgeoning of both the academic and performing aspects of College music, in addition writing the standard book in English on Messiaen, to whom the University gave an Honorary Doctorate of Music due to Robert's efforts.

Since Robert retired in 1999 (sadly, dying shortly afterwards), the writer of this brief chapter, a former post-graduate student of Robert's, has been in post. [*The editors add:* thus maintaining the tradition of the Tutorial Fellow being a distinguished composer, for Professor Saxton, formerly Head of Composition at first the Guildhall School of Music and then the Royal Academy of Music, has written works for the BBC, including the remarkable radio opera *The Wandering Jew* (2011), and for many of the country's leading symphony orchestras and choirs.] During the past decade, the College has appointed a fixed-term Junior Research Fellow/Lecturer, in addition to the Tutorial Fellow, who undertakes teaching and (post-) doctoral research; to date, five JRFs have held the post and all of these have gone on to distinguished professional academic careers. Apart from the achievements of organ scholars listed above, those reading Music as undergraduates at Worcester have achieved success in various fields (including law and arts administration) and academic results have been impressive. In recent years Worcester has been able to boast the highest number of applicants (per place) to read Music of any Oxbridge college. Furthermore, since the doctorate in Composition was initiated in 2000 and taught postgraduate courses in musicology at University-level have offered increasingly broad perspectives, Worcester has welcomed a healthy, and widening, intake of postgraduate musicians from international backgrounds, undertaking varied research projects. Three recent female DPhil composers have gone on to be commissioned internationally and, in all three cases, to teach in higher education, one at the University of Hong Kong, one as a college tutor at Oxford and another at the Conservatoire in Sydney.

In addition to the end-of-term concerts, the College Music Society (WCMS) organises weekly recitals during Full Term. Since 2012 the series has been enhanced by the enthusiastic and supportive Provost's termly invitation to hold one of these in the Lodgings, enabling the society to make use of the harpsichord (which came to the College with the Eland bequest of architectural books) in a wide range of repertoire. Music and sociability thus remain at the heart of College life.

Right: *Eland bequest harpsichord in the Provost's Lodgings.* Below: *The Worcester boys' and mixed choirs singing together.*

1960: The Buskins Reviewed in *Cherwell*

The Two Gentlemen of Verona by Worcester

What was Shakespeare's stage really like? According to Dr Leslie Hotson it was not situated at one end of an inn-yard or court-room with the audience facing it and did not contain either alcove or balcony. Instead he argues that the audience was seated all round an oblong stage, at either end of which were transparent houses under which were dressing-rooms and the tiring-house (our green-room).

All this occurs in Hotson's book *Shakespeare's Wooden O* and to put the theories into practice Worcester College Buskins have appropriately chosen Shakespeare's Wooden Play, *The Two Gentlemen of Verona* which they are presenting in the College Gardens this week.

Youthful Comedy

The Play, as Dr Johnson in a fit of politeness said, 'is not indeed one of Shakespeare's most powerful effusions'. It is a comedy of youth, preposterously romantic, raw and a trifle silly. There is some good light music in the verse, some tedious clowning, and a show-stopping dog. (Audiences always love animals just because of that touch of unpredictability they bring to the predictable world of theatre.)

And how does the play fit the new Elizabethan stage that the producer, Richard Proudfoot, has topically erected in Worcester? In some ways, quite well. Best of all it makes for speed with each scene following rapidly on the heels of the last.

Scenery does, however, have its uses, one of which is to indicate shift of locale. Here I would confidently wager it took the audience some little time to gather that the action moved from Vienna to Milan at the end of Act I. However the major theoretical objection to any sort of arena theatre, namely that speeches have to be shared out among the encircling audience, hardly once troubled me during the performance. I heard all that I wished to hear.

Academic

Thus the production was an interesting academic experiment but it didn't make one feel that this was the only way to appreciate and fully understand Shakespeare's plays as Hotson claims. You can perform them in a circus ring or the C.P.I., on a raft in the middle of the Channel or on a traffic island in Chelsea and they will still make their effect, given reasonable performances.

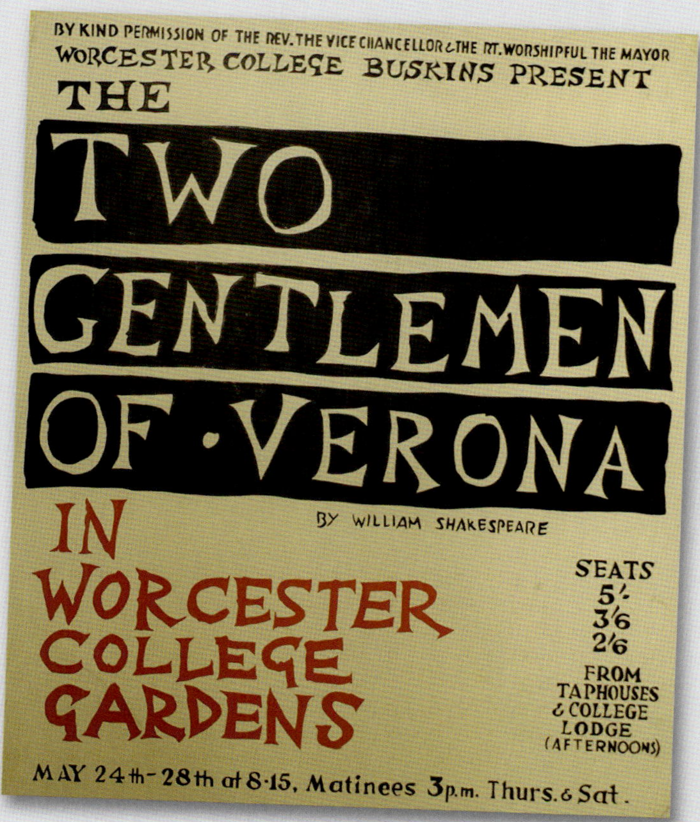

Poster for the 1960 Buskins production of The Two Gentlemen of Verona.

Mr Proudfoot's production was a little too brisk and direct and lacking in variety of pace, but it was all highly competent. There was an outstanding Launce from Mike Bawtree, violently grimacing like an Elizabethan Archie Rice. Not many of the other actors were likewise prepared to 'have a go' but I liked Austin Smith's upstanding passionate Valentine, Gordon Clark's toothy Thurio and Harriet Higgen's dignified Silvia.

Michael Billington

Director Richard Proudfoot went on to become one of the most distinguished Shakespeare scholars of the age and reviewer Michael Billington (St Catherine's) the most distinguished theatre critic. Michael Bawtree founded the Atlantic Theatre Festival in Canada.

24. 'Only a Librarian…': A Memoir of Worcester College

Lesley Le Claire †

Some years ago the editor of the **Oxford Magazine** *received a letter from an elderly Fellow of All Souls scolding him in no uncertain terms for the mixed metaphors and grammatical mistakes in an article he had published by a member of the English Faculty. Then, perhaps feeling he had gone too far, the correspondent made some very complimentary remarks about another article which had appeared in the same issue – 'although', he added dryly, 'the author is only a librarian … '*

He had a point. A librarian's job is in many ways distinctly curious, operating as it does at very different levels. I am sometimes reminded of the retort of the distinguished physician to his friends who reproached him for his own unhealthy life style. 'But my business', he said, 'is to be a signpost on the road to health – I don't necessarily have to go there myself!' It is very easy for a librarian, and even easier for the new breed of information technologist, to become a mere signpost on the road to knowledge. But if one has had the good fortune to have in one's care an extraordinary collection which attracts scholars from all over the world, and if those scholars are kind enough to take one by the hand down the roads they know so well, then the signpost analogy no longer holds water. That is what happened to me. My long connection with Worcester put me on the receiving end of a most liberal education and that is why I was able to write the article which met with the approval of the Fellow of All Souls.

However, it was long before I had any thought of being a librarian that I had my first taste of Oxford and of Worcester College. It was more than 60 years ago and it was very much the Oxford of romantic cliché that I encountered. The sun shone, there was a delicious picnic on the river and my brother and some of his friends had got up a party for the Merton Commemoration Ball. Post-war austerity was at last receding. We drank champagne – no more sickly fruit cup which tasted like melted down jelly babies – and for the first time I wore (such bliss) a dress which was not an ill-fitting hand-me-down. It has to be said my partners were not very good dancers but their manners were charming and I fell in love with at least two of them. I felt I was in the world of the books I had read: I identified with Holly Forsyte shyly meeting Val Dartie; I thought at any moment I might come across Sebastian with his teddy bear or overhear Lord Peter proposing to his Harriet in perfect Latin.

It was a magical weekend and the most magical event of all was Nevill Coghill's production of *The Tempest* in Worcester College garden. From the first moment until the final departure of Ariel, apparently running across the surface of the lake, we were caught in the enchanted web. And the magic of that production stayed with me long after the pretty frocks and the charming young men and the literary fantasies were forgotten. It was the beginning of my love affair with Worcester.

But it was a love affair put on hold for some years. In the interim, I followed family tradition by taking a degree at Glasgow University and after graduating became a library assistant in the University Library. When I returned to Oxford at the end of the 1950s it was to the post of Assistant Librarian at Lady Margaret Hall, where the building of a fine new library was reaching completion. Despite the richness of other library facilities in Oxford, the women's colleges from their beginnings realised the value to undergraduates of a well stocked working library on the spot. At LMH I learned how to run such a library. Some of the men's colleges on the other hand had paid little attention to their undergraduate libraries, although their historical collections were often a source of great pride. This was certainly true of Worcester. But Worcester had the good fortune to have a young energetic tutor in Medieval History who felt this state of affairs should not continue and he persuaded his colleagues to recruit a professional librarian to organise the undergraduate library and look after visiting scholars to the old library. And that is how I began my life in Worcester.

Opposite: *Lesley Le Claire.* Above: *Programme for the OUDS production of* The Tempest, *1949.*

I enjoyed my time at LMH and made good friends there. However, it intrigued me that women in Oxford still seemed to be slightly defensive about their right to be there; in Glasgow I don't think it ever occurred to us. Our grandmothers had won that battle long ago – but in Oxford it was mothers who had fought the good fight and the scars were not quite healed. (In Glasgow women were admitted as full members of the University in 1897 – in Oxford in 1920 – in Cambridge not until 1947!) But it was only when I went to work at Worcester that I fully understood why the women felt as they did. My move to Worcester was one of the most important – and in the event most rewarding – decisions of my life, but initially I wondered if I had made a bad mistake.

The Lake, *by Sydney H. Pavière, 1922.*

Shortly after my arrival I was given an inkling of the masculine world I was entering when I was invited to tea by Sir John Masterman. It was my first encounter with a Provost of the College – although strictly speaking he was already the ex-Provost. He was a charming host (a proper Edwardian tea – a choice of India or China and cucumber sandwiches *without* crusts and almond biscuits) and gentle talk about writers and books. In later years I was to learn more about Masterman – how he liked to win at games and manipulate events by 'a quiet word in the right place' and how he had the irritating habit of referring to 'my Fellows' and did not like to leave well alone after he had retired from the St Thomas's College, but I shall always remember a delightful afternoon long ago when a distinguished old man made a rather bemused young woman feel very welcome. Did he realise that his world was changing? Perhaps the answer lies in his own affectionate satire on the conversation and attitudes of the Worcester Senior Common Room, thinly disguised as the fictional St Thomas's in his 1952 *To Teach the Senators Wisdom or An Oxford Guidebook.* This extraordinarily comfortable society of bachelors is thrown into confusion and disarray when instead of the solemn American senators the dons were expecting to entertain, they are confronted by three feisty young women. His dons fight a skilful rearguard action, but the citadel had been breached. Did Masterman sense that the old Oxford – his Oxford – was beginning to fade?

It had not entirely faded when I started work in Worcester. Like most Oxford colleges Worcester was still run by men for men. Apart from scouts, two or three secretaries and bursary clerks, there were no women in the College. I was a new form of animal life and it was not at all clear where I fitted in. I was half an administrator and half an academic. There was of course no question of my being a member of the SCR – but was I, like the office staff, expected to use the formal mode of address to the Fellows while they called me by first name? In many ways my position at Worcester was rather curious; I felt like a governess in a 19th-century novel – neither above the salt nor below it.

However my immediate problems were practical. At LMH the library was a gleaming new building, airy, well-lit, well-heated and well-cleaned: at Worcester the 18th-century elegance of the Clarke Library contrasted sharply with the 20th-century squalor of the undergraduate library. On my first morning when I climbed the beautiful staircase (62 steps, up which all books arriving in the Lodge had to be carried) and entered the attic which housed the undergraduate library, my heart sank. There was a pervading smell of overcooked cabbage from the dining hall below; the floor linoleum was torn and patchy; the place was littered with the detritus adolescents tend to leave in their wake and everywhere there were overflowing ashtrays, for in those unregenerate days smoking was still regarded as an aid to study rather than a fire hazard or risk to health. My office was a dark little cell above the lobby of the Lower Library. It led to the other attic, the room over the Chapel, which housed not only the idiosyncratic book collection of the

19th-century Librarian Henry Pottinger but also, on occasion, the corpse of a dead pigeon trapped in the eaves. There was no plumbing in the building so the unfortunate scout whose duty it was to clean it had to carry buckets of water across the quad and up the stair. Moreover, the use of electrical equipment frequently proved too much for the antiquated wiring system and we would be plunged into darkness. Very early on I realised that while it was desirable to be on good terms with the Fellows, it was absolutely essential to make friends with the maintenance staff. One of my staunchest allies was an old man called Sam Berry. Sam had been the College bicycle boy in his youth and was promoted – on obscure reasoning – to College electrician. I was to discover later that he wielded considerable power because for reasons equally obscure he held the key for the cupboard containing the College store of toilet rolls.

All this must make Worcester in the 1960s seem closer to Gloucester College than to the institution we are celebrating in the 21st century. However, I learned to subdue my housewifely instincts and to laugh, albeit ruefully, at the College's medieval domestic arrangements. I did with difficulty manage to prohibit smoking, but the real cleanup of the Upper Library had to wait for more than a decade when funds were raised for a daring architectural scheme to create an extra floor in the roof space. Plumbing was installed and the reading room completely refurbished. The whole building had to be closed for nearly a year and the 30,000 books of the undergraduate library were transferred by a chain gang of stalwarts from the Bodleian to the Memorial Room in the Provost's yard. We managed this in the course of one hideous weekend. Undergraduates were deprived of any communal reading room but at least access to the books continued unimpeded. Mercifully, by this time I had got the catalogue on a reasonable footing

However there was one very pleasant aspect of my first year in Worcester. One of the concerns of Lord Franks, who was now Provost, was the lack of facilities for the increasing numbers of graduate students. A small Middle Common Room was therefore formed to meet their needs and some of its members, mostly modern linguists, adopted me unofficially, inviting me to coffee and discussion groups and occasionally to dine in Hall. On summer evenings we would play tennis (and no courts in Oxford have as beautiful a setting as those at Worcester with the background of the garden) and afterwards they would come and eat picnic suppers at my flat and tell me what modern French novels I should be reading. I remember them with great affection.

For my first few months I was really too busy to do much exploration of the Clarke Library although I was eager to do so. Richard Sayce, the Fellow Librarian, was a distinguished French scholar and bibliophile but markedly displayed the proprietorial feeling which is an occupational hazard for librarians in charge of rare collections. His knowledge was extensive but he only liked to share it with a chosen few. In this he was following the precedent set by his predecessor, the formidable Colonel Wilkinson. I never met Wilkinson, though the stories about him are legion. But I have rarely seated myself at his desk without feeling a cold breath of disapproval down my neck, that a mere female should have the temerity to take his place. However, by the time Richard Sayce became Fellow Librarian there was a steadily increasing awareness among 17th-century historians of the importance of our primary sources and a corresponding demand to consult them, so gradually he left it to me to look after most visitors to the Library.

One of my difficulties was that the catalogue was a splendid historical manuscript in its own right – so much so that some important shelf marks were themselves lost in the mists of history and completely out of date! Thankfully, help was on hand from an unexpected quarter. The head of the stack in the Bodleian, Jack Webster, a kindly, fatherly figure who had started work there when he left school aged 14, had done odd jobs in the Worcester Library for years and had total recall of where and when books had been moved. Had he been born a generation later, he would undoubtedly have become Librarian of one of our great city libraries. As it was, he was a first-rate library technician. Wilkinson, academic dinosaur though he was in many ways, recognised his quality and had the good sense and delicacy not to pay him for his services but saw to it that a case of best Highland malt was delivered to his house every Christmas. As for me, I would have been lost without him because he fell into the habit of dropping in to see me on his way home in the evening and answering the queries which had puzzled me that day. Mr Webster (I never called him 'Jack') was the first in a long series of mentors who became, in many cases, life-long friends.

I soon realised that the vague ideas I retained from school of the period which in those days we still called 'the-Tudors-and-the-Stuarts' were quite inadequate if I was to be any use to visiting scholars and research students. And so began my own historical investigations into the Worcester collections.

I could see that George Clarke had really left us a double bequest – not only his own magnificent collection but also the books and manuscripts of his father William Clarke. The two libraries are in many ways complementary. In the space of a generation they reflect the interests and preoccupations of two interlinked but contrasting worlds, and house both sides of the Civil War under

Colours of the regiments of horse, 1654, from William Clarke's library.

one roof. Yet the significance of William Clarke's collection in particular lay unremarked for many years until Henry Pottinger, then Fellow Librarian, mentioned, quite casually perhaps, to a young historian of his acquaintance, that we had some old documents that might be of interest. The historian was the future Regius Professor, Charles Firth.

Gerald Aylmer, founding Professor of History in the University of York and later Master of St Peter's College, author of magisterial volumes on the civil services of Charles I and the Commonwealth, was to be one of my most important guides up what has been called 'the Mount Everest of British History, the English Revolution of the 17th century'. But when he came to spend a sabbatical term working in the Worcester Library in 1967, I had barely reached base camp. I well remember that first meeting. I was more than a little in awe of him. But five minutes into our conversation he produced one of his marvellous Olympian laughs, and in no time we were having great fun imagining Firth's growing excitement as the full significance of the treasure-trove presented to him dawned on him.

The meeting with Gerald Aylmer was a turning point for me. About the same time Christopher Hill's *The World Turned Upside Down* appeared, intensifying the growing interest in the Leveller movement in the 17th century. From that moment I knew that a door had opened on an exciting new world of ideas and that from my vantage point in Worcester I would be able to watch research in progress and sometimes even contribute to it.

However, it was one of Clarke's pamphlets which has nothing to do with the Levellers that was to give me my first real thrill of discovery. As one might expect, the collection, like most such collections, contains one of the most famous of contemporary pamphlets – that describing the execution of the king. Having read it elsewhere, I barely glanced at Clarke's copy; but then my eye was caught by a small asterisk beside the phrase 'a Gentleman that touched the Ax' and in the margin another asterisk with – in his own hand – his initials 'W.C.' It seems almost certain that Clarke was on the scaffold in his secretarial capacity. He was very well aware, of course, of the horrible fate of men whose presence there could damn them as regicides – and yet, and yet – part of him wanted posterity to know. Elsewhere in this volume, the conservator Kate Colleran, talks of her sense of hearing 'hello' across the centuries when she touched the thumb mark of the 17th-century papermaker. I felt an identical shiver of recognition when I saw Clarke's initials.

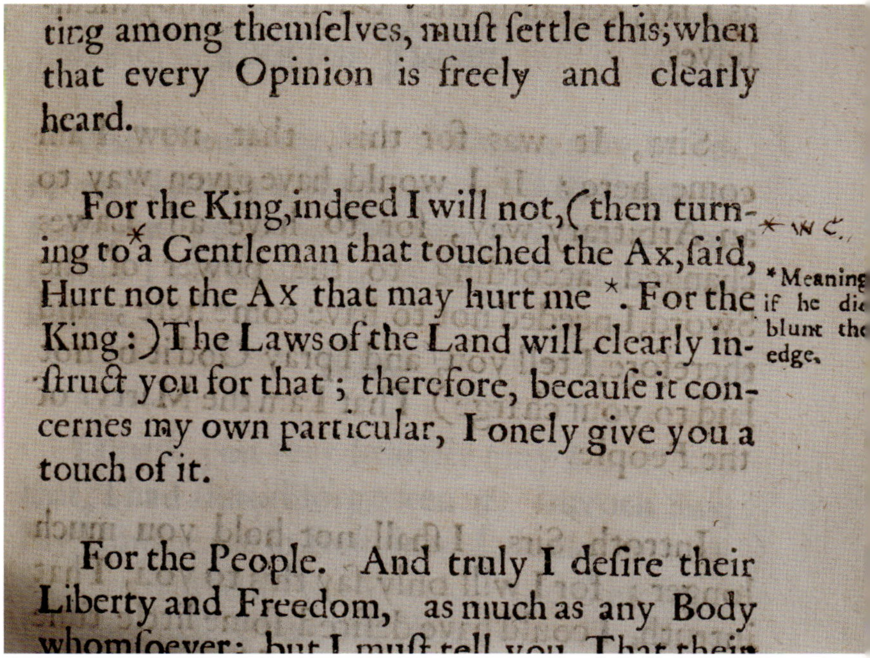
ting among themſelves, muſt ſettle this; when that every Opinion is freely and clearly heard.

For the King, indeed I will not, (then turning to a Gentleman that touched the Ax, ſaid, Hurt not the Ax that may hurt me *. For the King:) The Laws of the Land will clearly inſtruct you for that; therefore, becauſe it concernes my own particular, I onely give you a touch of it.

For the People. And truly I deſire their Liberty and Freedom, as much as any Body whomſoever: but I muſt tell you That their

*W.C.

*Meaning if he di blunt the edge.

From the pamphlet 'King Charles his speech made upon the scaffold'*, with William Clarke's initials in the margin.*

The study of Clarke's pamphlets and conversations with another set of friends in the MCR – mostly historians – and with some undergraduates whom I had managed to enthuse by showing them the text, led me to realising an idea which had been lurking in my mind for some time: the dramatisation of the Putney Debates. For me this was the second landmark. I soon discovered, of course, that a moment of dramatic history doesn't necessarily turn into good theatre, but by dint of using Clarke as the narrator and by using his pamphlets in a few background scenes, I think I created a reasonable narrative. Both Gerald Aylmer and Austin Woolrych went through my version with a small tooth comb: they could not have paid me a higher compliment and although occasionally Gerald looked over his spectacles and said 'Speculative, Lesley!' and Austin 'Only a very nit-picking academic could object to … ', to my great relief they approved of it.

I would like to end on the appreciation of very old friends in College, particularly to the loyal and enduring friendship and support of James Campbell, Fellow Librarian, who brought me to the College in the first place. A favourite colleague was the great Harry Pitt, and when he died we all felt he needed a very special memorial so another friend, Stuart Proffitt and I put together a book with tributes from people from all aspects of his life. My life at Worcester began with Shakespeare in the garden and I would like it to end with Jonathan Bate, a noted Shakespearean scholar. It was my great delight to get to know him a little and enjoy our conversations during his visits to me.

Looking back on my years at Worcester I can say, as Harry Pitt said at the end of his life, that what mattered most was 'laughter and the love of friends', referring to the lines of Hilaire Belloc:

From quiet homes and first beginning,
Out to the undiscovered ends,
There's nothing worth the wear of winning,
But laughter and the love of friends.

May Worcester always be a place that echoes to the sound of laughter and harbours lifelong friendships.

25. Modern Student Life

Jessica Goodman

Twenty-first century Worcester life is in many ways unrecognisable for an alumnus of the mid-20th century. All students are accommodated in modern, often en-suite rooms, clustered around large kitchens. The 'consumer-student', paying thousands of pounds a year to be at university, feels the pressure to make his or her time count, accumulating internships, club presidencies and community work for the CV alongside academic responsibilities. Most communication is conducted via email or text message: the libraries are more likely to resound to tapping laptops than scratching pens, and tutors now know the precise time at which the result of that early-hours essay crisis was finally submitted.

Sarah Murton, JCR President in the mid-1990s, arrived at the very start of this technological revolution, and recalls the lucky friend who owned a much-coveted and occasionally borrowed laptop: 'We didn't really have email, we still used pigeon post to communicate, and we mostly wrote our essays by hand, which I suppose is unthinkable now.' Since then every aspect of university life has become digitised. Library catalogues have almost all been transferred online, and books and articles can not only be ordered but also often consulted without leaving the comfort of an internet-connected study bedroom. Laptops, not exercise books, are the note-taking tool of choice in lectures, libraries and faculty buildings increasingly provide wi-fi networks, and everything from registration to reporting to Formal Hall booking takes place through a centralised online Student Self-Service Site. The extent of this revolution was unimaginable in 1990, when the JCR report in the *College Record* noted that 'the computer room has truly taken off this last year, with many undergraduates using newly-learnt word-processing skills for their essays, dissertations and correspondence'.

As university fees have increased, the vision of higher education as a service provided to student customers has intensified. Some institutions feel the pressure to prove the value of their degree in an increasingly competitive market. But 2011–12 JCR President Sam Barker thinks the merit of an Oxford degree speaks for itself.

> *It's so clearly worth it, it doesn't really play on the mind, I'm not being swindled. Whereas the increase in fees might encourage people to think more carefully about university as a general concept, I think here your degree is clearly worth the money and you will almost certainly earn it back.*

Nonetheless, Worcester takes the futures of its students seriously, and in the past few years has taken advantage of networks of former

ABOVE: *Worcester and its students today.* RIGHT: *Chalking in the Provost's Yard to commemorate Blades in Summer Eights Week.*

students to provide its newest members with advice and role models for their own burgeoning careers. Annual careers information evenings bring together current students and successful alumni from fields as diverse as filmmaking, law and scientific research, and both students and alumni find it rewarding and revealing.

But before students can even think about life after graduation, they have to earn a place at university. With the boom in university attendance in the 1980 and 1990s, and increasing numbers of top A-level grades awarded every year, pressure on places at all institutions has increased. At Oxford, applications have increased by 55 per cent over the past ten years, but the number of places has remained the same, creating ever more intense competition. In the context of an increasing focus nationally on widening access to higher education, the Oxford interview system has come in for particular scrutiny and often criticism. Yet the University spends over £2.5 million annually on outreach activities, and the interview system itself is designed to gain the most rounded possible view of all candidates. In the University as a whole, students from the state sector now make up 57.5 per cent of the undergraduate population, up from 42 per cent in 1990. The image of the old-boys' network is gradually dissolving, though there remains some distance to go in convincing the wider public that this is the case.

In 1995, the year that the first JCR Admissions Officer was appointed, the *College Record* notes a new JCR initiative of writing to all the state schools in the UK to invite applications from students who might not have considered applying to Oxford. Worcester today boasts the highest application rate of all the University colleges. Sam Barker puts that down to an inclusivity that makes it welcoming to applicants from any background:

> *Worcester doesn't put people off. Other colleges are maybe too grand, or too big, or too old, or too modern; we sit happily in the middle. It's so pretty, anyone who walks in the door really likes it, and as long as we keep along with that our welcoming, friendly atmosphere, I think in terms of access it's a really good college, because it doesn't conform to any one particular stereotype.*

And indeed, in 2012 67 per cent of Worcester's offers to UK applicants went to students from the maintained (as opposed to private) sector, the third-highest proportion of all colleges, and well up on the University average.

Things were not always thus. Sarah Murton's father had attended Worcester in the 1960s. One of her earliest memories is being brought to Worcester as a child, and told 'this is where you're going to come one day'. However, her Brighton sixth-form college nearly prevented her from fulfilling that prediction. 'When I told my school I wanted to apply they said "don't be so ridiculous"; they said I could apply for Oxford but not Worcester, because it was so public-school focused. But I went ahead anyway, and I did it, I proved them all wrong.'

In fact, students from the maintained sector were in a minority across the whole University in the 1990s: in 1994, the year of Sarah's matriculation, 65 per cent of offers went to the private sector. The precise figures for Worcester at this time are not known, but in 2001, the first year for which admissions by college are available, the three-year average for Worcester shows just 44 per cent of offers going to the state sector, in comparison to a University-wide average of 52.9 per cent. These figures suggest that Sarah's sense of a public-school bias has some basis in fact, and underline the enormous progress that has been made over the intervening decade.

In this early-1990s context, the election of Sarah, a state school student, as the JCR's second-ever female President was even more special. Ten years later, another JCR president-to-be, the Liverpudlian Dominic McKean, was to have quite a different experience, encouraged by his sixth-form theology teacher to give Oxford a chance:

ABOVE: *Student accommodation.* OPPOSITE: *Students celebrating 'Midway', the halfway point of their degrees, in 2006.*

> *Oxford had never been on my radar; I just didn't think it was for me. I went to visit not knowing anything about the College or its rich history. In fact, I didn't know much about Oxford, apart from having watched the Boat Race once or twice when I was younger. But being given that opportunity and encouragement to go and see everything first-hand convinced me that this was the place where I wanted to study. From the first moment I felt excited by Worcester, and as soon as I walked into the quad I knew it was also the place where I needed to be.*

Dominic spent his first year living in the then-infamous Staircase 24, a set of houses backing onto Worcester Place that were, at the time, a world away from the first-year hub that was the Goldfish Bowl (Staircases 17–20). By the early 2000s, accommodation had progressed beyond wood-panelled study sets with a bathroom across the quad: the rooms built during the 1990s were warm and bright, and shared ample bathroom facilities. But the revolution was really to come towards the end of the decade, when the new Earl Building, the development of the Beaumont Street complex and later the Ruskin Lane building brought over 200 new or updated en-suite rooms, all grouped around spacious, modern kitchens. Now, all undergraduates and a number of graduates can be accommodated on site, and even since the refurbishment of the Goldfish Bowl,

the new Staircase 24 has remained some of the most desirable undergraduate accommodation – a far cry from the 'ghetto' of Dominic's day.

One change brought about by the provision of kitchens was a drop in numbers of students attending informal Hall. With Formal Hall sittings also cut to four nights a week, it might appear that Worcester is at risk of losing its excellent reputation as one of Oxford's culinary capitals. Happily this is not the case: the 2012 academic year saw a resurgence in First Hall attendance, such that the hours were extended, and Formal Hall attendance is still strong, the food remaining one of Worcester's draws for potential applicants. While Old Members remember dubiously coloured, anonymous cuts of meat, and over-boiled vegetables, today's undergraduates are more likely to be served curry, lasagne or stir-fry at informal Hall, and delicately dressed venison or duck followed by an artistically decorated chocolate torte at the later sitting. A student-led Edible Garden initiative, established in 2010, now provides some of the produce cooked in Hall, and its first full Harvest Supper for 123 guests was held in Michaelmas Term 2011.

Yet for all the ways Worcester has changed over the decades, certain features remain unmistakably recognisable. Just as the fleets of subfusc-clad students cycling down the High Street every June could belong to any era, so there are many elements of Worcester life that hold a timeless quality, linking these smart-phone tapping students to their College ancestors. Part of what ties these generations of students together is the physicality of Worcester itself. Sarah Murton recalls ascending the Library stairs at night and wondering about the thousands of feet that had made the same journey over the previous two centuries. The crowds of students massing in the cloisters for Formal Hall, the Latin grace intoned by a scholar at the start of dinner, the nerves of a first tutorial, the camaraderie of Finals revision or a crucial sporting fixture, the haunting strains of a choral evensong drifting across the quad, or the magical spectacle of the College and its members transformed for the Commemoration Ball: any one of these moments, cherished by every Worcesterite as their own special memory of Oxford life, also belongs to the collectivity; to every time, and every generation. But as well as the physical proximity of so many gown-clad ghosts, Dominic McKean sees a certain Worcester spirit linking students through the ages. 'Meeting alumni from 30 years ago at a gaudy reaffirmed my belief that a certain type of person is attracted to Worcester, and that in a way we are all intrinsically linked. The older alumni seemed just like older versions of ourselves.'

And indeed, the resounding response when students are asked to characterise the College is as their home. 'It's friendly, relaxed, and – this might sound strange – cosy', says Sarah Murton, who describes the College as a 'total haven', and is still in touch with a close group of Worcester friends despite several years spent living abroad. Dominic McKean sees lifetime College membership as a real support network.

From the very beginning you are drawn into being part of the Worcester family. And as with all good families no matter how far you might stray, you are always welcomed back with open arms.

Football 1st XI 2010–11 Cuppers winners: Back row (l–r) B. Sloman, A. Titchen, A. Caio; Middle row (l–r) S. Poulson, M. Ward, T. Phelan, M. Isaacs, T. Chadwick, A. Taylor; Front row (l–r) O. Gee, J. Brown, T. Greene (captain), M. Sinnett, E. Thomas; Absent: L. Steward-George (vice-captain).

Ladies Hockey 2008–9 League Champions: Back row (l–r) J. Thompson, S. Gilkes, R. Burrows, J. Hamilton, A. Crothers; Front row (l–r) E. Braund, E. Reed, A. Yandle (captain), L. Magill, E. Halstead (vice captain).

> *When I meet up with Worcester friends we always simply carry on where we left off and it feels as if no time has passed at all. There is no artificiality, and the tangible feeling that everyone got on so well – students and staff – really makes the place feel at once genuine and warm.*

Sarah too recalls how her tenure as JCR President opened her eyes to the wider College community, while Sam fondly describes the cheerful rapport built up with senior staff members, in contrast to the combative relationships his fellow JCR Presidents reported with their College administration.

Certain College staff members are always held in the affection of the student body, and in the modern era the more notorious personalities have been Food Service Manager Marion McKenna and the much-missed bar manager, Tony Wilson. Dominic recalls the infamous barman:

> *I will always miss Tony, who looked after me during my time in Worcester and who was a special friend. The bar seems strange without his ubiquitous presence, forever shouting at students to hang their coats up! But Worcester will remain in essence what it always has been because there are always new people to take up the mantle and continue its traditions. Even though I can no longer see Tony I feel his spirit whenever I return to the bar.*

Tony was the football team's most ardent fan, but it was only after the first team finished runners up in the league one year that he decided he could no longer stand by on the side-lines. Under his guidance as coach, Worcester went on a run of three successive league titles (2006–8) and one cup win. Not only that, but Tony became (probably) the oldest player ever to score for Worcester during a brief cameo appearance in Doxbridge, the annual sports tournament held in Dublin. His dedication earned him a memorial shirt on the wall of his old domain.

Indeed, Worcester's sporting prowess across the board is held in awe by many an inferior college. The presence of the sports grounds on site is not only a draw for applicants, but also a secret weapon for intensive training. In 2010–11 alone both the Men's first XI football and the Cricket first XI won Cuppers, the Darts team won the league, the 1st novice boat won Christ Church regatta, and two women's VIIIs won blades at both Torpids and Summer Eights.

Other student societies continue to flourish, with Buskins producing at least two performances a year, including the annual summer garden production. Buskins output has often included

Above: *Worcester College Freshers, 2012.* Left: The Merchant of Venice, *2013.*

new writing by College members, and for the College's 250th Anniversary in 1964, students performed *The Passing of Gloucester Hall* by Michael Symes. The Woodroffe Society, founded in 1947, provides a discussion forum for ethical and moral issues, and a popular dining event each year, while the graduate Franks Society meets thrice termly for dinner and a presentation by a member of the MCR. Charity events have been a regular feature of the Worcester calendar, from the 1979 42-hour relay reading of the *Iliad* and the *Odyssey*, in aid of Cancer Research, to nearly 20 per cent of the MCR entering into the 2012 Oxford Town and Gown charity 10k race. Both the JCR and MCR run an active social calendar, including Bar Nights, Open Mic events, theatre trips, and the inevitable and ever-popular bops. Sam Barker describes the Worcester of the 2010s as 'just hitting its stride': it can only be hoped that there is plenty more to come.

But even when Finals are over, the bar is empty, the last library books have been handed back, and the subfusc has been tidied away in the back of a wardrobe, the impact of three or four years in Worcester leaves an important impression. Sarah Murton's determination to apply in the face of her teachers' advice had been the first step in a journey that saw her campaign for changes to housing provision in College and successfully persuade the

Students after matriculation.

local council to install a pedestrian crossing on Worcester Street, following a spate of accidents: 'My time in Worcester gave me the confidence to believe in myself. Being JCR President was something really special for me; it taught me that you can do anything if you set your mind to it.' In strikingly similar words, Dominic McKean echoes the view of College as a crucial place of self-development:

> *Worcester was the glue that kept my three years of experiences at Oxford together. It is no coincidence that most of my lasting friendships were made with Worcester students because the College was the place to which I returned constantly to draw from its well of encouragement, to go out again and become the person I needed to become. While staying loyal to my roots as an ordinary, sports-loving lad from Liverpool, Worcester gave me opportunities to meet exceptional people with all kinds of backgrounds different to mine and, ultimately, to take from that experience a belief and confidence that I had something special to offer the world.*

Hundreds of Old Members across the decades will empathise with Dominic's words. For all its wonderful buildings, stunning gardens, and fascinating history, Worcester will remain, for the majority of its alumni, their home. It is perhaps not surprising that Sam finds that Old Members still talk about the College almost in the present tense. Timeless, familial and inclusive, while still evolving and adapting to keep pace with changing times, Modern Worcester constantly brings together the past and the present in perfect balance, taking the very best from each.

A JCR Timeline

Some notable (and not-so-notable) moments from the modern history of the student body:

1979 Victory of the first Worcester female boat to enter Christ Church regatta.

1987 Demise of the committee position 'Captain of Bicycles'.

1989 As the student favourite *Neighbours* takes off in popularity, one of its stars is made an honorary member of the JCR and visits the College for lunch, attracting the attention of the local media.

1990 Introduction of the first recycling scheme into College, as well as the start of a controversial electronic payment system for food.

1991 JCR participation in the 'Send a cow' initiative, which buys cows for Ugandan villages. In honour of this initiative, a cow and calf are left grazing in the Orchard, Hester the cow is made an honorary member of the JCR, and the Blue Boat challenges a 'Provost's VIII' to a milk-drinking contest.

1994 First College Freshers' Week.

1995 First production of a Freshers' handbook, and the creation of the position of 'Admissions Officer'.

1996 Ban on smoking in the bar proposed; eventually implemented only during the broadcast of *Neighbours*.

1999 Introduction of Peer Support scheme.

2004 MCR associate membership extended to spouses/partners etc; 4th years entitled to full membership.

2005 Attempt to introduce Woostmas: an annual festival in Hilary Term, including the singing of Woostmas Carols, to be composed by the Arts Rep.

JCR President becomes the official Protector of the College Ducks.

2011 Tom, Ellie and Harry Bate (residents of the Provost's Lodgings, aged 13, 11 and five) voted honorary members of the JCR for their undying support of Worcester sport.

List of Subscribers

This book has been made possible by the generosity of the subscribers listed below. Those 300 subscribers who responded to the **First to 300** challenge are listed in **bold**. Single years represent year of matriculation, or the first year of Fellowship.

FT = Fellow and Tutor
PF = Professorial Fellow
F = Fellow
FB = Fellow and Bursar
SF = Sachs Fellow
EF = Emeritus Fellow
HF = Honorary Fellow

Roger Abbott 2006
A. Abdullah 1997
Dr Shanta Acharya 1979
Daryl Achilles 2002
Richard G. Adams 1938
Felicity Adi 2003
Professor Peter Aggleton 1971
Professor Jean Aitchison PF 1993; EF 2003
P.J. Aitken 1978
Dr M. Afifi Al-Akiti F 2001
Robert Alexander Albright FRPS 1968
John H. Alcock 1966
H.E.J. Aldridge 1961
Hugh Allan 1956
William Allen 1987
Richard Allnatt 1985
Dr A.J. Anderson 1964
E. Clive Anderson 1964
Giles Andreae 1985
Noël Annesley 1960
David Ansell 1968
Dr Gregory Ansell 1963
Nazli Arad-Osmond 1996
Sarah Archer 1999
Robin Arculus 1956
Robert G. Ardrey 1998
Viscount Ashbrook 1956
Philip Ashton 1966
R.J.A. Askew 1971
Dr Rob and Mrs Aida Atenstaedt 1995
David Attewell 1957
Philip James Baggley 2005
Carolyn Bagley 1979
Charles A Baker 1990
Sunil Bakrania 1986
Alasdair Balfour 1992
Martin John Banister 1959
G.H.A. Bankes 1963

Professor Peter Banks 1957
David Barbour 1972
Richard Barke 1996
David Barlow 1956
Laura Barnes 2002
Andrew Barnett 1979
Eva Barnett 1990
Katherine Barnett (née Ogilvie Thompson) 1987
Tom Barnsley 1968
Philip Barras 1971
Michael Barrett 1961
Ondine Barrow 1987
Christopher Barton 1975
Jonathan Batey 1968
J.J.R. Batstone 2006
Edward Batt 1944
Marc Baylis 1989
Sarah Bayliss and Dan Cook 1982
Philip Bean 1986
Dr K. Juliet A. Bedford 1998
Ian Beer 1965
Kathi Beier 2007
Alison Jane Bell 1982
Brian Bell 1965
J.R.S. Bell 1953
Paul Belok 1979
Terence Bendixson 1954
Michael Bendon 1960
Liz Benjamin 1995
John Bennett 1969
E.A. Benson FRCS 1956
Lars C. Bespolka 1984
Antonin Besse 1976
Dr P.G. Biddle OBE 1961
Andrew Bigham 1960
David Bigmore 1966
Terry Bird 1967
Stephan Bisse 2001

Richard Black 1966
Richard Blackburn 1958
Dennis Blair 1968
Martin Blake 1949
Elizabeth Blomfield (née Turner) 1991
Jeremy Blundell 1961
Robert G.C. Blyth 1974
Rachel Boak 1998
Tom Boardley 1975
Roger Bodley 1966
Kostas Bokos 1998
R.J. and L. Bomphrey 2000
Malcolm L. Booth 1958
Neil Booth 1990
Emily Boswell 1992
Christopher Bothwell 1997
Anthony Bourne 1961
Thomas Bowen Wright 1997
J. Bowman 2000
Andrew Boyle 1982
Professor David Bradshaw FT 1987
Robin Bradshaw 1956
Isabel Braham 1979
Gabrielle Branson 2000
David Breakell 1968
Simon Brew 1963
A.W. Brierley 1970
Robin Brighton 1956
Michelle Brigoli 2005
Robin Broadley 1954
Roger Brock 1977
Julie Brooker (née Starkey) 1991
Hannah Brooks 1998
A. St J. Brown 1974
Christopher Brown 1957
David Brown 1959
Lord Brown of Eaton-under-Heywood HF 1957

Lucy Brown 2003
Simon Richard Brown 2001
Stuart Brown QC 1969
Barbara Browne
Paul Browne 1987
William Broyles 1966
David Brunning 1962
Matthew Brunning 1992
Martin Bryan-Brown 1956
Jon Buchan 1958
Martin L Budd 1960
Ivor John Bufton 1954
Andrew Buglass 1984
John Buglass 1983
B.W. Bull 1977
Nick and Michelle Bullmore 1998
Robin C. Burgess 1978
Rhys Burriss 1970
George Burton 1966
Malcolm Bush 1964
Garrett Buxton 2006
Daisy Buzzoni 2012
T.W. Cain 1955
Andrea Caio 2009
Damian Caluori 2002
Iain Cameron 1983
James Cameron 1954
J.T. Campbell 1955
In memory of Kenneth Campbell
Stephen Campbell 1988
Professor Dr Nuno Ayres de Campos 1970
David Cane 1981
A.C.S. Carter 1957
David Carter 1975
Dr Lionel Cartwright 1974
Noel Casey 1994
Ronan Cassidy 1985
Celia Caughey 1982

Nigel Cave 1962
Robin Cave 1952
Sudhir Chadha 1969
Richard Chalmers 1970
James Chapman 1998
Naveed Chaudhry 2004
Sanjay Chauhan 1988
Michael L Chelk
Sai Wing Cheng 1989
Graham D Child 1961
Dennis Chiles 1967
D.A. Chilton 1966
J.T. Chirurg 1969
Hugh A.J. Chisholm 1995
John Church 1956
Mike Churchman 1970
John Cieslik-Bridgen 1992
Phil Clamp 1986
John D. Clark 1945
Dr Relf Clark 1973
Dr Richard Clark 1972
Steve Clarke 1970
Nicholas Cleobury 1968
Peter Clift 1984
David Close 2001
Antonia Coad 1999
Michael Coburn 1984
Francis Michael Cochrane 1969
Dr M.J. Cogbill 1982
Tony Coles 2005
His Honour John Colyer QC 1955
Joyce M Connell 1997
Mike Connolly 1955
Peter Connors 1979
Paul Conrad 1973
Dr P H Constable 1985
Dr Julian Cook 1974
M R Cook 1955
Michele Amos Cooke 1998
Nicholas Cooke 1963
H.N. Cookes 1975
Dr E.D.K. Coombe 1943
Andrew Cooper 1964
Colin Cooper 1955
Edward Cooper 1956
The Revd Derek Copeland 1959
Stevan P.G. Corbett 1975
Mary Anne Cordeiro 1979
Martin Cordey 1980
Charlotte Corkett (née Adams) 2002
Tim Cornick 1976
Andrew Corser 1973
David Cottrell 1971
Desmond Coulson 1953
Laila Courtney 2001
Rachael Cove 2006

Michael Coveney 1967
Alex Cox 1973
Geoffrey Cox 1959
Lynne and James Cox 2002
Tom Cox 2007
James Craig 1997
John Crellin 1968
Thomas Crewe 2009
Robert Crispe 1952
David Cronyn 1954
Martin Cross 1964
John Crowhurst 1956
Robert Crowter-Jones 2007
Francesca and Toby Crump 2001
Charlotte Cunningham (née Luxembourg) 1985
Martin G Cunningham 1969
John Curran 1986
John Curtis 1953
Sir John Curtiss 1942
Nicholas S.I. Daglish 1959
H. James Dalton 1952
T. Daly 1998
Clifford S. Dammers 1991
Mark R.G. Darbon 1997
Robin Darwall-Smith
Rhys David 1962
Catherine Davidson (née Wragg) 1998
Richard Davidson 1964
J.B. Davies 1955
Malcolm R.J. Davis 1968
Michelle Davis (née Winch) 1991
Michael Davison 1952
Tanera Dawkins 1987
Christopher Day 1952
Coleen Day, Director of Development
Peter H. Deacon 1966
Celia Deakin 2000
Nick Dean 1972
Jeremy Deane 1963
Masato Degawa 1976
Ben Delo 2002
David Denison 1991
Robert Dent 1965
Andrew Diament 1983
Matthew Dick 1995
Dr Nnamdi Dimgba 2000
Adam Dinwoodie 2005
Anthony Disney 1958
Dr Nick Dixon 2003
Matthew Dobbs Esq. 1978
Raymond Dodd 1946
Professor Paul Doe 1949
Anna Dominey 2011
Edward Donati 2004
Dr Kim Dora FT 2010

Martin Doughty 1967
Andrew Douglas 1974
David Douglas 1963
Gerald John Dowler 1985
Dr Anthony Dowling 1962
Teresa Dianne and John Michael Doyle
Thomas Doyle 1977
Alasdair Drake 1984
Robert Draper 1989
Iain Dresser 1957
Lt Col Alastair Drew 1961
Gregory Drew 1955
Barry Driver 1966
Dr Stuart Drummond 1949
Judge Brian Duckworth DL 1953
Matthew Duckworth 1978
Carsten Duke 1995
Robert Duncan 1970
Charles Dunn 1979
Matthew Dunning 1984
Nick Dwelly 1957
Peter R.S. Earl 1973
Richard Earl FT 1999
Lindsay East 1967
Jonathan Ebsworth 1980
Robin Eccles 1953
J.R.G. Edwards 1957
Olivia Egger 2006
Professor John Eland PF 1983; EF 2006
John Y. Ellis 1954
Katherine Ellis 2008
Pete Ellis 1973
Michael Robert England 1996
Dr Stefano Evangelisti 2011
David Evans 1975
Matt Evans 1992
Simon Evans 1982
Harry Everett 1970
Michael R J Everingham 1980
Edwin Famous 1999
Richard Faulkner 1964
Dylan and Sue Fenn
Andrew Ferguson 1965
John Fielden 1959
Joerg Filthaut 1990
Max Findlay 1970
David Fitt 1966
Richard Fitzjohn 1984
Alistair Fletcher 1975
Peter Fletcher 1952
Guy Foord-Kelcey 1993
Peter Forshaw 1993
Michael Foster 1949
Nicholas Foster 2002
John D Fox SF 1977

Noah Franklin 1978
Richard Frapwell 1967
Roger Freeman 1952
Christine French 1981
Terence Froggatt 1963
Ernest Frost 1913
Peter Fry 1986
Michael Fuller 1981
Ian R.G. Furnivall 1976
P.J. Gadsden 1949
Phillip Gale 2003
Adrian Gardner 1981
Brian Gardner 1966
Felicity Gardner 1983
Timothy Garland 1960
Douglas Garrad 1947
Michael J Geary 1968
Fred Gee 1956
T.E.D. Gee 1980
Peter Gell 1949
Thomas German 2012
Michael Gibbs 1955
Peter Gibson 1955
Dr K.E. Gilchrist 1988
Denis Gildea 1946
Ian Gillespie 1964
Gardar Gislason 1967
Charles Gladstone 1983
W. John Glancy 1964
Sir Iain Glidewell HF 1942
Seamus Goatley 1982
Jonathan Golub 1989
Barry Goodchild 1953
Vicki Goodwin 1995
John Gowar 1958
Trevor Charles Gower 1974
Alec Graham
Robert Graham 1964
Dr Alexander Grant 1965
Victoria Grant 1999
Michael Gray 1950
Andrei Grecu 2004
The Revd Prebendary Alan Green 1975
Raymond Greenburgh 1946
Henry Greenfield 1958
Jeremy Greenstock HF 1962
Kenneth M Greig 1978
David and Rosalind Grice
The Revd Rowland Powell Griffiths 1926
Hugo Grimston 1999
Jack Grimston 1987
Peter Grosvenor 1951
Douglas Grounds 1955
Catherine Grum 1998

Robert Gullifer 1980
Stuart Gulliver 1977
Gerald Gurney 1952
Peter Gutierrez 1981
Jessica Hadley 2009
John Hagestadt 1959
Nicholas Hagger 1958
Dr Roy Martin Haines 1954
The Revd Professor James Haire AC 1965
Heather Hall (née Murray) 1980
Jane Hall 1982
David Halls 1981
Dr Steven Halls 1976
The Rt Hon Lord Hamilton HF 1961
Kenneth Hamilton 1991
Benjamin Hammond 1998
Joanna Hampton 1991
Christopher Hancock 1944
Nick Harding 1978
Roger H. Harding-Smith 1957
Jonathan and Ellen Hardwick (née Shardlow) 1994
Simon Hargreaves QC 1986
Hugh J.W. Harper 1986
Jennifer Harper (née Noel) 1993
Keith D. Harrap 1959
Roger Harrington 1962
Roy Harrington 1963
David Harris 1981
Gerald Harris 1963
Richard J. Harris 1972
Steve Harrison 1974
Neil Hartley 1984
Roxby Hartley 1986
Tom Hartley 2006
Steve Hartnell OBE 1977
Ralph Hassall 1997
Martin Hatfull 1976
Nicholas Havers 1998
Ian Haworth 2008
Geoffrey John Hayhurst 1966
Jessica J. He 2004
Ron Heapy 1956
Roger Heath-Brown PF 1999
Harry Hecht 2005
Rhys and Jillian Hedges
Gregory Heibel 1992
Richard Hemingway 1962
Alexander Henderson 1985
Frances Henderson 1996
Hugo Herbert-Jones 1940
Pierre Hervy 1962
Nicholas Heywood-Waddington 1974
Ernest M. Hilditch 1958
M.J. Hill 1965

Rupert Hill 1972
John W. Hinchey 1976
R.K. Hindle 1956
Chris Hinze 1986
Peter Hirst 1999
Simon Hirst 2002
Mike Hoath 1966
Michael Hodgetts 1954
Dr Richard J Hodgkiss 1971
John Hodson 1964
Adam Hoffman 1992
Christopher Holder 1995
Michael Holdsworth 1957
Claire Hollinghurst and Paul Nicholls 1986, 1989
Paul F.O. Holloway 1986
Ben Holmes 1992
David Burton Homan 1952
Richard Hooper CBE 1959
Dermot Hope-Simpson 1949
Roger Hopkins 1965
Dr Alastair Horn 1984
Richard N. Horne 1945
Jeremy Horner 1980
Ralph Houlbrooke 1962
Clive Howard 1980
Jon Howard 1992
Richard Howell 1998
Roger Howes 1966
Ian Howlett 2004
Kathryn Howley 2005
Dr John Hudson 1961
W.J.S. Hudson 1948
Celia Hughes 1983
Delyth Hughes 2006
Bruce Hugman 1963
Alexander Hunt 2009
Henry Hunt 1981
Ian Hunt 2000
J.S.M. Hunt 1954
Tony Hunt 1962
John Huntriss 1967
Zoë Hurley (née Smith) 1992
John Hutchings 1957
Jill Ireland 1982
Lucinda Ireland 1981
Gregg Irwin 1990
Tim Isaac 1968
Carl Andreas Isaksson 1997
David Ives 1956
J. David Jackson 1960
Alexander T. James 2013
Andrew James 2001
Andrew Jardine, Estates Bursar FB 2010
Nicholas Jenni 1972
A.S. Jennings 1994

M.B. Jennings 1990
Dr Erik Jensen 1954
Dr Keith Johnson 1973
Lawrence Johnson 1969
Simon Johnson 1983
Alan Belford Jones 1976
E.B.D. Jones 1952
Gareth D. Jones 1970
Garry Peter Jones 1976
Geraint Jones 2001
Glyn Jones 1970
Iain R. Jones 1984
Mark Jones 1969
Rachael Jones 1992
Rick Jones 1991
Robert A. Jones 1996
S.G.S.S. Jones 1984
Sean Jones QC 1985
Albert Jordan 1955
Christopher Jose 1959
Dr Simon P. Joseph 1959
Samip H. Joshi 2005
Sophie Jourdier 1993
Anthony Julius 1989
Jeremy Robin Kaye 1958
John Kear 1958
Andrew and Dipika Keen 1994
Alexandra Lee Kelly 2007
Tom Kemp 1962
Ian Kennedy 1966
Stephen Kenny QC 1982
Melvin T. Kenyon 1975
Michael Kernan 1974
Andrew Kerr 1991
Jane Kerry, First Female Lodge Porter
Angelika Ketzer 2009
David Kidd-May 1952
David Kilmister 1955
Dr Andrew King 1979
Colonel David King FB 1986
The Revd M.C. King 1953
Nick King 1984
Paul Kingsbury 1979
Harry Kinmonth 2002
Nicholas Knight 1994
Christine Knight-Maunder 1988
Sir John Knox 1947
Peter Kosminsky 1976
Martin Kyle 1960
Alexandra Kyrke-Smith 2008
Neville Kyrke-Smith 1976
Dr Evan LaBuzetta 2004
Ioannis Ladas 2010
Peter Laing 1966
Ian Laird 1966
Francis Lamport FT 1996; EF 2001

Philip Landon 1985
Jeremy J Lang 1956
Mark Lanier 1980
Richard Lawrence 1964
Michael K Lawson 1974
Tony Ledgard 1960
Aimee-Jane Lee 1997
Freddie Lee 1995
James Lee 1998
M.L.H. Lee 1942
Peter Lee 1960
Elizabeth Leeding 1999
David R. Leigh 1964
Julian Leong 1994
J.R. Lester 1971
Andrew and Sarah Lewis 1983, 1984
David Lewis 1988
Diana Lewis 1993
John W Lewis 1952
Tim Lewis 2002
C.P. Liddell 1980
Katie Liddell 2002
David Lilley 1969
John C. Lin 1984
Ian Lindsay 1976
Nick Lines 1971
Stephen Lipton 1977
James Little 1984
Niel Livingstone 1956
Sarah Livingstone 1981
Gary Lloyd 1997
Major C.A.R. Lockhart 1954
Richard Longworth 1973
Andrew Lorenz 1974
James Lorenz 2012
Keith Louis 1951
Dr John Lourie 1962
Serge Lourie 1965
John Love 1965
Andrew Luff 1976
Heather Clare Luff 1989
Cameron Dean Boase Luke 2001
H. John Lush 1957
Sue Lush
John Tao-Che Ma 1970
John and Rebecca MacDonald 1997, 1998
Alan Macfarlane 1960
Alastair Mackeown 1998
James Macnaughton 1956
Angus Macpherson 1952
Tristan Mahoney 1996
John Mainstone 1953
John Mair 1950
Kristina Maria Manalo 2007
James Maple 1952

Anthony Marsh 1977
Bruce Marshall AM 1973
W.J. Marshall 1980
Peter Martin 1972
Robin Martin 1965
The Revd Rupert Martin 1975
Don Mathew 1961
Alan Matthias 1956
Hon Henry C. Maude 1950
The Rt Hon Sir Anthony May HF 1960
Martin May 1984
Paul and Imogene Z. Mayhew 1989, 1991
Antony Mays 1993
James and Jackie McCallum
Robert McCracken QC 1968
John McEachern 2008
Richard McGrane 1976
Grant McIntyre 1964
Anne Meadows (née Clayton) 1994
John Meeson 1958
Jenny Messenger 2008
Benjamin Meuli 1974
Paul and Lisa Miller 1995, 1996
The Revd Graham Mitchell 1971
Ross Mitchell 1977
Sarah Mold 2009
Alex Money 2010
R.D. Montgomerie 1958
Richard Moore 1982
Benedict Morgan 1980
N.P. Ll Morgan 1958
R.B. Ll Morgan 1954
Kerry Morley (née Leach) 1997
James Mossop 1981
Luther Munford 1971
Mike and Lucy Munro (née Sharman) 1987, 1989
Bill Murdie 1969
Fergus and Rosanne Murison 1977, 1979
Nick Murphy 1962
A.M. Murray 1959
Paul M. Murray 1986
Lisa Neanor (née Cosgrove) 1989
George Needham 1963
Josephus Nelson 1987
Rowan Neslen 2001
Tracey Neuman 2000
Michael Newbold 1959
S.B. Newey 1957
Brooks Newmark MP 1980
Roger Nicholls 1955
Paul Nixon 1956
Ben Norman 1991
The Marquis of Normanby 1972
Humphrey Norrington 1956
Steve Norris 1964
Edward Nugee TD QC 1949
The Revd Dr C.J.B. O'Neill 1972
Christopher Oakley 1976
Dr Christopher Oliver CBE 1959
Richard Olsen 1962
Professor Mark Ormrod 1979
Nigel Osborne 1984
J.T. Otto-Jones 1983
Kenneth J. Ovey 1944
David Oxley CBE 1958
Malcolm Padgett 1971
Kenneth Painter 1956
Mike Palfreman 1978
Lord Peter Palumbo 1956
Neil Papworth 2008
Karen Park 2007
Simon Park 2007
Joanna Parker
Gerald Parsons 1972
John Parsons 1969
Ruth Partington
Daniel Paul 2004
Basil Payne 1949
Kenneth Pearce 1949
Christopher T. Pears 1984
Frederick E. Pearson 1956
Marilyn Peddie, Accounts Manager
Malcolm Peel 1953
Thomas Geoffrey Peet 1977
John Peirce 1956
Ian Pemberton 1967
Christopher Pennell 1965
Geoffrey Perrin 1967
M.G. Perry 1963
Russell Lee Perry 1957
David J. Phillips 1957
Mark Phillips 1959
John Philpott 1972
Mark S. Philps 1970
J.M. Pickard 1962
Alan E. Pickup 1971
Dr Martin 'Trucky' Pickup 2002
Arthur Picton 1961
Andrew Pierssené 1949
Anthony Pitt-Rivers 1951
Kate Pointer 2003
The Revd Prebendary Michael Pollit 1951
Michael Polonsky 1963
The Revd Ray Porter 1963
Tom Porter 2005
Daniel Poser 1985
Professor Barry V.L. Potter 1973
Lillie Potter 1997
D.G. Preddy 1957
Benjamin Jan Price 1998
James Edward Price 2010
John Price 1961
Michael Price 1969
Tom Price 1967
Roger Prior 1963
John Kenneth Pritchard 1989
S.G. Proffitt 1979
G.R. Proudfoot 1955
Mark John Puttick 2007
David Christopher Quirke 1969
Michael Rallings 1996
Mark Rathbone 1975
E Alastair Rattray 1957
Owain Raw-Rees 1978
Rob Rawlins 1968
Patrick Rawnsley 1983
The Revd Charles Razzall 1973
David Read 1965
Emily Read 1996
Dr David N. Redman 1968
Laurence Reed 1950
Emily Rees Jones 2005
Margarida Lima Rego 1999
Katie Reisz 2007
Charlotte Rendle 1996
Rebecca Rennison 2001
James Reynolds 1997
David Richardson 1956
Andrea Richter 1991
Sarah Rickard (née Flynn) 1994
Jonathan Ridgway 1997
John Rivers 1964
David Roberts 1967
John T. Roberts 1973
Julian V. Roberts PF 2005
Karen Elizabeth Roberts (née Fry) 1980
Raymond Roberts 1969
Alan Robertson 1970
Colin Robertson 1972
David Robins 1964
Henry Robinson 1972
Philip Robinson 1981
Edward Roche 2004
Charles Rodway 1989
His Honour D.A.H. Rodwell QC 1956
Professor Warwick Rodwell OBE 1972
Philip Rooney 1974
Nick Rose 1976
Stephen Rose 1950
In memory of M.J. Rowe 1956
Colin Rowland 1963
Gavin Roynon 1956
Dr Colin Ruck 1948
Philip Rundle 1953
Rt Hon Sir Timothy Sainsbury HF 1953
Dr Matthew Salisbury and Jennifer Rushworth 2007, 2005
Peter Salter 1957
Professor James Sambrook 1952
Michael R.S. Sanderson 1958
David Sandys-Renton 1956
Jim Sanger 1959
Dr Tony Saul 1964
Malcolm Saunders 1975
Charles Savage 1957
Matthew Savage 1984
Simon Savage 1987
John M. Sayers 1961
Jean-Pierre Schweitzer 2009
Jürg Schwyter
Henry Sclater 1965
David Scutt 1943
Graham Searle 1958
John Seawright 1970
David Sefton 1990
Keval Shah 1996
Damis Shaharudin 1988
Sunkalp Sharma 2007
A.G. Sharp 1950
Christopher F. Sharp QC 1971
William F. Sharp 1953
Colin Sheaf 1971
Martin Sheeter 1968
Paul Shelton 1971
John Shephard 1969
F. Ronald Shimmin 1953
Gareth R. Shires 2001
P.K. Sidenius 1988
Geoffrey Simm 1966
Dr Helen Simmons 1986
David Skinner 1978
Mark Slater 1974
Professor Simon Smail CBE 1964
Alastair Small 1960
Graham Smallbone 1954
The Revd Austin Smith 1959
Alistair P. Somerville 2012
Dr Ramon M.G. Soriano 1986
Christopher Sparkhall 1995
Robert Spicer 1982
Professor William Stafford 1964
Henry Stanford 1984
Julian Stanford 1953
Dr Richard van der Star 1970
Roland Stedeford 1949
The Venerable Gordon John Steele 1980
Kenneth Stern 1949
Jennie Stevens 2009

Tim Stevenson OBE 1967
Andy Stewart 2003
Peter Stewart 1965
Chip Stidolph 1961
Theo Stocker 2001
Dr Mark Stoker 1985
Dr Tom and Cheryl Stone 2002, 1999
Evan Stone QC 1949
John Storey 1975
Richard Stovin-Bradford 1976
James Stow 1959
Caroline Megan Stratton 1996
Carmy Strzelecki, Accounts Assistant
Paul G. Stubley 2008
Stephanie Studer 2007
Bernard Sufrin FT 1983; EF 2010
John Sumiga 1969
Andrew Sutcliffe 1979
Philip Sutterby 1996
C.J. Sutton 1963
M.A. Sutton MC KCSG 1945
Christopher Swain 1964
William Swinbank 1970
Terence R. Swinn 1965
Col Charlie Sykes PWRR 1987
Sir John Sykes Bt 1960
Michael Symes 1962
Yasuzo Takeno 1990
Dr Stephen Tapril 1999
Greg Tarr 2004

Graham Taylor 1960
H. John H. Taylor 1960
Mostyn H.J. Taylor 2003
Charles Thatcher 1953
John Theakston 1970
Samuel Thomas 2011
Anthony Ogilvie Thompson 1984
Henry Thompson 1959
Julian Ogilvie Thompson 1953
Sir Richard Thompson HF 1958
David Thomson 1955
Dr Robert Gregory Thorne 1969
Malcolm Todd 1985
Robert Richard Toomey 1968
Dr Estee Torok 1988
Stephen Tough 1977
Edward Towne 2000
Rebecca Trentham 1989
Jeremy Triggs 1950
P.A. Trower 1967
A.R. (Toby) Turl 1957
Professor J.A. Turner 1967
Lucy Turner 1999
Neil Turner, SCR Butler
Nigel Urwin 1969
Peter Valder 1951
John Waite 1961
Sir Harold Walker 1952
Christopher Walls 1967
David Walser 1958

John Walters 1959
Richard Walton 1990
G.A. Ward 1948
Dr Nigel Ward 1972
Justin Wark 1979
C.F.G. Warman 1958
Katy and Edmond Warner 1982
Steve Warren-Smith 1982
Richard John Waterhouse 1989
Brian Watkins CMG 1958
J.D. Watson 1953
Matthew Watson 1993
Daniel Waxman 2006
A.P. Weale PF 1982–2005; EF 2006–
Naomi Webb 2007
Peter Webber 1966
Ernest Wedgwood 1970
Lucy Welch 2011
Professor Ian Wells 1965
Sir John Weston HF 1958
James A.D. Wetenhall 1949
Richard Wetenhall 1980
Simon Wethered 1964
John Whicker 1955
David White 1959
Duncan Trevor White 1974
S.J. White 1954
Rodney Whittaker 1967
Barrie A. Wigmore HF 1964
Katy Wilcock 2007

J.G. Willcox 1959
John Williams 1980
Michael Williams 1961
Robert Williams 1968
Sean Williams 1982
Tom Williams 1997
Mat Williamson 1999
Neil Williamson 1962
R.J. Williamson 1957
Adam Martin Willman 2001
E.P. Wilson FT 1975; EF 2008
Peter Wilson 1959
Nicholas Winsor 1980
Michael Winterbottom FT 1967; EF 1993
Dr G.C.S. Wise 1999
Christa and Richard Wiseman 1984, 1983
David Wood 1963
Hon Justice Mark Woolford 1979
Edward Wray 1987
Jeremy Wright 1965
Dr Derek Wyatt 1942
Rupert Yardley 1980
Ian Yenney 2005
Wallace Yip 1988
Laura Jane Young 2007
Rabbi Roderick Young 1979
Paul Zisman 1978

Index

Bold indicates authorship. *Italics* indicate for images.

Select Bibliography

Alton, R., 'The New Model Patrons: the JCR Picture Collections', *Apollo*, 1997, 145 (423, May), pp. 63–6

Amphlett, J., *An Index to Dr Nash's Collections for a History of Worcestershire*, 2 vols, Oxford, Worcestershire Historical Society, 1894–5

Ballantyne, A., *Architecture, Landscape and Liberty: Richard Payne Knight and the Picturesque*, Cambridge, CUP, 1997

Barrett, A.H., *'Richard Blechinden: The First Provost of Worcester College, Oxford'*, Oxoniensia, 1986, 51, pp. 139–69

———, *'The Naming of Worcester College'*, Worcester *College Record*, 1991, pp. 24–5

Bean, A., *The Patronage and Architectural Activities of Dr George Clarke (1661–1736)*, MA report, University of London, 1972

Bell, N., *Music in Medieval Manuscripts*, Toronto, University of Toronto Press, 2001

Bradshaw, D., 'The American Chaplain and the Modernist Poets: William Force Stead, W.B. Yeats and T.S. Eliot', *Worcester College Record*, 2011, pp. 103–33

Briggs, A., *Special Relationships: People and Places*, London, Frontline Books, 2012

Burgon, J.W., *Lives of Twelve Good Men*, London, John Murray, 1889

Bushell, D., *William Law Pope and Henry Bishop: Two Clerics in Victorian Tunbridge Wells*, London, FWPC, 2009

Campbell, J., *'Worcester College and the University Election of 1865'*, Worcester *College Record*, 1957–9, pp. 13–16

Chapman, J., ed., *Reminiscences of Three Oxford Worthies: Rev J. Keble*...Rev. J. Miller... to which is prefixed a memoir by the late Rev. J. Wilson...and Rev. C.A. Ogilvie, Oxford, J. Parker, 1875

Childers, James Saxon, *Laurel and Straw*, New York, D. Appleton & Co., 1927

Church, R.W., *The Oxford Movement. Twelve Years*, London, Macmillan, 1891

Clayton, T., 'Clarke: father and son', in S.J. Green and P. Horden, *All Souls under the Ancien Regime*, Oxford, OUP, 2007, pp. 117–31

———, *'The print collection of George Clarke at Worcester College, Oxford'*, Print Quarterly, 1992, 9 (2), pp. 123–141.

Cocks, A.H., *The War History of the 6th Tank Battalion*, Uckfield, N&M Press, 2003

Daniel, C.H.O. and Barker, W.R., *Worcester College*, London, Robinson & Co, 1900

de Hamel, C., *A History of Illuminated Manuscripts*, London, Phaidon Press Ltd, 1986

Devereux, R.A. and Griffiths, D.N., *Worcester College, Oxford*, Oxford, Oxford University Archaeological Society, 1951

Eidelberg, M., *' "Landskips ... dark and gloomy": reintroducing Henry Ferguson'*, Apollo, 2000, 152 (461, July), pp. 27–36

Elmhirst, P.B., ed., *The Family Budget*, York, Elmyrste Press, 2011

Elmhirst, W., *A Freshman's Diary*, Oxford, Blackwell, 1969

Engel, A.J., *From Clergyman to Don: the Rise of the Academic Profession in Nineteenth-Century Oxford*, Oxford, Clarendon Press, 1983

Foster, P.G.M., *'William Sheffield: four letters to Gilbert White'*, Archives of Natural History, 1985, 12 (1), pp. 1–21

Gillingham, S.E., *Encountering Burges: Reflections on the Art and Architecture of the Chapel at Worcester College*, Oxford, London, Millennium Publishing, 2009

———, *Psalms through the Centuries Volume One*, Oxford, Wiley-Blackwell, 2008

Griffiths, M., 'In an Oxford country garden?', *Country Life*, August 9 2007, 201 (32) pp. 64–8

———, 'Is this England's oldest garden?', *Country Life*, September 18 2013, 207 (38) pp. 98–102

Hanley-Read, C., 'William Burges', in Ferriday, P., ed., *Victorian Architecture*, London, Jonathan Cape, 1963, pp. 185–220

Harris, J. and Higgott, G., *Inigo Jones: the Complete Architectural Drawings*, London, Zwemmer, 1989

Henderson, F., 'Reading, and writing, the text of the Putney debates', in Mendle, M., ed., *The Putney Debates of 1647*, Cambridge, CUP, 2001, pp. 36–50

Henderson, P., 'A Shared Passion: The Cecils and their Gardens', in Croft, P., ed., *Patronage, Culture and Power: The Early Cecils* (Yale University Press, New Haven and London, 2002), pp. 99–120

Hunt, J., 'An aesthete among the hearties: Jocelyn Brooke at Worcester College, 1927–28', *Worcester College Record*, 2004, pp. 51–60

Keynes, S., *'The Cult of King Alfred the Great', in Keynes*, S., ed., Anglo-Saxon England, Cambridge, Dept. of Anglo-Saxon, 1999, pp. 225–356

Lamport, F., 'H.T. Gerrans: Man of Many Parts', *Worcester College Record*, 2002, pp. 54–60

Le Claire, L., 'The survival of the manuscript', in Mendle, M., ed., *The Putney Debates of 1647*, Cambridge, CUP, 2001, pp. 19–50

Lièvre, A., *Miss Willmott of Warley Place: Her Life and Her Gardens*, Faber & Faber, London and Boston, 1980

Lowden, J., 'Manuscript Illumination in Byzantium, 1261–1557' in Evans, H.C., ed., *Byzantium. Faith and Power, Yale*, Yale University Press, 2004, pp. 259–93

Lys, F.J., *Worcester College 1882–1943 and Some Account of a Stewardship*, Oxford, Hall, 1944

MacCulloch , D., *A History of Christianity*, London, Allen Lane, 2009

Masterman, J.C., *On the Chariot Wheel*, London, OUP, 1975

———, *To Teach the Senators Wisdom or An Oxford Guidebook*, London, Hodder & Staughton, 1952

Mordaunt Crook, J., *William Burges and the High Victorian Dream*, London, John Murray, 1981

Nockles, P.B., *The Oxford Movement in Context*, Cambridge, CUP, 1994

Oskala, A., '"Our Versatile Dean": W.H. Hadow's Musical Activities at Oxford', *Worcester College Record*, 2004, pp. 65–73

Philpot, O.L.S., *Stolen Journey*, London, Hodder & Stoughton, 1950

Ramsay, G., 'Un collège d'ancien régime – Worcester between the Wars', *Worcester College Record*, 1988, pp. 24–33

Sayce, R., 'Les livres français d'un collectionneur anglais: George Clarke (1661–1736)', *Revue français d'histoire du livre*, 1979, 24, pp. 3–13.

Sheppard, E., 'Shepilinda's Memoirs of the City and University of Oxford', Bodleian Library, Oxford, MS.Top.Oxon.d.287

Smith, M.A., 'Caduceus porcelain and palette: John Wall of Worcester', *Worcester College Record*, 2000, pp. 52–5

Sutherland, L., 'The Foundation of Worcester College, Oxford', *Oxoniensia*, 1979, 44, pp. 62–80

Wilkinson, C.H., 'Worcester College Library', *Transactions of the Oxford Bibliographical Society*, 1927, pp. 263–326

Williams, M., *William Burges, Pitkin Guides*, Norwich, Jarrold Publishing, 2004

Wilson, E., 'The Gardens', *Worcester College Record*, 2008, pp. 38–44

———, 'The Provost's Rose Garden', *Worcester College Record*, 2007, pp. 41–7

Wood, J., 'Inigo Jones, Italian Art, and the Practice of Drawing', *Art Bulletin*, 1992, 74 (2), pp. 247–70

Select primary documents:

A Catalogue of Books, to be Sold ... 1755 ... being a Choice Collection late belonging to Roger Bourchier, of Worcester-College, Deceased [Oxford,1755]

Report and Evidence upon the Recommendations of Her Majesty's Commissioners for Inquiring into the State of the University of Oxford, presented to the Board of Heads of Houses and Proctors, Oxford, at the University Press, 1853

Correspondence respecting the Proposed Measures of Improvement in the Universities and Colleges of Oxford and Cambridge, London, 1854

University of Oxford Commission. Part I: Minutes of evidence taken by the Commissioners, London, HMSO, 1881

House of Lords Committee Minutes, 21 March 1701[/2], Parliamentary Archives, HL/PO/CO/1/6

Acknowledgements

Producing this book would not have been possible without the indefatigable work of many people, especially Dr Joanna Parker, College Librarian, Emma Goodrum, Archivist, and Coleen Day, Director of Development and Alumni Relations. Grateful thanks are due to the trustees of the Wilkinson Trust for a contribution towards the cost of illustrations and the research time of Jessica Goodman, and to Michael Biggs, the Worcester College Society and the Wilkinson Trust for generously funding the position of Archivist. Thanks also to Neil Turner, SCR Butler, for cleaning the College silver prior to its being photographed.

For permission to reproduce extracts from documents, we are grateful to the Imperial War Museum (letters from Charles Crichton, p. 72), the Elmhirst family (letter from Willie Elmhirst, p. 68), the Parliamentary Archives (p. 34) and the Tate Gallery (letter from Paul Nash, p. 170).

Picture acknowledgements

We would like to thank all of those who supplied images for the book, in particular our superb photographers, Roy and Alex Fox, Fine Art Photographers, and Coleen Day, who between them supplied the majority of new photography, 2013.

The copyright for the majority of images is held by Worcester College. Other images are reproduced with the kind permission of (in alphabetical order): Ashmolean Museum (29); The Warden and Fellows of All Souls College, Oxford (166L); K.T. Bruce (198B); Keith Barnes, Photographers Workshop, Oxford, www.photographersworkshop.co.uk (9,13,36R, 66, 83–89 except 88–9C); Angelika Benz (8R, 211B, back coverTR); Bodleian Library (146); British Library (20); Trustees of the British Museum (29L); Nick Cistone (57,99T); Country Life (105BL); Colin Dunn (Scriptura) (35); Paul Draper (42BL); Maggie Faultless (98, bottom); Gillman & Soame (155; 161; 211T); Jeff Goodman (106–7); Simon Joseph (213); Andrew and Martin Knapp (137R); Norman McBeath (2,6); Jennifer McRae (166R); Oberon Books/Chester Performs (148L); Penguin Photography (210TB); The Master, Fellows and Scholars of Pembroke College, Oxford (34); Sean Pham (57); Random House (146R); Rothenstein Estate and Bridgeman Art Library (72L, 116, 130R); Blair Rogers (148R); The President and Fellows of St John's College, Oxford (22); Matt Wilson (Cover, 4, 10–11, 36TL); Yale University Press (117R). B = Bottom, C = Centre, T = Top, L = Left, R = Right.

Photographs credited Gillman & Soame have been reproduced by kind permission of Gillman & Soame Photography, and can be reordered by visiting www.gillmanandsoame.co.uk/archive or by telephoning 01869 328200.

Every effort has been made to trace copyright holders and credit pictures correctly. We would also like to thank all those that sent in photos or memories that we were not able to include.

Worcester: Portrait of an Oxford College

First published in 2014 by Third Millennium Publishing Limited, a subsidiary of Third Millennium Information Limited.

2–5 Benjamin Street
London
United Kingdom
EC1M 5QL
www.tmiltd.com

ISBN: 978 1 906507 72 5

British Library Cataloguing in Publication Data
A CIP catalogue record for this book is available from the British Library.

Design	Susan Pugsley
Production	Bonnie Murray
Reprographics	Studio Fasoli, Verona, Italy
Printing	Gorenjski Tisk, Slovenia

Photographs for the section openers:

History: *Signatures on the College statutes, including that of the first Provost Richard Blechinden.*

Place: *William Roxby Beverly, watercolour 1846, given by Michael Pirie, 2013.*

People: *College gaudy.*

Things: *Silver given to Richard Greswell on his retirement.*

Life: *Production of* The Merchant of Venice *by Lucy Dawkins, 2013.*

Front endpapers: *David Loggan, Gloucester Hall, from* Oxonia Illustrata, *1675.*

Back endpapers: *Edmund Hort New, Worcester College 1931, bird's-eye view made for* The New Loggan Guide to Oxford Colleges, *1932.*

The Front Quadrangle & the Library with the buildings of Gloucester Coll:
The Lake
Kitchens
Fives Court
Worcester Street
1·Hall c·1720-84. 7·Ancient Entrance.
2·Chapel c·1720-56. to Gloucester College.
3·Library c·1720. 8·Pump Quad:
4.5.6·Buildings of 9·Ancient Kitchen.
Gloucester College. 10·Drive to the Provost's Lodgings.
WORCESTER·COLLEGE·OXFORD·Endowed A·D·
Originally founded for Benedictine Students A·D·1283,
GLOUCESTER·COLLEGE·Re-established after the
Published by Edmund Hort New, Hon: M.A. & A·R·I·B·A at 17 Worcester Place, Oxford A·D·1931